ABOUT THIS PUBLICATION

FOR SERVICE ASSISTANCE

Customer Service
1.704.898.0770

North Carolina General Statues is published by The Muliti-Media Group of Greater Charlotte in Charlotte, North Carolina. Copyright 2015 by the Multi-Media Group of Greater Charlotte. This book or parts thereof may not be reproduced in any form, stored in a retrieval system, or transmitted in any form by any means—electronic, mechanical, photocopy, recording or otherwise—without prior written permission of the publisher, except as provided by United States of America copyright law.

The records required by U.S. Code 2257(a) through (c) and the pertinent regulations 28 C.F.R. Cli. 1, Part 75 with respect to this publication and all materials associated with such records are maintained by The Multi-Media Group of Greater Charlotte, Publisher and available for review by Attorney General.

www.visionbooks.org

Copyright © 2015 by MMGGC
All rights reserved!

TID: 5072137
ISBN (10) digit: 1502990571
ISBN (13) digit: 978-1502990570

123-4-56789-01239-Paperback
123-4-56789-01239-Hardback

First Edition

090520140547

Printed in the United States of America

2015 EDITION

North Carolina Criminal Law And Procedure-Pamphlet # 69

Printed In conjunction with the Administration of the Courts

North Carolina Criminal Law and Procedure
Pamphlet Reference Guide

Chapters	Pamphlet
Chapter 1 Civil Procedure	1
Chapter 1 Civil Procedure (Continue)	2
Chapter 1A Rules of Civil Procedure	2
Chapter 1B Contribution.	2
Chapter 1C Enforcement of Judgments.	2
Chapter 1D Punitive Damages.	2
Chapter 1E Eastern Band of Cherokee Indians.	2
Chapter 1F North Carolina Uniform Interstate Depositions and Discovery Act.	2
Chapter 2 - Clerk of Superior Court [Repealed and Transferred.]	3
Chapter 3 - Commissioners of Affidavits and Deeds [Repealed.]	3
Chapter 4 - Common Law	3
Chapter 5 - Contempt [Repealed.]	3
Chapter 5A - Contempt	3
Chapter 6 - Liability for Court Costs	3
Chapter 7 - Courts [Repealed and Transferred.]	3
Chapter 7A – Judicial Department	3
Chapter 7A – Continuation (Judicial Department)	4
Chapter 7A – Continuation (Judicial Department)	5
Chapter 7B - Juvenile Code	5
Chapter 8 - Evidence	6
Chapter 8A - Interpreters for Deaf Persons [Recodified.]	6
Chapter 8B - Interpreters for Deaf Persons	6
Chapter 8C - Evidence Code	6
Chapter 9 - Jurors	6
Chapter 10 - Notaries [Repealed.]	6
Chapter 10A - Notaries [Recodified.]	6
Chapter 10B - Notaries	6
Chapter 11 - Oaths	6
Chapter 12 - Statutory Construction	6
Chapter 13 - Citizenship Restored	6
Chapter 14 - Criminal Law	7
Chapter 14 –Criminal Law (Continuation)	8
Chapter 15 - Criminal Procedure	9
Chapter 15A - Criminal Procedure Act (Continuation)	10
Chapter 15A - Criminal Procedure Act (Continuation)	11
Chapter 15B - Victims Compensation	11
Chapter 15C - Address Confidentiality Program	11
Chapter 16 - Gaming Contracts and Futures	11
Chapter 17 - Habeas Corpus	11

Chapter 17A - Law-Enforcement Officers [Recodified.]	11
Chapter 17B - North Carolina Criminal Justice Education and Training System [Recodified.] Chapter 17C - North Carolina Criminal Justice Education and Training Standards Commission	11 11
Chapter 17D - North Carolina Justice Academy	11
Chapter 17E - North Carolina Sheriffs' Education and Training Standards Commission	11
Chapter 18 - Regulation of Intoxicating Liquors [Repealed.]	12
Chapter 18A - Regulation of Intoxicating Liquors [Repealed.]	12
Chapter 18B - Regulation of Alcoholic Beverages	12
Chapter 18C - North Carolina State Lottery	12
Chapter 19 - Offenses against Public Morals	12
Chapter 19A - Protection of Animals	12
Chapter 20 - Motor Vehicles	13
Chapter 20 - Motor Vehicles (Continuation)	14
Chapter 20 - Motor Vehicles (Continuation)	15
Chapter 20 - Motor Vehicles (Continuation)	16
Chapter 21 - Bills of Lading	17
Chapter 22 - Contracts Requiring Writing	17
Chapter 22A - Signatures	17
Chapter 22B - Contracts Against Public Policy	17
Chapter 22C - Payments to Subcontractors	17
Chapter 23 - Debtor and Creditor	17
Chapter 24 – Interest	17
Chapter 25 – Uniform Commercial Code	18
Chapter 25 – Uniform Commercial Code (Continuation)	19
Chapter 25A – Retail Installment Sales Act	20
Chapter 25B - Credit	20
Chapter 25C - Sales of Artwork	20
Chapter 26 - Suretyship	20
Chapter 27 - Warehouse Receipts [Repealed.]	20
Chapter 28 - Administration [Repealed.]	20
Chapter 28A - Administration of Decedents' Estates	20
Chapter 28B - Estates of Absentees in Military Service	20
Chapter 28C - Estates of Missing Persons	20
Chapter 29 - Intestate Succession	21
Chapter 30 - Surviving Spouses	21
Chapter 31 - Wills	21
Chapter 31A - Acts Barring Property Rights	21
Chapter 31B - Renunciation of Property and Renunciation of Fiduciary Powers Act	21
Chapter 31C - Uniform Disposition of Community Property Rights at Death Act	21
Chapter 32 - Fiduciaries	21
Chapter 32A - Powers of Attorney	21
Chapter 33 - Guardian and Ward [Repealed and Recodified.]	21

Chapter 33A - North Carolina Uniform Transfers to Minors Act	21
Chapter 33B - North Carolina Uniform Custodial Trust Act	21
Chapter 34 - Veterans' Guardianship Act	22
Chapter 35 - Sterilization Procedures	22
Chapter 35A - Incompetency and Guardianship	22
Chapter 36 - Trusts and Trustees [Repealed.]	22
Chapter 36A - Trusts and Trustees	22
Chapter 36B - Uniform Management of Institutional Funds Act [Repealed.]	22
Chapter 36C - North Carolina Uniform Trust Code	22
Chapter 36D - North Carolina Community Third Party Trusts, Pooled Trusts	23
Chapter 36E - Uniform Prudent Management of Institutional Funds Act	23
Chapter 37 - Allocation of Principal and Income [Repealed.]	23
Chapter 37A - Uniform Principal and Income Act	23
Chapter 38 - Boundaries	23
Chapter 38A - Landowner Liability	23
Chapter 39 - Conveyances	23
Chapter 39A - Transfer Fee Covenants Prohibited	23
Chapter 40 - Eminent Domain [Repealed.]	23
Chapter 40A - Eminent Domain	23
Chapter 41 - Estates	23
Chapter 41A - State Fair Housing Act	23
Chapter 42 - Landlord and Tenant	23
Chapter 42A - Vacation Rental Act	23
Chapter 43 - Land Registration	23
Chapter 44 - Liens	24
Chapter 44A - Statutory Liens and Charges	24
Chapter 45 - Mortgages and Deeds of Trust	24
Chapter 45A - Good Funds Settlement Act	24
Chapter 46 - Partition	24
Chapter 47 - Probate and Registration	25
Chapter 47A - Unit Ownership	25
Chapter 47B - Real Property Marketable Title Act	25
Chapter 47C - North Carolina Condominium Act	25
Chapter 47D - Notice of Settlement Act [Expired.]	25
Chapter 47E - Residential Property Disclosure Act	25
Chapter 47F - North Carolina Planned Community Act	25
Chapter 47G - Option to Purchase Contracts	25
Chapter 47H - Contracts for Deed	25
Chapter 48 - Adoptions +	26
Chapter 48A - Minors	26
Chapter 49 - Bastardy	26
Chapter 49A - Rights of Children	26
Chapter 50 - Divorce and Alimony	26
Chapter 50A - Uniform Child-Custody Jurisdiction and	

Enforcement Act	26
Chapter 50B - Domestic Violence	26
Chapter 50C - Civil No-Contact Orders	26
Chapter 51 - Marriage	26
Chapter 52 - Powers and Liabilities of Married Persons	27
Chapter 52A - Uniform Reciprocal Enforcement of Support Act [Repealed.]	27
Chapter 52B - Uniform Premarital Agreement Act	27
Chapter 52C - Uniform Interstate Family Support Act	27
Chapter 53 - Banks	27
Chapter 53A - Business Development Corporations and North Carolina Capital Resource Corporations	28
Chapter 53B - Financial Privacy Act	28
Chapter 54 - Cooperative Organizations	28
Chapter 54A - Capital Stock Savings and Loan Associations [Repealed.]	28
Chapter 54B - Savings and Loan Associations	29
Chapter 54C - Savings Banks	29
Chapter 55 - North Carolina Business Corporation Act	30
Chapter 55A - North Carolina Nonprofit Corporation Act	31
Chapter 55B - Professional Corporation Act	31
Chapter 55C - Foreign Trade Zones	31
Chapter 55D - Filings, Names, and Registered Agents for Corporations, Nonprofit Corporations, and Partnerships	31
Chapter 56 - Electric, Telegraph and Power Companies [Repealed.]	31
Chapter 57 - Hospital, Medical and Dental Service Corporations [Recodified.]	31
Chapter 57A - Health Maintenance Organization Act [Recodified.]	31
Chapter 57B - Health Maintenance Organization Act [Recodified.]	31
Chapter 57C - North Carolina Limited Liability Company Act.	31
Chapter 58 - Insurance.	32
Chapter 58 - Insurance (Continuation)	33
Chapter 58 - Insurance (Continuation)	34
Chapter 58 - Insurance (Continuation)	35
Chapter 58 - Insurance (Continuation)	36
Chapter 58 - Insurance (Continuation)	37
Chapter 58 - Insurance (Continuation)	38
Chapter 58A - North Carolina Health Insurance Trust Commission [Recodified.]	38
Chapter 59 - Partnership.	39
Chapter 59B - Uniform Unincorporated Nonprofit Association Act.	39
Chapter 60 - Railroads and Other Carriers [Repealed and Transferred.]	39
Chapter 61 - Religious Societies	39
Chapter 62 - Public Utilities	39

Chapter 62 - Public Utilities (Continuation)	40
Chapter 62A - Public Safety Telephone Service And Wireless Telephone Service	40
Chapter 63 - Aeronautics	40
Chapter 63A - North Carolina Global TransPark Authority	40
Chapter 64 - Aliens	40
Chapter 65 – Cemeteries	40
Chapter 66 - Commerce and Business	41
Chapter 67 - Dogs	41
Chapter 68 - Fences and Stock Law	41
Chapter 69 - Fire Protection	41
Chapter 70 - Indian Antiquities, Archaeological Resources and Unmarked Human Skeletal Remains Protection	42
Chapter 71 - Indians [Repealed.]	42
Chapter 71A - Indians	42
Chapter 72 - Inns, Hotels and Restaurants	42
Chapter 73 - Mills	42
Chapter 74 - Mines and Quarries	42
Chapter 74A - Company Police [Repealed.]	42
Chapter 74B - Private Protective Services Act [Repealed.]	42
Chapter 74C - Private Protective Services	42
Chapter 74D - Alarm Systems	42
Chapter 74E - Company Police Act	42
Chapter 74F - Locksmith Licensing Act	42
Chapter 74G - Campus Police Act	42
Chapter 75 - Monopolies, Trusts and Consumer Protection	42
Chapter 75A - Boating and Water Safety	43
Chapter 75B - Discrimination in Business	43
Chapter 75C - Motion Picture Fair Competition Act	43
Chapter 75D - Racketeer Influenced and Corrupt Organizations	43
Chapter 75E - Unlawful Activities in Connection With Certain Corporate Transactions	43
Chapter 76 - Navigation	43
Chapter 76A - Navigation and Pilotage Commissions	43
Chapter 77 - Rivers, Creeks, and Coastal Waters	43
Chapter 78 - Securities Law [Repealed.]	43
Chapter 78A - North Carolina Securities Act	43
Chapter 78B - Tender Offer Disclosure Act [Repealed.]	43
Chapter 78C - Investment Advisers	43
Chapter 78D - Commodities Act	43
Chapter 79 - Strays [Repealed.]	43
Chapter 80 - Trademarks, Brands, etc.	44
Chapter 81 - Weights and Measures [Recodified.]	44
Chapter 81A - Weights and Measures Act of 1975.	44
Chapter 82 - Wrecks [Repealed.]	44
Chapter 83 - Architects [Recodified.]	44

Chapter 83A - Architects	44
Chapter 84 - Attorneys-at-Law	44
Chapter 84A - Foreign Legal Consultants	44
Chapter 85 - Auctions and Auctioneers [Repealed.]	44
Chapter 85A - Bail Bondsmen and Runners [Recodified.]	44
Chapter 85B - Auctions and Auctioneers	44
Chapter 85C - Bail Bondsmen and Runners [Recodified.]	44
Chapter 86 - Barbers [Recodified.]	44
Chapter 86A - Barbers	44
Chapter 87 - Contractors	44
Chapter 88 - Cosmetic Art [Repealed.]	44
Chapter 88A - Electrolysis Practice Act	44
Chapter 88B - Cosmetic Art	45
Chapter 89 - Engineering and Land Surveying [Recodified.]	45
Chapter 89A - Landscape Architects	45
Chapter 89B - Foresters	45
Chapter 89C - Engineering and Land Surveying	45
Chapter 89D - Landscape Contractors	45
Chapter 89E - Geologists Licensing Act	45
Chapter 89F - North Carolina Soil Scientist Licensing Act	45
Chapter 89G - Irrigation Contractors	45
Chapter 90 - Medicine and Allied Occupations	45
Chapter 90 - Medicine and Allied Occupations (Continuation)	46
Chapter 90 - Medicine and Allied Occupations (Continuation)	47
Chapter 90 - Medicine and Allied Occupations (Continuation)	48
Chapter 90A - Sanitarians and Water and Wastewater Treatment Facility Operators	48
Chapter 90B - Social Worker Certification and Licensure Act	48
Chapter 90C - North Carolina Recreational Therapy Licensure Act	48
Chapter 90D - Interpreters and Transliterators	48
Chapter 91 - Pawnbrokers [Repealed.]	48
Chapter 91A - Pawnbrokers Modernization Act of 1989	48
Chapter 92 - Photographers [Deleted.]	48
Chapter 93 - Certified Public Accountants	48
Chapter 93A - Real Estate License Law	49
Chapter 93B - Occupational Licensing Boards	49
Chapter 93C - Watchmakers [Repealed.]	49
Chapter 93D - North Carolina State Hearing Aid Dealers and Fitters Board.	49
Chapter 93E - North Carolina Appraisers Act	49
Chapter 94 - Apprenticeship	49
Chapter 95 - Department of Labor and Labor Regulations	49
Chapter 95 - Department of Labor and Labor Regulations (Continuation)	50
Chapter 96 - Employment Security	50
Chapter 97 - Workers' Compensation Act	50
Chapter 97 - Workers' Compensation Act (Continuation)	51

Chapter 98 - Burnt and Lost Records	51
Chapter 99 - Libel and Slander	51
Chapter 99A - Civil Remedies for Criminal Actions	51
Chapter 99B - Products Liability	51
Chapter 99C - Actions Relating to Winter Sports Safety and Accidents	51
Chapter 99D - Civil Rights	51
Chapter 99E - Special Liability Provisions	51
Chapter 100 - Monuments, Memorials and Parks	51
Chapter 101 - Names of Persons	51
Chapter 102 - Official Survey Base	51
Chapter 103 - Sundays, Holidays and Special Days	51
Chapter 104 - United States Lands	51
Chapter 104A - Degrees of Kinship	51
Chapter 104B - Hurricanes or Other Acts of Nature	51
Chapter 104C - Atomic Energy, Radioactivity and Ionizing Radiation [Repealed and Recodified.]	51
Chapter 104D - Southern States Energy Compact	51
Chapter 104E - North Carolina Radiation Protection Act	51
Chapter 104F - Southeast Interstate Low-Level Radioactive Waste Management Compact [Repealed]	51
Chapter 104G - North Carolina Low-Level Radioactive Waste Management Authority Act of 1987 [Repealed]	51
Chapter 105 - Taxation	51
Chapter 105 - Taxation (Continuation)	52
Chapter 105 - Taxation (Continuation)	53
Chapter 105 - Taxation (Continuation)	54
Chapter 105A - Setoff Debt Collection Act	55
Chapter 105B - Defaulted Student Loan Recovery Act	55
Chapter 106 - Agriculture	55
Chapter 106 - Agriculture (Continue)	56
Chapter 106 - Agriculture (Continue)	57
Chapter 107 - Agricultural Development Districts [Repealed.]	57
Chapter 108 - Social Services [Repealed and Recodified.]	57
Chapter 108A - Social Services	57
Chapter 108B - Community Action Programs	58
Chapter 108C Medicaid and Health Choice Provider Requirements.	58
Chapter 108D Medicaid Managed Care for Behavioral Health Services.	58
Chapter 109 - Bonds [Recodified.]	58
Chapter 110 - Child Welfare	58
Chapter 111 - Aid to the Blind	58
Chapter 112 - Confederate Homes and Pensions [Repealed.]	58
Chapter 113 - Conservation and Development	58
Chapter 113 - Conservation and Development (Continuation)	59

Chapter 113A - Pollution Control and Environment	59
Chapter 113A - Pollution Control and Environment (Continuation)	60
Chapter 113B - North Carolina Energy Policy Act of 1975	60
Chapter 114 - Department of Justice	60
Chapter 115 - Elementary and Secondary Education [Repealed.]	60
Chapter 115A - Community Colleges, Technical Institutes, and Industrial Education Centers [Repealed.]	60
Chapter 115B - Tuition and Fee Waivers	60
Chapter 115C - Elementary and Secondary Education	60
Chapter 115C - Elementary and Secondary Education (Continuation)	61
Chapter 115C - Elementary and Secondary Education (Continuation)	62
Chapter 115C - Elementary and Secondary Education (Continuation)	63
Chapter 115D - Community Colleges	63
Chapter 115E - Private Educational Facilities Finance Act [Recodified]	63
Chapter 116 - Higher Education	63
Chapter 116 - Higher Education (Continuation)	63
Chapter 116A - Escheats and Abandoned Property [Repealed.]	64
Chapter 116B - Escheats and Abandoned Property	64
Chapter 116C - Continuum of Education Programs	64
Chapter 116D - Higher Education Bonds	64
Chapter 116E -Education Longitudinal Data System	64
Chapter 117 - Electrification	64
Chapter 118 - Firemen's and Rescue Squad Workers' Relief and Pension Funds [Recodified.]	64
Chapter 118A - Firemen's Death Benefit Act [Repealed.]	64
Chapter 118B - Members of a Rescue Squad Death Benefit Act [Repealed.]	64
Chapter 119 - Gasoline and Oil Inspection and Regulation	64
Chapter 120 - General Assembly	65
Chapter 120 - General Assembly (Continuation)	66
Chapter 120 - General Assembly (Continuation)	67
Chapter 120C - Lobbying	67
Chapter 121 - Archives and History	67
Chapter 122 - Hospitals for the Mentally Disordered [Repealed.]	67
Chapter 122A - North Carolina Housing Finance Agency	67
Chapter 122B - North Carolina Agricultural Facilities Finance Act [Repealed.]	67
Chapter 122C - Mental Health, Developmental Disabilities, and Substance Abuse Act of 1985	67
Chapter 122C - Mental Health, Developmental Disabilities, and Substance Abuse Act of 1985 (Continuation)	68

Chapter 122D - North Carolina Agricultural Finance Act	68
Chapter 122E - North Carolina Housing Trust and Oil Overcharge Act	68
Chapter 123 - Impeachment	69
Chapter 123A - Industrial Development [Repealed.]	69
Chapter 124 - Internal Improvements	69
Chapter 125 - Libraries	69
Chapter 126 - State Personnel System	69
Chapter 127 - Militia [Repealed.]	69
Chapter 127A - Militia	69
Chapter 127B - Military Affairs	69
Chapter 127C - Advisory Commission on Military Affairs	69
Chapter 128 - Offices and Public Officers	69
Chapter 128 - Offices and Public Officers (Continuation)	70
Chapter 129 - Public Buildings and Grounds	70
Chapter 130 - Public Health [Repealed.]	70
Chapter 130A - Public Health	70
Chapter 130A - Public Health (Continuation)	71
Chapter 130A - Public Health (Continuation)	72
Chapter 130B - Hazardous Waste Management Commission [Repealed.]	72
Chapter 131 - Public Hospitals [Repealed.]	72
Chapter 131A - Health Care Facilities Finance Act	72
Chapter 131B - Licensing of Ambulatory Surgical Facilities [Repealed.]	72
Chapter 131C - Charitable Solicitation Licensure Act [Repealed.]	72
Chapter 131D - Inspection and Licensing of Facilities	72
Chapter 131E - Health Care Facilities and Services	72
Chapter 131E - Health Care Facilities and Services (Continuation)	73
Chapter 131F - Solicitation of Contributions	73
Chapter 132 - Public Records	73
Chapter 133 - Public Works	74
Chapter 134 - Youth Development [Recodified.]	74
Chapter 134A - Youth Services [Repealed.]	74
Chapter 135 - Retirement System for Teachers and State Employees; Social Security; Health Insurance Program for Children	74
Chapter 135 - Retirement System for Teachers and State Employees; Social Security; Health Insurance Program for Children	75
Chapter 136 - Transportation	75
Chapter 136 - Transportation (Continuation)	76
Chapter 137 - Rural Rehabilitation [Repealed.]	76
Chapter 138 - Salaries, Fees and Allowances	76
Chapter 138A - State Government Ethics Act	76

Chapter 139 - Soil and Water Conservation Districts	76
Chapter 140 - State Art Museum; Symphony and Art Societies	76
Chapter 140A - State Awards System	76
Chapter 141 - State Boundaries	76
Chapter 142 - State Debt	76
Chapter 143 - State Departments, Institutions, and Commissions	77
Chapter 143 - State Departments, Institutions, and Commissions (Continuation)	78
Chapter 143 - State Departments, Institutions, and Commissions (Continuation)	79
Chapter 143 - State Departments, Institutions, and Commissions (Continuation)	80
Chapter 143A - State Government Reorganization	80
Chapter 143B - Executive Organization Act of 1973	80
Chapter 143B - Executive Organization Act of 1973 (Continuation)	81
Chapter 143B - Executive Organization Act of 1973 (Continuation)	82
Chapter 143C - State Budget Act	83
Chapter 143D - The State Governmental Accountability and Internal Control Act	83
Chapter 144 - State Flag, Official Governmental Flags, Motto, and Colors	83
Chapter 145 - State Symbols and Other Official Adoptions.	83
Chapter 146 - State Lands	83
Chapter 147 - State Officers	83
Chapter 148 - State Prison System	84
Chapter 149 - State Song and Toast	84
Chapter 150 - Uniform Revocation of Licenses [Repealed.]	84
Chapter 150A - Administrative Procedure Act [Recodified.]	84
Chapter 150B - Administrative Procedure Act	84
Chapter 151 - Constables [Repealed.]	84
Chapter 152 - Coroners	84
Chapter 152A - County Medical Examiner [Repealed.]	84
Chapter 152A - County Medical Examiner [Repealed.] (Continuation)	85
Chapter 153 - Counties and County Commissioners [Repealed.]	85
Chapter 153A - Counties	85
Chapter 153B - Mountain Resources Planning Act	85
Chapter 153C - Uwharrie Regional Resources Act	85
Chapter 154 - County Surveyor [Repealed.]	85
Chapter 155 - County Treasurer [Repealed.]	85
Chapter 156 - Drainage	85

Chapter 156 – Drainage (Continuation)	86
Chapter 157 - Housing Authorities and Projects	86
Chapter 157A - Historic Properties Commissions [Transferred.]	86
Chapter 158 - Local Development	86
Chapter 159 - Local Government Finance	86
Chapter 159 - Local Government Finance (Continuation)	87
Chapter 159A - Pollution Abatement and Industrial Facilities Financing Act [Unconstitutional.]	87
Chapter 159B - Joint Municipal Electric Power and Energy Act	87
Chapter 159C - Industrial and Pollution Control Facilities Financing Act	87
Chapter 159D - The North Carolina Capital Facilities Financing Act	87
Chapter 159E - Registered Public Obligations Act	87
Chapter 159F - North Carolina Energy Development Authority [Repealed.]	87
Chapter 159G - Water Infrastructure	87
Chapter 159H - [Reserved.]	87
Chapter 159I - Solid Waste Management Loan Program and Local Government Special Obligation Bonds	87
Chapter 160 - Municipal Corporations [Repealed And Transferred.]	87
Chapter 160A - Cities and Towns	88
Chapter 160A - Cities and Towns (Continuation)	89
Chapter 160B - Consolidated City-County Act	89
Chapter 160C - Baseball Park Districts [Repealed.]	90
Chapter 161 - Register of Deeds	90
Chapter 162 - Sheriff	90
Chapter 162A - Water and Sewer Systems	90
Chapter 162B Continuity of Local Government in Emergency.	90
Chapter 163 Elections and Election Laws.	90
Chapter 163 Elections and Election Laws. (Continuation)	91
Chapter 164 Concerning the General Statutes of North Carolina.	92
Chapter 165 Veterans.	92
Chapter 166 Civil Preparedness Agencies [Repealed.]	92
Chapter 166A North Carolina Emergency Management Act.	92
Chapter 167 State Civil Air Patrol [Repealed.]	92
Chapter 168 Persons with Disabilities.	92
Chapter 168A Persons With Disabilities Protection Act.	92
Chapter 123.	

Impeachment.

Article 1.

The Court.

§ 123-1. Senate is court of impeachment; quorum.

The court for the trial of impeachments shall be the Senate. A majority of the members shall be necessary to constitute a quorum. (Const., art. 4, s. 3; 1868-9, c. 168, s. 1; Code, ss. 2923, 2924; Rev., s. 4623; C.S., s. 6244.)

§ 123-2. Chief Justice presides in impeachment of Governor.

When the Governor of the State, or Lieutenant Governor, upon whom the powers and duties of the office of Governor have devolved, is impeached, the Chief Justice of the Supreme Court shall preside; and in a case requiring the Chief Justice to preside, notice shall be given him, by order of the Senate, of the time and place fixed for the consideration of the articles of impeachment, with a request to attend; and the Chief Justice shall preside over the Senate during the consideration of said articles upon the trial of the person impeached. But the Chief Justice shall not vote on any question during the trial, and shall pronounce decision only as the organ of the Senate with its assent. (Const., art. 4, s. 4; 1868-9, c. 168, s. 6; Code, s. 2927; Rev., s. 4624; C.S., s. 6245.)

§ 123-3. Power of the Senate as a court.

The Senate, as a court, shall have power to compel the attendance of parties and witnesses, to enforce obedience to its orders, mandates, writs, precepts, and judgments, to preserve order, to punish, in a summary way, contempts of its authority, orders, mandates, writs, precepts, or judgments, to adjourn from time to time, and to make all lawful rules and regulations which it may deem essential or conducive to the ends of justice. (1868-9, c. 168, s. 4; Code, s. 2926; Rev., s. 4626; C.S., s. 6246.)

§ 123-4. Power of presiding officer.

The presiding officer of the Senate shall have power:

(1)   To direct all necessary preparations in the Senate chamber.

(2)   To make and issue by himself or by the clerk of the Senate all orders, mandates, writs, and precepts authorized by law or by the Senate.

(3)   To direct all the forms of procedure during the trial not otherwise specially provided for.

(4)   To decide in the first instance, without a division, all questions of evidence and incidental questions; but the same shall, on demand of one fifth of the members present, be decided by yeas and nays. (1868-9, c. 168, s. 5; Code, s. 2927; Rev., s. 4627; C.S., s. 6247.)

§ 123-5. Causes for impeachment.

Each member of the Council of State, each justice of the General Court of Justice, and each judge of the General Court of Justice shall be liable to impeachment for the commission of any felony, or the commission of any misdemeanor involving moral turpitude, or for malfeasance in office, or for willful neglect of duty. (1868-9, c. 168, s. 16; Code, s. 2937; Rev., s. 4628; C.S., s. 6248; 1973, c. 1420.)

Article 2.

Procedure in Impeachment.

§ 123-6. Articles of impeachment preferred.

All impeachments must be delivered by the House of Representatives to the presiding officer of the Senate, who shall thereupon cause proclamation to be made in the following words:

"All persons are commanded to keep silence, on pain of imprisonment, while the House of Representatives is exhibiting to the Senate of North Carolina articles of impeachment against _____."

After which the articles shall be exhibited, and then the presiding officer of the Senate shall inform the House of Representatives that the Senate will take proper order on the subject of impeachment, of which due notice shall be given to the House of Representatives. (1868-9, c. 168, ss. 2, 3; Code, s. 2925; Rev., s. 4630; C.S., s. 6249.)

§ 123-7. When President of Senate impeached, another officer chosen.

If the President of the Senate be impeached, notice thereof shall immediately be given to the Senate by the House of Representatives, in order that another President may be chosen. (1868-9, c. 168, s. 14; Code, s. 2935; Rev., s. 4631; C.S., s. 6250.)

§ 123-8. Notice given to the accused.

The Senate, upon the presentation of articles of impeachment and its organization as a court, shall forthwith cause the person impeached to appear and answer the articles exhibited, either in person or by attorney. He shall be entitled to a copy of the impeachment and have a reasonable time to answer the same. (1868-9, c. 168, s. 7; Code, s. 2928; Rev., s. 4632; C.S., s. 6251.)

§ 123-9. Accused entitled to counsel.

The person accused is entitled on the trial of impeachment to the aid of counsel. (1868-9, c. 168, s. 8; Code, s. 2929; Rev., s. 4629; C.S., s. 6252.)

§ 123-10. Time of hearing fixed.

When issue is joined in the trial of an impeachment the court shall fix a time and place for the trial thereof. (1868-9, c. 168, s. 9; Code, s. 2930; Rev., s. 4633; C.S., s. 6253.)

§ 123-11. Oath administered to members.

At the time and place appointed, and before the commencement of the trial, the presiding officer of the Senate shall administer to each member of the court then present, and to other members as they appear, an oath or affirmation truly and impartially to try and determine the charge in question, under the Constitution and laws, according to the evidence. No member of the court shall sit or give his vote upon the trial until he shall have taken such oath or affirmation. (1868-9, c. 168, s. 10; Code, s. 2931; Rev., s. 4625; C.S., s. 6254.)

Article 3.

Effect of Impeachment.

§ 123-12. Accused suspended during trial.

Every officer impeached shall be suspended from the exercise of his office until his acquittal. (1868-9, c. 168, s. 13; Code, s. 2934; Rev., s. 4634; C.S., s. 6255.)

§ 123-13. Manner of conviction; judgment; indictment.

No person shall be convicted on an impeachment without the concurrence of two thirds of the Senators present. Upon a conviction of the person impeached, judgment may be given that he be removed from office, or that he be disqualified to hold any office of honor, trust, or profit under this State, or both. Every person convicted on impeachment shall, nevertheless, be liable to indictment and punishment according to law. (Const., art. 4, ss. 3, 4; 1868-9, c. 168, ss. 11, 12, 15; Code, ss. 2932, 2933, 2936; Rev., s. 4635; C.S., s. 6256.)

Chapter 123A.

Industrial Development.

§§ 123A-1 through 123A-27: Repealed by Session Laws 1983, c. 717, s. 39.

Chapter 124.

Internal Improvements.

Article 1.

General Provisions.

§ 124-1. Control of internal improvements.

The Governor and Council of State shall have charge of all the State's interest in all railroads, canals and other works of internal improvements. The Board of Directors of a State-owned railroad company shall be responsible for managing its affairs and for reporting as set forth in G.S. 124-17. (1925, c. 157, s. 1; 2000-146, s. 2; 2013-360, s. 34.14(a).)

§ 124-2. State deemed shareholder in corporation accepting appropriation.

When an appropriation is made by the State to any work of internal improvement conducted by a corporation, the State shall be considered, if so directed in the act making the appropriation, a stockholder in such corporation, and shall have as many shares as may correspond with the amount of money appropriated; and the acceptance of such money shall be deemed to be a consent of the corporation to the terms herein expressed. (1925, c. 157, s. 2; 1985, c. 792, s. 13.21.)

§ 124-3. Report of railroad, canal, etc.; contents.

(a) The president or other chief officer of every railroad, canal, or other public work of internal improvement in which the State owns an interest, shall, report annually to the Joint Legislative Commission on Governmental Operations. This report shall include:

(1) Number of shares owned by the State.

(2) Number of shares owned otherwise.

(3) Par value of the shares.

(4) Repealed by Session Laws 2000-146, s. 3, effective July 1, 2000.

(5) Amount of bonded debt, and for what purpose contracted.

(6) Amount of other debt, and how incurred.

(7) If interest on bonded debt has been punctually paid as agreed; if not, how much in arrears.

(8) Amount of gross receipts for past year, and from what sources derived.

(9) An itemized account of expenditures for past year.

(10) A summary of all leases, sales, or acquisitions of real property to which the company has been a party since the last report.

(11) Suits at law pending against his company concerning its bonded debt, or in which title to all or any part of such road or canal is concerned.

(12) Any sales of stock owned by the State, by whose order made, and disposition of the proceeds.

(13) Annual financial statements, including notes, audited by an independent certified public accounting firm.

(b) Recodified as G.S. 124-17(b) by Session Laws 2013-360, s. 34.14(d), effective July 1, 2013.

(c) Recodified as G.S. 124-17(c) by Session Laws 2013-360, s. 34.14(d), effective July 1, 2013. (1925, c. 157, s. 3; 1993, c. 539, s. 928; 1994, Ex. Sess., c. 24, s. 14(c); 2000-67, s. 7.2(b); 2000-146, s. 3; 2013-360, s. 34.14(d).)

§ 124-4: Repealed by Session Laws 2000-146, s. 4.

§ 124-5. Approval of encumbrance on State's interest in corporations.

(a) No corporation or company in which the State owns the majority of any class of voting stock shall sell, lease, mortgage, or otherwise encumber its franchise, right-of-way, or other property, except by and with the approval and consent of the Governor and Council of State.

(b) Recodified as G.S. 124-15(b) by Session Laws 2013-360, s. 34.14(b), effective July 1, 2013. (1925, c. 157, s. 5; 1981 (Reg. Sess., 1982), c. 1372, s. 5; 1983, c. 905, ss. 10, 11; 1985, c. 792, ss. 13.25, 13.26; 2000-146, s. 5; 2013-360, s. 34.14(b).)

§ 124-5.1. North Carolina Railroad Company dividends deposited to Highway Fund.

Any dividends of the North Carolina Railroad Company received by the State shall be deposited into the Freight Rail & Rail Crossing Safety Improvement Fund within the Highway Fund and administered by the Rail Division of the Department of Transportation. The Fund shall be used for the enhancement of freight rail service and railroad-roadway crossing safety, which may include the following project types:

(1) Track and associated infrastructure improvements for freight service.

(2) Grade crossing protection, elimination, and hazard removal.

(3) Signalization improvements.

(4) Assistance for projects to improve rail access to industrial, port, and military facilities and for freight intermodal facility improvements, provided that funding assistance under this subdivision shall be subject to the same limits as that for short-line railroads under G.S. 136-44.39.

The Fund may also be used to supplement funds allocated for freight rail or railroad-roadway crossing safety projects approved as part of the Transportation Improvement Program. (2000-67, s. 7.2(a); 2005-276, s. 28.7; 2013-360, s. 34.14(g).)

§ 124-6. Appointment of proxies, director of railroad companies, etc.

(a) The Governor shall appoint on behalf of the State all such officers or agents as, by any act, incorporating a company for the purpose of internal improvement, are allowed to represent the stock or other interests which the State may have in such company; and such person or persons shall cast the vote to which the State may be entitled in all the meetings of the stockholders of such company under the direction of said Governor; and the said Governor may, if in his opinion the public interest so requires, remove or suspend such persons, officers, agents, proxies, or directors in his discretion.

(b) Recodified as G.S. 124-15(a) by Session Laws 2013-360, s. 34.14(b), effective July 1, 2013. (1925, c. 157, s. 6; 1997-443, s. 32.30(k); 1999-431, s. 3.3(a); 2013-360, s. 34.14(b).)

§ 124-7. Power of investigation of corporations.

The Governor and Council of State shall have the power to investigate the affairs of any corporation or association described in G.S. 124-3 and may require the Attorney General or the Utilities Commission to assist in making such investigation under the rules and regulations prescribed in Chapter 62. (1925, c. 157, s. 7; 1933, c. 134, s. 8; 1941, c. 97, s. 1.)

§ 124-8. Reserved for future codification purposes.

§ 124-9. Reserved for future codification purposes.

§ 124-10. Reserved for future codification purposes.

Article 2.

State-Owned Railroad Company.

§ 124-11. Definition.

As used in this Chapter, the term "State-Owned Railroad Company" shall mean a railroad company in which the State owns all of the voting stock. (2000-146, s. 7.)

§ 124-12. Powers of a State-owned railroad company.

A State-owned railroad company shall have, in addition to the powers of any railroad corporation, the power to:

(1) Lease, license, or improve property. - A State-owned railroad company may lease, license, or improve its right-of-way and property, whether held by easement, presumptive grant, express grant, or otherwise, for the purpose of preserving and protecting its railroad corridor and franchise.

(2) Condemnation in fee simple. - A State-owned railroad company may exercise the power of eminent domain to acquire property in fee simple for the purposes specified in G.S. 40A-3(a)(4). The procedures of Article 2 of Chapter 40A of the General Statutes shall apply to the exercise of the power of eminent domain under this subdivision. (2000-146, s. 7.)

§ 124-13. Effect on State-owned railroad company charter.

Nothing in this Chapter repeals or modifies any State-owned railroad company charter or limits the rights of the shareholders of the company as provided in Chapter 55 of the General Statutes. (2000-146, s. 7.)

§ 124-14: Reserved for future codification purposes.

§ 124-15. Board of directors; appointment and approval of encumbrances.

(a) Notwithstanding subsection (a) of G.S. 124-6, for any State-owned railroad company that has trackage in more than two counties, seven of the members of the Board of Directors shall be appointed by the Governor, three of the members of the Board of Directors shall be appointed by the General Assembly upon the recommendation of the Speaker of the House of Representatives in accordance with G.S. 120-121, and three of the members of the Board of Directors shall be appointed by the General Assembly upon the recommendation of the President Pro Tempore of the Senate in accordance with G.S. 120-121. The Board of Directors shall consist of 13 members. Of the Governor's seven appointments, one shall be from the appointees to the Board of Transportation and one shall be the Secretary of Commerce or the Secretary's designee. Of the initial members appointed by the Governor, three shall be appointed for terms of four years and four shall be appointed for terms of two years. Of the initial members recommended to the General Assembly by the Speaker of the House of Representatives, two shall be appointed for terms of four years and one shall be appointed for a term of two years. Of the initial members recommended to the General Assembly by the President Pro Tempore of the Senate, two shall be appointed for terms of four years and one shall be appointed for a term of two years. Thereafter all Board members shall serve four-year terms. The Board shall elect the chairman from among its membership.

(b) No State-owned railroad company shall sell, lease, mortgage, or otherwise encumber its franchise, right-of-way, or other property, except by and with the approval and consent of the Board of Directors of that corporation. The president or other chief officer of the State-owned railroad company shall report any acquisitions and dispositions in accordance with G.S. 124-3(10). (1997-443, s. 32.30(k); 1999-431, s. 3.3(a); 2000-146, s. 5; 2013-360, s. 34.14(b).)

§ 124-16. Strategic plan and capital investment plan required of State-owned railroad company; performance management system.

(a) Any State-owned railroad company shall prepare and maintain a comprehensive strategic plan and a capital investment plan. The strategic plan shall include a mission statement describing the purpose of the company and clear goals that address the strategic issues facing the company.

(b) Any State-owned railroad company shall develop and implement a formalized performance management system based on its strategic plan. The performance management system shall measure and monitor progress toward achieving strategic objectives. When performance fails to achieve strategic objectives within the time period established in the plan, a State-owned railroad company shall take corrective action. (2013-360, s. 34.14(c).)

§ 124-17. Enhanced annual report of State-owned railroad company; additional reporting requirements to Governor and General Assembly.

(a)   A State-owned railroad company shall submit an annual report to the Joint Legislative Commission on Governmental Operations and the Joint Legislative Transportation Oversight Committee. The report shall include the following:

(1)   The information required under G.S. 124-3.

(2)   A copy of the strategic plan and the capital investment plan required under G.S. 124-16.

(3)   Any failures to meet strategic objectives and what corrective actions were taken under G.S. 124-16(b).

(4)   Anticipated dividends for the next three fiscal years.

(5)   A description of the State-owned railroad company's business, subsidiaries, and markets in which it operates.

(6)   A list of the properties owned by the State-owned railroad company.

(7)   A list of the directors and executive officers of the State-owned railroad company and a description of the background and experience of each.

(8)   A description of the State-owned railroad company's code of ethics and conflicts of interest policy.

(9)   A summary of the fees paid to an accounting firm during the year.

(10)   A list of the compensation paid to directors and officers of the State-owned railroad company.

(11)   A description of the State-owned railroad company's disagreements with its accountants if there has been a change in accountants.

(12) A description of any transactions between the State-owned railroad company and its directors, officers, and their family members.

(b) Upon the request of the Governor or any committee of the General Assembly, a State-owned railroad company shall provide all additional information and data within its possession or ascertainable from its records. The State-owned railroad company shall not be deemed to have waived any attorney-client privilege when complying with this subsection. At the time a State-owned railroad company provides information under this section, it shall indicate whether the information is confidential. Confidential information shall be subject to subsection (c) of this section.

(c) Confidential information includes (i) information related to a proposed specific business transaction where inspection, examination, or copying of the records would frustrate the purpose for which the records were created, or (ii) information that is subject to confidentiality obligations of a railroad company. Confidential information is exempt from Chapter 132 of the General Statutes and shall not be subject to a request under G.S. 132-6(a). (2000-146, s. 3; 2013-360, s. 34.14(d).)

§ 124-18. Dividends required of State-owned railroad company.

Any State-owned railroad company that has trackage in more than two counties shall issue an annual cash dividend to the State. The amount of the annual dividend is twenty-five percent (25%) of the company's income from the prior year's trackage rights agreements. The dividend is due by January 15 of each year, and interest shall accrue at the annual rate of prime plus one percent (1%) if the payment is not paid by the due date. The Directors of any State-owned railroad company who vote for or assent to the dividend required under this section shall not be held liable under G.S. 55-8-33. (2013-360, s. 34.14(h).)

Chapter 125.

Libraries.

Article 1.

State Library Agency.

§ 125-1. State library agency.

The library agency of the State of North Carolina shall be the Department of Cultural Resources. (1955, c. 505, s. 3; 1973, c. 476, s. 84.)

§ 125-2. Powers and duties of Department of Cultural Resources.

The Department of Cultural Resources shall have the following powers and duties:

(1) To adopt a seal for use in official business.

(2) To make to the Governor a biennial report of its activities and needs, including recommendations for improving its services to the State, to be transmitted by the Governor to the General Assembly.

(3) To accept gifts, devises, and endowments for the purposes which fall within the general legal powers and duties of the Department of Cultural Resources. Unless otherwise specified by the donor or testator, the Department of Cultural Resources may either expend both the principal and interest of any gift or devise or may invest such sums in whole or in part, by and with the consent of the State Treasurer, in securities in which sinking funds may be invested under the provisions of G.S. 142-34.

(4) To purchase and maintain collections of books, periodicals, newspapers, maps, films, audiovisual and other materials; to subscribe to computerized databases; to provide other resources, services and programs; and to serve as an information distribution center for State government and the people of the State as a means for the promotion of knowledge, education, commerce and business in the State. The scope of the library's collections, resources and services should be determined by the Secretary of Cultural Resources upon consideration of the recommendations of the State Library Commission; and in making these decisions, the Secretary shall take into account the collections, resources and services of other libraries throughout the State and the availability of such collections, resources and services to the general public. All materials owned by the State Library shall be available for free circulation to libraries and to all citizens of the State under rules and regulations fixed by the librarian, except that the librarian may restrict the circulation of books and other materials which, because they are rare or are

used intensively in the library for reference purposes or for other good reasons, should be retained in the library at all times. The public schools shall be given equal priority in borrowing all films which are available for circulation.

(5) To give assistance, advice and counsel to other State agencies maintaining special reference collections as to the best means of establishing and administering such libraries and collections.

(5a) To provide for the establishment and maintenance of union catalogs.

(6) To fix reasonable penalties for damage to or failure to return any book, periodical or other material owned by the Department of Cultural Resources, or for violation of any rule or regulation concerning the use of books, periodicals, and other materials in the custody of the Department of Cultural Resources.

(7) Repealed by Session Laws 1987, c. 199, s. 4.

(8) To give assistance, advice and counsel to all libraries in the State, to all communities which may propose to establish libraries, and to all persons interested in public libraries, as to the best means of establishing and administering such libraries, as to the selection of books, cataloguing, maintenance and other details of library management.

(9) To provide library services to blind and physically handicapped readers of North Carolina by making available to them books and other reading materials in braille, or sound recordings or any other medium used by the blind and physically handicapped; to enter into contracts and agreements with appropriate libraries and other organizations for the purposes of serving the blind and physically handicapped; to enter into contracts with library agencies of other states for providing library service to the blind and physically handicapped of those states, provided adequate compensation is paid for such service and such contract is otherwise advantageous to this State.

(10) To plan and coordinate cooperative programs between the various types of libraries within the State of North Carolina, and to coordinate State development with regional and national cooperative library programs; and to assist nonprofit corporations in organization and operation for the purposes of cooperative programs. (1955, c. 505, s. 3; 1961, c. 1161; 1973, c. 476, s. 84; 1977, c. 645, s. 1; 1981, c. 918, s. 4; 1983, c. 819; 1987, c. 199; 2011-284, s. 88.)

§§ 125-3 through 125-4. Repealed by Session Laws 1973, c. 476, s. 84.

§ 125-5. Public libraries to report to Department of Cultural Resources.

Every public library in the State shall make an annual report to the Department of Cultural Resources in such form as may be prescribed by the Department. The term "public library" shall, for the purpose of this section, include subscription libraries, college and university libraries, legal association, medical association, Supreme Court, and other special libraries. (1955, c. 505, s. 3; 1973, c. 476, s. 84.)

§ 125-6. Librarian's seal.

It shall be the duty of the Secretary of State to furnish the State Librarian with a seal of office. The State Librarian is authorized to certify to the authenticity and genuineness of any document, paper, or extract from any document, paper, or book or other writing which may be on file in the Library. When a certificate is made under his hand and attested by his official seal, it shall be received as prima facie evidence of the correctness of the matter therein contained, and as such shall receive full faith and credit. (1955, c. 505, s. 3.)

§ 125-7. State policy as to public library service; annual appropriation therefor; administration of funds.

(a) It is hereby declared the policy of the State to promote the establishment and development of public library service throughout all sections of the State.

(b) For promoting, aiding, and equalizing public library service in North Carolina a sum shall annually be appropriated out of the moneys within the State treasury to be known as the Aid to Public Libraries Fund.

(c) The fund herein provided shall be administered by the Department of Cultural Resources, which shall frame bylaws, rules and regulations for the allocation and administration of such funds. The funds shall be used to improve, stimulate, increase and equalize public library service to the people of the whole State, shall be used for no other purpose, except as herein provided, and shall be allocated among the legally established municipal, county or regional libraries in the State taking into consideration local needs, area and population to be served, local interest and such other factors as may affect the State program of public library service.

(d) For the necessary expenses of administration, allocation, and supervision, a sum not to exceed seven percent (7%) of the annual appropriation may annually be used by the Department of Cultural Resources.

(e) The fund appropriated under this section shall be separate and apart from the appropriations of the Department of Cultural Resources, which appropriation shall not be affected by this section or the appropriation hereunder.

(f) Repealed by Session Laws 1973, c. 476, s. 84. (1955, c. 505, s. 3; 1973, c. 476, s. 84; 1979, c. 578.)

§ 125-8. Department of Cultural Resources authorized to accept and administer funds from federal government and other agencies.

The Department of Cultural Resources is hereby authorized and empowered to receive, accept and administer any money or moneys appropriated or granted to it, separate and apart from the appropriation by the State for the Department of Cultural Resources, for providing and equalizing public library service in North Carolina:

(1) By the federal government and,

(2) By any other agencies, private and/or otherwise.

The fund herein provided for shall be administered by the Department of Cultural Resources, which Department shall frame bylaws, rules and regulations for the allocation and administration of this fund. This fund shall be used to increase, improve, stimulate and equalize library service to people of the whole State, and shall be used for no other purpose whatsoever except as hereinafter provided, and shall be allocated among the counties of the State, taking into consideration local needs, area and population to be served, local interests as evidenced by local appropriations, and such other factors as may affect the State program of library service. Any gift or grant from the federal government or other sources shall become a part of said funds, to be used as part of the State fund, or may be invested as the Department of Cultural Resources may deem advisable, according to provisions of G.S. 125-5(5), the income to be used for the promotion of libraries as stated in this section. (1955, c. 505, s. 3; 1973, c. 476, s. 84.)

§ 125-9. Librarian certification.

The Secretary of Cultural Resources shall issue librarian certificates to public librarians under such reasonable rules and regulations as the Public Librarian Certification Commission may adopt. A complete record of the transaction of the Department in the issuance of librarian certificates shall be kept at all times in the office of the North Carolina State Library. (1955, c. 505, s. 3; 1973, c. 476, s. 53.)

§ 125-10. Temporary certificates for public librarians.

Upon the submission of satisfactory evidence that no qualified librarian is available for appointment as chief librarian, and upon written application by the Department of Cultural Resources for issuance of a temporary certificate to an unqualified person who is available for the position, a temporary certificate, valid for one year only, may be issued to such persons by the Public Librarian Certification Commission. (1955, c. 505, s. 3; 1973, c. 476, ss. 53, 84.)

§ 125-11. Failure to return books.

Any person who shall fail to return any book, periodical, or other material withdrawn by him from the Library shall be guilty of a Class 3 misdemeanor if he shall fail to return the borrowed material within 30 days after receiving a notice from the State Librarian that the material is overdue. The provisions of this section shall not be in effect unless a copy of this section is attached to the overdue notice by the State Librarian. (1955, c. 505, s. 3; 1993, c. 539, s. 929; 1994, Ex. Sess., c. 24, s. 14(c).)

§§ 125-11.1 through 125-11.4. Reserved for future codification purposes.

Article 1A.

State Depository Library System.

§ 125-11.5. Purpose.

The purpose of this Article is to establish a depository system for the distribution of State publications to designated libraries throughout the State in order to facilitate public access to publications issued by State agencies. (1987, c. 771, s. 2.)

§ 125-11.6. Definitions.

As used in this Article:

(1) "Depository library" means a library designated to receive and maintain State publications and make them available to the public.

(2) "Document" means any printed document including any report, directory, statistical compendium, bibliography, map, regulation, newsletter, pamphlet, brochure, periodical, bulletin, compilation, or register, regardless of whether the printed document is in paper, film, tape, disk, or any other format.

(3) "State agency" means every State department, institution, board, and commission.

(4) "State publication" means any document prepared by a State agency or private organization, consultant, or research firm, under contract with or under the supervision of a State agency: Provided, however, the term "State publication" does not include administrative documents used only within the issuing agency, documents produced for instructional purposes that are not intended for sale or publication, appellate division reports and advance sheets distributed by the Administrative Office of the Courts, the S.B.I. Investigative "Bulletin", documents that will be reproduced in the Senate or House of Representatives Journals, or documents that are confidential pursuant to Article 17 of Chapter 120 of the General Statutes. (1987, c. 771, s. 2.)

§ 125-11.7. State Library designated the official depository for all State publications.

The State Library shall be the official, complete, and permanent depository for all State publications, and shall receive five copies of all State publications in addition to the copies required for the depository system: Provided, however, the State Library shall receive only five copies of any State publication offered for sale by a State agency at a price at least high enough to recover production costs: Provided, further, the State Library, notwithstanding the definition of "State publication" contained in this Article, shall have authority to exclude from required deposit in the State Library any items or materials which it finds are not appropriate for deposit. (1987, c. 771, s. 2.)

§ 125-11.8. State Publications Clearinghouse created.

(a)   A State Publications Clearinghouse is created within the Department of Cultural Resources, the Division of State Library.

(b)   The Clearinghouse shall:

(1)   Advise State agencies annually of the number of copies of State publications needed for distribution.

(2)   Advise State agencies annually that they are required to submit only five copies of any State publication offered for sale at a price at least high enough to recover production costs.

(3)   Receive from State agencies promptly after publication the number of copies of State publications specified, and distribute these to the depository libraries.

(4)   Prepare on microfiche one or more copies of each State publication that is printed on paper for reference and interlibrary loan purposes.

(5)   Publish a checklist of State publications and distribute the checklist without charge to all requesting North Carolina libraries.

(6)   Forward two copies of all State publications that are printed on paper to the Library of Congress. (1987, c. 771, s. 2.)

§ 125-11.9. Powers and duties of the State Library.

The State Library:

(1)   Shall carry out the provisions of this Article.

(2)   Develop and maintain standards for depository libraries. The standards shall include the ability to receive, process, organize, retain, and make available State publications and the ability to provide reference assistance and interlibrary loan service for depository publications.

(3)   Shall designate depository libraries, taking into account regional distribution and number of persons served, such that State publications will be conveniently accessible to residents in all areas of the State. The State Library may designate at least one library in each congressional district.

(4)   May designate as selective depository libraries those institutions that wish to receive less than the full deposit. Selective depository libraries shall meet the same standards for reference and interlibrary loan service as full depository libraries.

(5)   May enter into depository contracts with public libraries and community, technical, special, college and university libraries that meet the standards for depository eligibility adopted by the Clearinghouse.

(6)   Shall determine how many copies of State publications each State agency must submit for the State depository system. The State Library may permit a State agency to submit fewer copies of a document if the State Library determines that fewer copies are adequate in light of the cost of the document and the projected public interest in the document.

(7)   Shall adopt rules to administer the depository program. These rules may include the State Library's priorities and resulting schedules for collecting, maintaining, and making available State publications in various formats. (1987, c. 771, s. 2; 1991, c. 636, s. 14.)

§ 125-11.10. Duties of State agencies.

(a) State agencies shall send the requested number of copies of each of their publications to the Clearinghouse within 10 days of issuance.

(b) The head of each State agency shall designate a publications officer who shall be responsible for supplying the requested number of copies of each State publication of that agency to the Clearinghouse. Each agency shall notify the Clearinghouse of the identity of its publications officer before October 1, 1987, and within 30 days of any change of publications officer. The publications officer shall supply the Clearinghouse semiannually a complete list of the agency's State publications issued within the previous six months and any other information regarding the publications of the agency requested by the Clearinghouse.

(c) State agencies may request permission from the State Library to submit fewer than the requested number of copies of a document. The request shall include information on the cost of the document and the projected public interest in the document. (1987, c. 771, s. 2.)

§ 125-11.11. Advisory Committee.

The Secretary of Cultural Resources may appoint an advisory committee of State officials and depository librarians to review and advise on the operation of the depository system. (1987, c. 771, s. 2.)

§ 125-11.12: Repealed by Session Laws 1993, c. 447, s. 1.

§ 125-11.13. Alkaline paper required for government publications.

(a) State publications that are of historical or enduring value and importance to the citizens of North Carolina shall be printed on alkaline (acid-free) paper. These publications shall be designated on an annual basis by the State Librarian and the University Librarian at the University of North Carolina at Chapel Hill and shall include publications of an historical, biographical, legal, or statistical nature relating to the State of North Carolina, past, present, or future. These publications shall identify thereon, adjacent to the name of the agency responsible for publication, a statement that the publication is printed on permanent paper.

(b) By November 1 of each year, the State Librarian and the University Librarian at the University of North Carolina at Chapel Hill shall designate the titles for publication on alkaline paper and shall notify each State agency that is responsible for the publication of a designated title. An agency so notified shall begin printing the designated title on alkaline paper within one year after receipt of the notification or at the awarding of the contract for the publication, whichever event occurs first. The Coordinator of the North Carolina State Publications Clearinghouse shall monitor compliance with this requirement and shall transmit a copy of the compliance report to the State Librarian and to the University Librarian at the University of North Carolina at Chapel Hill by October 1 of each year.

(c) The State Librarian and the University Librarian at the University of North Carolina at Chapel Hill shall report by November 1 of each year to the Joint Legislative Commission on Governmental Operations regarding the titles designated for printing on alkaline paper and shall include in the report the compliance report received from the Coordinator of the North Carolina State Publications Clearinghouse. (1991, c. 224, s. 1.)

Article 2.

Interstate Library Compact.

§ 125-12. Compact enacted into law; form.

The Interstate Library Compact is hereby enacted into law and entered into by this State with all states legally joining therein in the form substantially as follows:

INTERSTATE LIBRARY COMPACT.

Article I. POLICY AND PURPOSE.

Because the desire for the services provided by libraries transcends governmental boundaries and can most effectively be satisfied by giving such services to communities and people regardless of jurisdictional lines, it is the policy of the states party to this Compact to cooperate and share their responsibilities; to authorize cooperation and sharing with respect to those types of library facilities and services which can be more economically or efficiently developed and maintained on a cooperative basis, and to authorize cooperation and sharing among localities, states and others in providing joint or cooperative library services in areas where the distribution of population or of existing and potential library resources make the provision of library service on an interstate basis the most effective way of providing adequate and efficient service.

Article II. DEFINITIONS.

As used in this Compact: (a) "Public library agency" means any unit or agency of local or state government operating or having power to operate a library.

(b)   "Private library agency" means any nongovernmental entity which operates or assumes a legal obligation to operate a library.

(c)   "Library agreement" means a contract establishing an interstate library district pursuant to this Compact or providing for the joint or cooperative furnishing of library services.

Article III. INTERSTATE LIBRARY DISTRICTS.

(a)   Any one or more public library agencies in a party state in cooperation with any public library agency or agencies in one or more other party states may establish and maintain an interstate library district. Subject to the provisions of this Compact and any other laws of the party states which pursuant hereto remain applicable, such district may establish, maintain and operate some or all of the library facilities and services for the area concerned in accordance with the terms of a library agreement therefor. Any private library agency or agencies within an interstate library district may cooperate therewith, assume duties, responsibilities and obligations thereto, and receive benefits therefrom as provided in any library agreement to which such agency or agencies become party.

(b)   Within an interstate library district, and as provided by a library agreement, the performance of library functions may be undertaken on a joint or cooperative basis or may be undertaken by means of one or more arrangements between or among public or private library agencies for the extension of library privileges to the use of facilities or services operated or rendered by one or more of the individual library agencies.

(c)   If a library agreement provides for joint establishment, maintenance or operation of library facilities or services by an interstate library district, such district shall have power to do any one or more of the following in accordance with such library agreement:

(1)   Undertake, administer and participate in programs or arrangements for securing, lending or servicing of books and other publications, any other materials suitable to be kept or made available by libraries, library equipment or for the dissemination of information about libraries, the value and significance of particular items therein, and the use thereof.

(2)   Accept for any of its purposes under this Compact any and all donations, and grants of money, equipment, supplies, materials, and services, (conditional or otherwise), from any state or the United States or any subdivision or agency thereof, or interstate agency, or from any institution, person, firm or corporation, and receive, utilize and dispose of the same.

(3)   Operate mobile library units or equipment for the purpose of rendering bookmobile service within the district.

(4)   Employ professional, technical, clerical and other personnel, and fix terms of employment, compensation and other appropriate benefits; and where desirable, provide for the in-service training of such personnel.

(5)   Sue and be sued in any court of competent jurisdiction.

(6)   Acquire, hold, and dispose of any real or personal property or any interest or interests therein as may be appropriate to the rendering of library service.

(7) Construct, maintain and operate a library, including any appropriate branches thereof.

(8) Do such other things as may be incidental to or appropriate for the carrying out of any of the foregoing powers.

Article IV. INTERSTATE LIBRARY DISTRICTS, GOVERNING BOARD.

(a) An interstate library district which establishes, maintains or operates any facilities or services in its own right shall have a governing board which shall direct the affairs of the district and act for it in all matters relating to its business. Each participating public library agency in the district shall be represented on the governing board which shall be organized and conduct its business in accordance with provision therefor in the library agreement. But in no event shall a governing board meet less often than twice a year.

(b) Any private library agency or agencies party to a library agreement establishing an interstate library district may be represented on or advise with the governing board of the district in such manner as the library agreement may provide.

Article V. STATE LIBRARY AGENCY COOPERATION.

Any two or more state library agencies of two or more of the party states may undertake and conduct joint or cooperative library programs, render joint or cooperative library services, and enter into and perform arrangements for the cooperative or joint acquisition, use, housing and disposition of items or collections of materials which, by reason of expense, rarity, specialized nature, or infrequency of demand therefor would be appropriate for central collection and shared use. Any such programs, services or arrangements may include provision for the exercise on a cooperative or joint basis of any power exercisable by an interstate library district and an agreement embodying any such program, service or arrangement shall contain provisions covering the subjects detailed in Article VI of this Compact for interstate library agreements.

Article VI. LIBRARY AGREEMENTS.

(a) In order to provide for any joint or cooperative undertaking pursuant to this Compact, public and private library agencies may enter into library agreements. Any agreement executed pursuant to the provisions of this Compact shall, as among the parties to the agreement:

(1) Detail the specific nature of the services, programs, facilities, arrangements or properties to which it is applicable.

(2) Provide for the allocation of costs and other financial responsibilities.

(3) Specify the respective rights, duties, obligations and liabilities of the parties.

(4) Set forth the terms and conditions for duration, renewal, termination, abrogation, disposal of joint or common property, if any, and all other matters which may be appropriate to the proper effectuation and performance of the agreement.

(b) No public or private library agency shall undertake to exercise itself, or jointly with any other library agency, by means of a library agreement any power prohibited to such agency by the constitution or statutes of its state.

(c) No library agreement shall become effective until filed with the Compact Administrator of each state involved, and approved in accordance with Article VII of this Compact.

Article VII. APPROVAL OF LIBRARY AGREEMENTS.

(a)   Every library agreement made pursuant to this Compact shall, prior to and as a condition precedent to its entry into force, be submitted to the attorney general of each state in which a public library agency party thereto is situated, who shall determine whether the agreement is in proper form and compatible with the laws of his state. The attorneys general shall approve any agreement submitted to them unless they shall find that it does not meet the conditions set forth herein and shall detail in writing addressed to the governing bodies of the public library agencies concerned the specific respects in which the proposed agreement fails to meet the requirements of law. Failure to disapprove an agreement submitted hereunder within 90 days of its submission shall constitute approval thereof.

(b)   In the event that a library agreement made pursuant to this Compact shall deal in whole or in part with the provision of services or facilities with regard to which an officer or agency of the state government has constitutional or statutory powers of control, the agreement shall, as a condition precedent to its entry into force, be submitted to the state officer or agency having such power of control and shall be approved or disapproved by him or it as to all matters within his or its jurisdiction in the same manner and subject to the same requirements governing the action of the attorneys general pursuant to subsection (a) of this Article. This requirement of submission and approval shall be in addition to and not in substitution for the requirement of submission to and approval by the attorneys general.

Article VIII. OTHER LAWS APPLICABLE.

Nothing in this Compact or in any library agreement shall be construed to supersede, alter or otherwise impair any obligation imposed on any library by otherwise applicable law, nor to authorize the transfer or disposition of any property held in trust by a library agency in a manner contrary to the terms of such trust.

Article IX. APPROPRIATIONS AND AID.

(a) Any public library agency party to a library agreement may appropriate funds to the interstate library district established thereby in the same manner and to the same extent as to a library wholly maintained by it and, subject to the laws of the state in which such public library agency is situated, may pledge its credit in support of an interstate library district established by the agreement.

(b) Subject to the provisions of the library agreement pursuant to which it functions and the laws of the states in which such district is situated, an interstate library district may claim and receive any state and federal aid which may be available to library agencies.

Article X. COMPACT ADMINISTRATOR.

Each state shall designate a Compact Administrator with whom copies of all library agreements to which his state or any public library agency thereof is party shall be filed. The Administrator shall have such other powers as may be conferred upon him by the laws of his state and may consult and cooperate with the compact administrators of other party states and take such steps as may effectuate the purposes of this Compact. If the laws of a party state so provide, such state may designate one or more deputy Compact administrators in addition to its Compact Administrator.

Article XI. ENTRY INTO FORCE AND WITHDRAWAL.

(a) This Compact shall enter into force and effect immediately upon its enactment into law by any two states. Thereafter, it shall enter into force and effect as to any other state upon the enactment thereof by such state.

(b) This Compact shall continue in force with respect to a party state and remain binding upon such state until six months after such state has given notice to each other party state of the repeal thereof. Such withdrawal shall not be construed to relieve any party to a library agreement entered into pursuant to this Compact from any obligation of that agreement prior to the end of its duration as provided therein.

Article XII. CONSTRUCTION AND SEVERABILITY.

This Compact shall be liberally construed so as to effectuate the purposes thereof. The provisions of this Compact shall be severable and if any phrase, clause, sentence or provision of this Compact is declared to be contrary to the constitution of any party state or of the United States or the applicability thereof to any government, agency, person or circumstance is held invalid, the validity of the remainder of this Compact and the applicability thereof to any government, agency, person or circumstance shall not be affected thereby. If this Compact shall be held contrary to the constitution of any state party thereto, the Compact shall remain in full force and effect as to the remaining states and in full force and effect as to the state affected as to all severable matters. (1967, c. 190, s. 1.)

§ 125-13. Political subdivisions to comply with laws governing capital outlay and pledging of credit.

No county, municipality, or other political subdivision of this State shall be party to a library agreement which provides for the construction or maintenance of a library pursuant to Article III, subdivision (c)(7) of the Compact, nor pledge its credit in support of such a library, or contribute to the capital financing thereof, except after compliance with any laws applicable to such counties, municipalities, or other political subdivisions relating to or governing capital outlays and the pledging of credit. (1967, c. 190, s. 2.)

§ 125-14. "State library agency" defined.

As used in the Compact, "state library agency," with reference to this State, means the Department of Cultural Resources. (1967, c. 190, s. 3; 1973, c. 476, s. 84.)

§ 125-15. State and federal aid to interstate library districts.

An interstate library district lying partly within this State may claim and be entitled to receive State aid in support of any of its functions to the same extent and in the same manner as such functions are eligible for support when carried on by entities wholly within this State. For the purposes of computing and apportioning State aid to an interstate library district, this State will consider that portion of the area which lies within this State as an independent entity for the performance of the aided function or functions and compute and apportion the aid accordingly. Subject to any applicable laws of this State, such a district also may apply for and be entitled to receive any federal aid for which it may be eligible. (1967, c. 190, s. 4.)

§ 125-16. Compact Administrator and deputies.

The State Librarian shall be the Compact Administrator pursuant to Article X of the Compact. The State Librarian may appoint one or more deputy Compact Administrators pursuant to said Article. (1967, c. 190, s. 5.)

§ 125-17. Withdrawal from Compact.

In the event of withdrawal from the Compact the Governor shall send and receive any notices required by Article XI(b) of the Compact. (1967, c. 190, s. 6.)

Article 3.

Library Records.

§ 125-18. Definitions.

As used in this Article, unless the context requires otherwise:

(1) "Library" means a library established by the State; a county, city, township, village, school district, or other local unit of government or authority or

combination of local units of governments and authorities; community college or university; or any private library open to the public.

(2)   "Library record" means a document, record, or other method of storing information retained by a library that identifies a person as having requested or obtained specific information or materials from a library. "Library record" does not include nonidentifying material that may be retained for the purpose of studying or evaluating the circulation of library materials in general. (1985, c. 486, s. 2.)

§ 125-19. Confidentiality of library user records.

(a)   Disclosure. - A library shall not disclose any library record that identifies a person as having requested or obtained specific materials, information, or services, or as otherwise having used the library, except as provided for in subsection (b).

(b)   Exceptions. - Library records may be disclosed in the following instances:

(1)   When necessary for the reasonable operation of the library;

(2)   Upon written consent of the user; or

(3)   Pursuant to subpoena, court order, or where otherwise required by law. (1985, c. 486, s. 2.)

Chapter 126.

State Personnel System [State Human Resources System].

Article 1.

State Personnel System [State Human Resources System] Established.

§ 126-1. Purpose of Chapter; application to local employees.

It is the intent and purpose of this Chapter to establish for the government of the State a system of personnel administration under the Governor, based on accepted principles of personnel administration and applying the best methods as evolved in government and industry. It is also the intent of this Chapter that this system of personnel administration shall apply to local employees paid entirely or in part from federal funds, except to the extent that local governing boards are authorized by this Chapter to establish local rules, local pay plans, and local personnel systems. It is also the intent of this Chapter to make provisions for a decentralized system of personnel administration, where appropriate, and without additional cost to the State, with the State Human Resources Commission as the policy and rule-making body. The Office of State Human Resources shall make recommendations for policies and rules to the Commission based on research and study in the field of personnel management, develop and administer statewide standards and criteria for good personnel management, provide training and technical assistance to all agencies, departments, and institutions, provide oversight, which includes conducting audits to monitor compliance with established State Human Resources Commission policies and rules, administer a system for implementing necessary corrective actions when the rule, standards, or criteria are not met, and serve as the central repository for State Personnel System [State Human Resources System] data. The agency, department, and institution heads shall be responsible and accountable for execution of Commission policies and rules for their employees. (1965, c. 640, s. 2; 1997-349, s. 1; 2013-382, s. 9.1(c).)

§ 126-1.1. Career State employee defined.

(a) For the purposes of this Chapter, unless the context clearly indicates otherwise, "career State employee" means a State employee or an employee of a local entity who is covered by this Chapter pursuant to G.S. 126-5(a)(2) who:

(1) Is in a permanent position, and

(2) Has been continuously employed by the State of North Carolina or a local entity as provided in G.S. 126-5(a)(2) in a position subject to the North Carolina Human Resources Act for the immediate 24 preceding months.

(b) As used in this Chapter, "probationary State employee" means a State employee who is in a probationary appointment and is exempt from the provisions of the North Carolina Human Resources Act only because the employee has not been continuously employed by the State for the time period required by subsection (a) of this section. (1995, c. 141, s. 1; 2007-372, s. 1; 2013-382, ss. 3.1, 9.1(c).)

§ 126-1A: Repealed by Session Laws 1995, c. 141, s. 2.

§ 126-2. State Human Resources Commission.

(a)   There is hereby established the State Human Resources Commission (hereinafter referred to as "the Commission").

(b)   Repealed by Session Laws 2013-382, s. 2.1, effective August 21, 2013.

(b1)   The Commission shall consist of nine members, appointed as follows:

(1)   One member appointed by the General Assembly upon the recommendation of the Speaker of the House of Representatives who shall be an attorney licensed to practice law in North Carolina.

(2)   One member appointed by the General Assembly upon the recommendation of the President Pro Tempore of the Senate who shall be an attorney licensed to practice law in North Carolina.

(3)   One member appointed by the General Assembly upon the recommendation of the Speaker of the House of Representatives who shall be from private business or industry and who shall have a working knowledge of, or practical experience in, human resources management.

(4)   One member appointed by the General Assembly upon the recommendation of the President Pro Tempore of the Senate who shall be from private business or industry and who shall have a working knowledge of, or practical experience in, human resources management.

(5)   One member who is a veteran of the Armed Forces of the United States appointed by the Governor upon the nomination of the Veterans Affairs Commission and who is a State employee subject to this Chapter serving in a nonexempt supervisory position. The member may not be a human resources professional.

(6) One member appointed by the Governor who is a State employee subject to this Chapter serving in a nonexempt nonsupervisory position. The member may not be a human resources professional. The Governor shall consider nominations submitted by the State Employees Association of North Carolina.

(7) One member appointed by the Governor upon the recommendation of the North Carolina Association of County Commissioners who is a local government employee subject to this Chapter serving in a supervisory position. The member may not be a human resources professional.

(8) One member appointed by the Governor upon the recommendation of the North Carolina Association of County Commissioners who is a local government employee subject to this Chapter serving in a nonsupervisory position. The member may not be a human resources professional.

(9) One member of the public at large appointed by the Governor.

(c) Each member of the Commission shall be appointed for a term of four years. Members of the Commission may serve no more than two consecutive terms. Appointments by the General Assembly shall be made in accordance with G.S. 120-121, and vacancies in those appointments shall be filled in accordance with G.S. 120-122. Vacancies in appointments made by the Governor occurring prior to the expiration of a term shall be filled by appointment for the unexpired term.

(d) No member of the Commission may serve on a case where there would be a conflict of interest. The appointing authority may at any time remove any Commission member for cause.

(e) Members of the Commission who are State or local government employees subject to this Chapter shall be entitled to administrative leave without loss of pay for all periods of time required to conduct the business of the Commission.

(f) Five members of the Commission shall constitute a quorum.

(g) The Governor shall designate one member of the Commission as chair.

(h) The Commission shall meet quarterly, and at other times at the call of the chair. (1965, c. 640, s. 2; 1975, c. 667, ss. 2-4; 1989, c. 540; 1998-181, s.

1(a), (b); 2000-140, s. 29; 2007-287, s. 1; 2011-183, s. 90; 2013-382, ss. 2.1, 9.1(c).)

§ 126-3. Office of State Human Resources established and responsibilities outlined; administration and supervision; appointment, compensation and tenure of Director.

(a) There is hereby established the Office of State Human Resources (hereinafter referred to as "the Office") which shall be placed for organizational purposes within the Office of the Governor. Notwithstanding the provisions of North Carolina State government reorganization as of January 1, 1975, and specifically notwithstanding the provisions of Chapter 864 of the 1971 North Carolina Session Laws, Chapter 143A of the General Statutes, the Office of State Human Resources shall exercise all of its statutory powers in this Chapter, which shall be under the administration and supervision of a Director of the Office of State Human Resources (hereinafter referred to as "the Director") appointed by the Governor and subject to the supervision of the Commission for purposes of this Chapter. The salary of the Director shall be fixed by the Governor. The Director shall serve at the pleasure of the Governor.

(b) The Office shall be responsible for the following activities, and such other activities as specified in this Chapter:

(1) Providing policy and rule development for the Commission and implementing and administering all policies, rules, and procedures established by the Commission.

(2) Providing training in personnel management to agencies, departments, and institutions including train-the-trainer programs for those agencies, departments, and institutions who request such training and where sufficient staff and expertise exist to provide the training within their respective agencies, departments, and institutions.

(3) Providing technical assistance in the management of personnel programs and activities to agencies, departments, and institutions.

(4) Negotiating decentralization agreements with all agencies, departments, and institutions where it is cost-effective to include delegation of authority for

certain classification and corresponding salary administration actions and other personnel programs to be specified in the agreements.

(5) Administering such centralized programs and providing services as approved by the Commission which have not been transferred to agencies, departments, and institutions or where this authority has been rescinded for noncompliance.

(6) Providing approval authority of personnel actions involving classification and compensation where such approval authority has not been transferred by the Commission to agencies, departments, and institutions or where such authority has been rescinded for noncompliance.

(7) Maintaining a computer database of all relevant and necessary information on employees and positions within agencies, departments, and institutions in the State's personnel system.

(8) Developing criteria and standards to measure the level of compliance or noncompliance with established Commission policies, rules, procedures, criteria, and standards in agencies, departments, and institutions to which authority has been delegated for classification, salary administration, performance management, development, evaluation, and other decentralized programs, and determining through routine monitoring and periodic review process, that agencies, departments, and institutions are in compliance or noncompliance with established Commission policies, rules, procedures, criteria, and standards.

(9) Implementing corrective actions in cases of noncompliance.

(10) Administering the State employee suggestion program (NC-Thinks). (1965, c. 640, s. 2; 1975, c. 667, s. 5; 1983, c. 717, s. 40; 1983 (Reg. Sess., 1984), c. 1034, s. 164; 1997-349, s. 2; 2011-224, s. 5; 2012-142, s. 25.1(c); 2012-194, s. 25; 2013-382, ss. 1.1, 1.2, 9.1(c).)

§ 126-4. Powers and duties of State Human Resources Commission.

Subject to the approval of the Governor, the State Human Resources Commission shall establish policies and rules governing each of the following:

(1) Position classification plans which shall provide for the classification and reclassification of all positions subject to this Chapter according to the duties and responsibilities of the positions.

(2) Compensation plans which shall provide for minimum, maximum, and intermediate rates of pay for all employees subject to the provisions of this Chapter.

(3) For each class of positions, reasonable qualifications as to education, experience, specialized training, licenses, certifications, and other job-related requirements pertinent to the work to be performed.

(4) Recruitment programs designed to promote public employment, communicate current hiring activities within State government, and attract a sufficient flow of internal and external applicants; and determine the relative fitness of applicants for the respective positions.

(5) Hours and days of work, holidays, vacation, sick leave, and other matters pertaining to the conditions of employment. The legal public holidays established by the Commission as paid holidays for State employees shall include Martin Luther King, Jr.'s Birthday and Veterans Day. The Commission shall not provide for more than 12 paid holidays per year, with three paid holidays being given for Christmas.

(5a) In years in which New Year's Day falls on Saturday, the Commission may designate December 31 of the previous calendar year as the New Year's holiday, provided that the number of holidays for the previous calendar year does not exceed 12 and the number of holidays for the current year does not exceed 10. When New Year's Day falls on either Saturday or Sunday, the constituent institutions of The University of North Carolina that adopt alternative dates to recognize the legal public holidays set forth in subdivision (5) of this section and established by the Commission may designate, in accordance with the rules of the Commission and the requirements of this subdivision, December 31 of the previous calendar year as the New Year's holiday.

(5b) A leave program that allows employees to volunteer in a literacy program in a public school for up to five hours each month.

(6) The appointment, promotion, transfer, demotion and suspension of employees.

(7) Cooperation with the State Board of Education, the Department of Public Instruction, the University of North Carolina, and the Community Colleges of the State and other appropriate resources in developing programs in, including but not limited to, management and supervisory skills, performance evaluation, specialized employee skills, accident prevention, equal employment opportunity awareness, and customer service; and to maintain an accredited Certified Public Manager program.

(7a) The separation of employees.

(8) A program of meritorious service awards.

(9) The investigation of complaints and the issuing of such binding corrective orders or such other appropriate action concerning employment, promotion, demotion, transfer, discharge, reinstatement, and any other issue defined as a contested case issue by this Chapter in all cases as the Commission shall find justified.

(10) Programs of employee assistance, productivity incentives, equal opportunity, safety and health as required by Part 1 of Article 63 of Chapter 143 of the General Statutes, and such other programs and procedures as may be necessary to promote efficiency of administration and provide for a fair and modern system of personnel administration. This subdivision may not be construed to authorize the establishment of an incentive pay program.

(11) In cases where the Commission finds discrimination, harassment, or orders reinstatement or back pay whether (i) heard by the Commission or (ii) appealed for limited review after settlement or (iii) resolved at the agency level, the assessment of reasonable attorneys' fees and witnesses' fees against the State agency involved.

(12) Repealed by Session Laws 1987, c. 320, s. 2.

(13) Repealed by Session Laws 1987, c. 320, s. 3.

(14) The implementation of G.S. 126-5(e).

(15) Recognition of State employees, public personnel management, and management excellence.

(16) The implementation of G.S. 126-7.

(17) An alternative dispute resolution procedure.

(18) Delegation of authority for approval of personnel actions through decentralization agreements with the heads of State agencies, departments, and institutions.

a. Decentralization agreements with Executive Branch agencies shall require a person, designated in the agency, to be accountable to the Director of the Office of State Human Resources for the compliance of all personnel actions taken pursuant to the delegated authority of the agency. Such agreements shall specify the required rules and standards for agency personnel administration.

b. The Director of the Office of State Human Resources shall have the authority to take appropriate corrective actions including adjusting employee salaries and changing employee classifications that are not in compliance with policy or standards and to suspend decentralization agreements for agency noncompliance with the required personnel administration standards.

The policies and rules of the Commission shall not limit the power of any elected or appointed department head, in the department head's discretion and upon the department head's determination that it is in the best interest of the Department, to transfer, demote, or separate a State employee who is not a career State employee as defined by this Chapter. (1965, c. 640, s. 2; 1971, c. 1244, s. 14; 1975, c. 667, ss. 6, 7; 1977, c. 288, s. 1; c. 866, ss. 1, 17, 20; 1985, c. 617, ss. 2, 3; c. 791, s. 50(b); 1985 (Reg. Sess., 1986), c. 1028, s. 6; 1987, c. 25, s. 2; c. 320, ss. 1-3; 1991, c. 65, s. 1; c. 354, s. 2; c. 750, s. 1; 1991 (Reg. Sess., 1992), c. 994, s. 2; 1993, c. 388, s. 2; c. 522, s. 10; 1995, c. 141, s. 4; 1997-349, s. 3; 1998-135, s. 1; 2013-360, s. 9.1; 2013-382, ss. 1.3, 9.1(c).)

§ 126-4.1: Repealed by Session Laws 2011-398, s. 41, effective January 1, 2012, and applicable to contested cases commenced on or after that date.

§ 126-5. Employees subject to Chapter; exemptions.

(a) The provisions of this Chapter shall apply to:

(1) All State employees not herein exempt, and

(2) All employees of the following local entities:

a. Area mental health, developmental disabilities, and substance abuse authorities, except as otherwise provided in Chapter 122C of the General Statutes.

b. Local social services departments.

c. County health departments and district health departments.

d. Local emergency management agencies that receive federal grant-in-aid funds.

An employee of a consolidated county human services agency created pursuant to G.S. 153A-77(b) is not considered an employee of an entity listed in this subdivision.

(3) County employees not included under subdivision (2) of this subsection as the several boards of county commissioners may from time to time determine.

(b) As used in this section:

(1) "Exempt position" means an exempt managerial position or an exempt policymaking position.

(2) "Exempt managerial position" means a position delegated with significant managerial or programmatic responsibility that is essential to the successful operation of a State department, agency, or division, so that the application of G.S. 126-35 to an employee in the position would cause undue disruption to the operations of the agency, department, institution, or division.

(3) "Exempt policymaking position" means a position delegated with the authority to impose the final decision as to a settled course of action to be followed within a department, agency, or division, so that a loyalty to the Governor or other elected department head in their respective offices is reasonably necessary to implement the policies of their offices. The term shall not include personnel professionals.

(4) "Personnel professional" means any employee in a State department, agency, institution, or division whose primary job duties involve administrative

personnel and human resources functions for that State department, agency, institution, or division.

(c) Except as to the policies, rules, and plans established by the Commission pursuant to G.S. 126-4(1), 126-4(2), 126-4(3), 126-4(4), 126-4(5), 126-4(6), and 126-7, and except as to the provisions of Articles 6 and 7 of this Chapter, the provisions of this Chapter shall not apply to:

(1) A State employee who is not a career State employee as defined by this Chapter.

(2) One confidential assistant and two confidential secretaries for each elected or appointed department head and one confidential secretary for each chief deputy or chief administrative assistant.

(3) Employees in exempt policymaking positions designated pursuant to G.S. 126-5(d).

(4) The chief deputy or chief administrative assistant to the head of each State department who is designated either by statute or by the department head to act for and perform all of the duties of such department head during his absence or incapacity.

(c1) Except as to the provisions of Articles 6 and 7 of this Chapter, the provisions of this Chapter shall not apply to:

(1) Constitutional officers of the State.

(2) Officers and employees of the Judicial Department.

(3) Officers and employees of the General Assembly.

(4) Members of boards, committees, commissions, councils, and advisory councils compensated on a per diem basis.

(5) Officials or employees whose salaries are fixed by the General Assembly, or by the Governor, or by the Governor and Council of State, or by the Governor subject to the approval of the Council of State.

(6) Employees of the Office of the Governor that the Governor, at any time, in the Governor's discretion, exempts from the application of the provisions of

this Chapter by means of a letter to the Director of the Office of State Human Resources designating these employees.

(7)   Employees of the Office of the Lieutenant Governor, that the Lieutenant Governor, at any time, in the Lieutenant Governor's discretion, exempts from the application of the provisions of this Chapter by means of a letter to the Director of the Office of State Human Resources designating these employees.

(8)   Instructional and research staff, physicians, and dentists of The University of North Carolina, including the faculty of the North Carolina School of Science and Mathematics.

(8a)   Employees of a regional school established pursuant to Part 10 of Article 16 of Chapter 115C of the General Statutes.

(9)   Employees whose salaries are fixed under the authority vested in the Board of Governors of The University of North Carolina by the provisions of G.S. 116-11(4), 116-11(5), and 116-14.

(9a)   Employees of the North Carolina Cooperative Extension Service of North Carolina State University who are employed in county operations and who are not exempt pursuant to subdivision (8) or (9) of this subsection.

(10)   Repealed by Session Laws 1991, c. 84, s. 1.

(11)   Repealed by Session Laws 2006-66, s. 9.11(z), effective July 1, 2007.

(12),   (13) Repealed by Session Laws 2001-474, s. 15, effective November 29, 2001.

(14)   Employees of the North Carolina State Ports Authority.

(15)   Employees of the North Carolina Global TransPark Authority.

(16)   The executive director and one associate director of the North Carolina Center for Nursing established under Article 9F of Chapter 90 of the General Statutes.

(17)   Repealed by Session Laws 2004-129, s. 37, effective July 1, 2004.

(18) Employees of the Tobacco Trust Fund Commission established in Article 75 of Chapter 143 of the General Statutes.

(19) Employees of the Health and Wellness Trust Fund Commission established in Article 21 of Chapter 130A of the General Statutes.

(20) Repealed by Session Laws 2008-134, s. 73(d), effective July 28, 2008.

(21) Employees of the Clean Water Management Trust Fund.

(22) Employees of the North Carolina Turnpike Authority.

(23) The Executive Administrator and the Deputy Executive Administrator of the State Health Plan for Teachers and State Employees.

(24) Employees of the State Health Plan for Teachers and State Employees as designated by law or by the Executive Administrator of the Plan.

(25) The North Carolina State Lottery Director and employees of the North Carolina State Lottery.

(26) Repealed by Session Laws 2011-145, s. 7.31(c), as added by Session Laws 2011-391, s. 17, and by Session Laws 2011-266, s. 1.37(c), effective July 1, 2011.

(27) The Chief Administrative Law Judge of the Office of Administrative Hearings.

(28) The Executive Director and the Assistant Director of the U.S.S. North Carolina Battleship Commission.

(29) The Executive Director, Deputy Director, all other directors, assistant and associate directors, and center fellows of the North Carolina Center for the Advancement of Teaching.

(30) Employees of the Department of Commerce employed in the Rural Economic Development Division.

(c2) The provisions of this Chapter shall not apply to:

(1) Public school superintendents, principals, teachers, and other public school employees.

(2) Recodified as G.S. 126-5(c)(4) by Session Laws 1985 (Regular Session, 1986), c. 1014, s. 41.

(3) Employees of community colleges whose salaries are fixed in accordance with the provisions of G.S. 115D-5 and G.S. 115D-20, and employees of the Community Colleges System Office whose salaries are fixed by the State Board of Community Colleges in accordance with the provisions of G.S. 115D-3.

(4) Employees of the Office of Proprietary Schools whose salaries are fixed by the State Board of Proprietary Schools in accordance with the provisions of G.S. 115D-89.2.

(c3) Except as to the policies, rules, and plans established by the Commission pursuant to G.S. 126-4(5) and the provisions of Article 6 of this Chapter, the provisions of this Chapter shall not apply to: Teaching and related educational classes of employees of the Division of Adult Correction of the Department of Public Safety, the Department of Health and Human Services, and any other State department, agency or institution, whose salaries shall be set in the same manner as set for corresponding public school employees in accordance with Chapter 115C of the General Statutes.

(c4) Repealed by Session Laws 1993, c. 321, s. 145(b).

(c5) Notwithstanding any other provision of this Chapter, Article 14 of this Chapter shall apply to all State employees, public school employees, and community college employees.

(c6) Article 15 of this Chapter shall apply to all State employees, public school employees, and community college employees.

(c7) Except as to the policies, rules, and plans established by the Commission pursuant to G.S. 126-4(1), 126-4(2), 126-4(3), 126-4(4), 126-4(5), 126-4(6), 126-7, 126-14.3, and except as to the provisions of G.S. 126-14.2, G.S. 126-34.1(a)(2), and Articles 6 and 7 of this Chapter, the provisions of this Chapter shall not apply to exempt managerial positions.

(c8) Except as to the provisions of Articles 5, 6, 7, and 14 of this Chapter, the provisions of this Chapter shall not apply to:

(1) Employees of the University of North Carolina Health Care System.

(2) Employees of the University of North Carolina Hospitals at Chapel Hill, as may be provided pursuant to G.S. 116-37(a)(4).

(3) Employees of the clinical patient care programs of the School of Medicine of the University of North Carolina at Chapel Hill as may be provided pursuant to G.S. 116-37(a)(4).

(4) Employees of the Medical Faculty Practice Plan, a division of the School of Medicine of East Carolina University.

(c9) Notwithstanding any other provision of this section, the provisions of Article 16 of this Chapter shall apply to all exempt and nonexempt State employees in the executive, legislative, and judicial branches unless provided otherwise by Article 16 of this Chapter. The provisions of Article 16 of this Chapter shall not apply to employees described in subdivisions (2) and (3) of subsection (a) of this section.

(c10) Notwithstanding any other provision of this section, the provisions of G.S. 126-8.5 shall apply to all exempt and nonexempt State employees in the executive, legislative, and judicial branch unless provided otherwise by G.S. 126-8.5. The provisions of G.S. 126-8.5 shall not apply to employees described in subdivisions (2) and (3) of subsection (a) of this section.

(c11) The following are exempt from: (i) the classification and compensation rules established by the State Human Resources Commission pursuant to G.S. 126-4(1) through (4); (ii) G.S. 126-4(5) only as it applies to hours and days of work, vacation, and sick leave; (iii) G.S. 126-4(6) only as it applies to promotion and transfer; (iv) G.S. 126-4(10) only as it applies to the prohibition of the establishment of incentive pay programs; and (v) Article 2 of Chapter 126 of the General Statutes, except for G.S. 126-7.1:

(1) The Office of the Commissioner of Banks and its employees; and

(2) The following employees of the Department of Cultural Resources:

a. Director and Associate Directors of the North Carolina Museum of History.

b. Program Chiefs and Curators.

c. Regional History Museum Administrators and Curators.

d. North Carolina Symphony.

e. Director, Associate Directors, and Curators of Tryon Palace.

f. Director, Associate Directors, and Curators of Transportation Museum.

g. Director and Associate Directors of the North Carolina Arts Council.

h. Director, Assistant Directors, and Curators of the Division of State Historic Sites.

(d) (1) Exempt Positions in Cabinet Department. - Subject to the provisions of this Chapter, which is known as the North Carolina Human Resources Act, the Governor may designate a total of 1,500 exempt positions throughout the following departments and offices:

a. Department of Administration.

b. Department of Commerce.

c. Repealed by Session Laws 2012-83, s. 7, effective June 26, 2012, and by Session Laws 2012-142, s. 25.2E(a), effective January 1, 2013.

d. Department of Public Safety.

e. Department of Cultural Resources.

f. Department of Health and Human Services.

g. Department of Environment and Natural Resources.

h. Department of Revenue.

i. Department of Transportation.

j.   Repealed by Session Laws 2012-83, s. 7, effective June 26, 2012, and by Session Laws 2012-142, s. 25.2E(a), effective January 1, 2013.

k.   Office of Information Technology Services.

l.   Office of State Budget and Management.

m.   Office of State Human Resources.

(2)   Exempt Positions in Council of State Departments and Offices. -

The Secretary of State, the Auditor, the Treasurer, the Attorney General, the Commissioner of Agriculture, the Commissioner of Insurance, and the Labor Commissioner may designate exempt positions. The State Board of Education may designate exempt positions in the Department of Public Instruction. The number of exempt policymaking positions in each department headed by an elected department head listed above in this sub-subdivision shall be limited to 20 exempt policymaking positions or one percent (1%) of the total number of full-time positions in the department, whichever is greater. The number of exempt managerial positions shall be limited to 20 positions or one percent (1%) of the total number of full-time positions in the department, whichever is greater.

(2a)   Designation of Additional Positions. - The Governor, elected department head, or State Board of Education may request that additional positions be designated as exempt. The request shall be made by sending a list of exempt positions that exceed the limit imposed by this subsection to the Speaker of the North Carolina House of Representatives and the President of the North Carolina Senate. A copy of the list also shall be sent to the Director of the Office of State Human Resources. The General Assembly may authorize all, or part of, the additional positions to be designated as exempt positions. If the General Assembly is in session when the list is submitted and does not act within 30 days after the list is submitted, the list shall be deemed approved by the General Assembly, and the positions shall be designated as exempt positions. If the General Assembly is not in session when the list is submitted, the 30-day period shall not begin to run until the next date that the

General Assembly convenes or reconvenes, other than for a special session called for a specific purpose not involving the approval of the list of additional positions to be designated as exempt positions; the policymaking positions shall not be designated as exempt during the interim.

(3) Letter. - These positions shall be designated in a letter to the Director of the Office of State Human Resources, the Speaker of the House of Representatives, and the President of the Senate by July 1 of the year in which the oath of office is administered to each Governor unless the provisions of subsection (d)(4) apply.

(4) Vacancies. - In the event of a vacancy in the Office of Governor or in the office of a member of the Council of State, the person who succeeds to or is appointed or elected to fill the unexpired term shall make such designations in a letter to the Director of the Office of State Human Resources, the Speaker of the House of Representatives, and the President of the Senate within 180 days after the oath of office is administered to that person. In the event of a vacancy in the Office of Governor, the State Board of Education shall make these designations in a letter to the Director of the Office of State Human Resources, the Speaker of the House of Representatives, and the President of the Senate within 180 days after the oath of office is administered to the Governor.

(5) Creation, Transfer, or Reorganization. - The Governor, elected department head, or State Board of Education may designate as exempt a position that is created or transferred to a different department, or is located in a department in which reorganization has occurred, after October 1 of the year in which the oath of office is administered to the Governor. The designation must be made in a letter to the Director of the Office of State Human Resources, the Speaker of the North Carolina House of Representatives, and the President of the North Carolina Senate within 180 days after such position is created, transferred, or in which reorganization has occurred.

(6) Reversal. - Subsequent to the designation of a position as an exempt position as hereinabove provided, the status of the position may be reversed and made subject to the provisions of this Chapter by the Governor, by an elected department head, or by the State Board of Education in a letter to the Director of the Office of State Human Resources, the Speaker of the North Carolina House of Representatives, and the President of the North Carolina Senate.

(7) Hearing Officers. - Except as otherwise specifically provided by this section, no employee, by whatever title, whose primary duties include the power to conduct hearings, take evidence, and enter a decision based on findings of fact and conclusions of law based on statutes and legal precedents shall be designated as exempt. This subdivision shall apply beginning July 1, 1985, and

no list submitted after that date shall designate as exempt any employee described in this subdivision.

(e) (Repealed for State employees hired on or after August 21, 2013) An exempt employee may be transferred, demoted, or separated from his or her position by the department head authorized to designate the exempt position except:

(1) When an employee who has the minimum service requirements described in G.S. 126-1.1 but less than 10 years of cumulative service in subject positions prior to placement in an exempt position is removed from an exempt position, for reasons other than just cause, the employee shall have priority to any position that becomes available for which the employee is qualified, according to rules and regulations regulating and defining priority as promulgated by the State Human Resources Commission; or

(2) When an employee who has 10 years or more cumulative service, including the immediately preceding 12 months, in subject positions prior to placement in an exempt position is removed from an exempt position, for reasons other than just cause, the employee shall be reassigned to a subject position within the same department or agency, or if necessary within another agency, and within a 35 mile radius of the exempt position, at the same grade and salary, including all across-the-board increases since placement in the position designated as exempt, as his most recent subject position.

(f) (Repealed for State employees hired on or after August 21, 2013) A department head is authorized to use existing budgeted positions within his department in order to carry out the provisions of subsection (e) of this section. If it is necessary to meet the requirements of subsection (e) of this section, a department head may use salary reserve funds authorized for his department.

(g) No employee shall be placed in an exempt position without 10 working days prior written notification that such position is so designated. A person applying for a position that is designated as exempt must be notified in writing at the time he makes the application that the position is designated as exempt.

(h) In case of dispute as to whether an employee is subject to the provisions of this Chapter, the dispute shall be resolved as provided in Article 3 of Chapter 150B. (1965, c. 640, s. 2; 1967, c. 24, s. 20; cc. 1038, 1143; 1969, c. 982; 1971, c. 1025, s. 2; 1973, c. 476, s. 143; 1975, c. 667, ss. 8, 9; 1977, c. 866, ss. 2-5; 1979, 2nd Sess., c. 1137, s. 40; 1983, c. 717, s. 41; c. 867, s. 2;

1985, c. 589, s. 38; c. 617, s. 1; c. 757, s. 206(c); 1985 (Reg. Sess., 1986), c. 955, s. 43; c. 1014, ss. 41, 235; c. 1022, s. 9; 1987, c. 320, s. 4; c. 395, s. 1; c. 809, s. 1; c. 850, s. 19; 1987 (Reg. Sess., 1988), c. 1064, s. 3; 1989, c. 168, s. 9; c. 236, s. 3; c. 484; c. 727, s. 218(85); c. 751, s. 7(13); 1991, c. 65, s. 2; c. 84, ss. 1, 2; c. 354, s. 3; c. 749, s. 4; 1991 (Reg. Sess., 1992), c. 879, s. 5; c. 959, s. 85; 1993, c. 145, s. 1; c. 321, s. 145(b); c. 553, ss. 39, 40; 1993 (Reg. Sess., 1994), c. 777, s. 4(g); 1995, c. 141, ss. 3, 5; c. 393, s. 1; 1995 (Reg. Sess., 1996), c. 690, s. 15; 1997-443, ss. 11A.118(a), 11A.119(a), 22.2(b); 1997-520, s. 3; 1998-212, s. 11.8(b); 1999-84, s. 21; 1999-253, s. 1; 1999-434, s. 25; 2000-137, s. 4(nn); 200

0-147, s. 4; 2000-148, s. 3; 2001-92, s. 2; 2001-424, s. 32.16(a); 2001-474, s. 15; 2001-487, ss. 21(d), 30(a), (b); 2002-126, s. 28.4; 2002-133, s. 4; 2004-124, s. 31.27(b); 2004-129, s. 37; 2005-276, s. 29.34(b); 2005-344, s. 9; 2006-66, ss. 9.11(y), (z), 9.17(e), 18.2(e); 2006-204, s. 2; 2006-221, s. 20; 2006-259, s. 49; 2006-264, s. 11; 2007-117, s. 3(b); 2007-195, s. 1; 2007-323, s. 28.22A(o); 2007-345, s. 12; 2007-484, s. 9(c); 2008-134, s. 73(d); 2009-451, ss. 9.13(f), 27.31(c); 2011-145, ss. 7.31(c), 19.1(g), (h), (l); 2011-241, s. 5; 2011-266, s. 1.37(c); 2011-391, s. 17; 2012-83, s. 7; 2012-142, ss. 8.9A(c), 25.2E(a); 2012-151, s. 11(a); 2013-360, s. 15.10(d); 2013-382, ss. 4.1, 4.3, 4.4, 4.5, 9.1(c); 2013-410, s. 47.2(b).)

§ 126-6: Repealed by Session Laws 1991, c. 65, s. 3.

§ 126-6.1: Repealed by Session Laws 1993, c. 397, s. 1.

§ 126-6.2. Reports.

(a) Beginning January 1, 1998, and quarterly thereafter, the head of each State agency, department, or institution employing State employees subject to the North Carolina Human Resources Act shall report to the Office of State Human Resources on the following:

(1) The costs associated with the defense or settlement of administrative grievances and lawsuits filed by current or former State employees and applicants for State employment, including the costs of settlements, attorneys' fees, litigation expenses, damages, or awards incurred by the respective State agencies, departments, and institutions. The report shall include an explanation

of the fiscal impact of these costs upon the operations of the State agency, department, or institution.

(2) Any other human resources functions or actions as may be requested by the Director of the Office of State Human Resources in order for the Office to evaluate the efficiency, productivity, and compliance of a State agency, department, or institution with policies, including, but not limited to, the compensation of State employees, voluntary shared-leave programs, equal employment opportunity plans and programs, and work options programs.

(b) Beginning May 1, 1998, and annually thereafter, the State Human Resources Commission shall report to the Joint Legislative Commission on Governmental Operations on the costs associated with the defense or settlement of lawsuits, and upon request, on the results of any other reports regarding human resources action or functions pursuant to subsection (a) of this section.

(c) Repealed by Session Laws 2013-382, s. 7.5, effective August 21, 2013. (1997-520, s. 8(a)-(c); 2013-382, ss. 7.5, 9.1(c).)

Article 2.

Salaries, Promotions, and Leave of State Employees.

§ 126-7: Repealed. See editor's note.

§ 126-7.1. Posting requirement; State employees receive priority consideration; reduction-in-force; Work First hiring.

(a) All vacancies for which any State agency, department, or institution openly recruit shall be posted in a place readily accessible to employees within at least the following:

(1) The personnel office of the agency, department, or institution having the vacancy; and

(2) The particular work unit of the agency, department, or institution having the vacancy.

If the decision is made, initially or at any time while the vacancy remains open, to receive applicants from outside the recruiting agency, department, or institution, the vacancy shall also be listed on a website maintained by the Office of State Human Resources for the purpose of informing current State employees and the public of such vacancy. The State agency, department, or institution may not receive approval from the Office of State Human Resources to fill a job vacancy if the agency, department, or institution cannot prove to the satisfaction of the Office of State Human Resources that it complied with these posting requirements. The agency, department, or institution which hires any person in violation of these posting requirements shall pay such person when employment is discontinued as a result of such violation for the work performed during the period of time between his initial employment and separation.

(b) State employees to be affected by a reduction in force shall be notified of the reduction in force as soon as practicable, and in any event, no less than 30 days prior to the effective date of the reduction in force.

(c) The State Human Resources Commission shall adopt rules to provide that State employees separated from State employment as the result of reductions in force who accept a position in State government shall be paid a salary no higher than the maximum of the salary grade of the position accepted.

(d) Subsection (a) of this section does not apply to vacancies which must be filled immediately to prevent work stoppage or the protection of the public health, safety, or security.

(e) If a State employee subject to this section:

(1) Applies for another position of State employment that would constitute a promotion; and

(2) Has substantially equal qualifications as an applicant who is not a State employee;

then the State employee shall receive priority consideration over the applicant who is not a State employee. This priority consideration shall not apply when the only applicants considered for the vacancy are current State employees.

(f) If a State employee who has been separated due to reduction in force or who has been given notice of imminent separation due to reduction in force:

(1) Applies for another position of State employment equal to or lower in salary grade than the position held by the employee at the time of notification or separation; and

(2) Has substantially equal qualifications as any other applicant;

then within all State agencies, the State employee who has been notified of or separated due to a reduction in force shall receive priority consideration over all other applicants. This priority shall remain in effect for a period of 12 months from the date the employee receives notification of separation by reduction in force. State employees separated due to reduction in force shall receive higher priority than other applicants with employment or reemployment priorities, except that the reemployment priority created by G.S. 126-5(e)(1) shall be considered as equal.

(f1) If a State employee who has been separated due to reduction in force or who has been given notice of imminent separation due to reduction in force accepts or rejects an offer for a position of State employment that is equal to or higher than the position held or equal to or higher than the salary earned by the employee at the time of separation or notification, then the employee's acceptance or rejection of that offer shall satisfy and terminate the one-time, 12-month priority granted by subsection (f) of this section.

(g) "Qualifications" within the meaning of subsection (e) of this section shall consist of:

(1) Training or education;

(2) Years of experience; and

(3) Other skills, knowledge, and abilities that bear a reasonable functional relationship to the abilities and skills required in the job vacancy applied for.

(h) Each State agency, department, and institution is encouraged to hire into State government employment qualified applicants who are current or former Work First Program participants.

(i) Each State agency, department, institution, university, community college, and local education agency shall verify, in accordance with the Basic Pilot Program administered by the United States Department of Homeland Security pursuant to 8 U.S.C. § 1101, et seq, each individual's legal status or authorization to work in the United States after hiring the individual as an employee to work in the United States. (1987, c. 689, s. 2; 1991, c. 65, s. 4; c. 474, s. 1; 1995, c. 141, s. 9; c. 507, s. 7.20(a); 1997-443, s. 12.7(d); 2006-259, s. 23.1(a); 2011-145, s. 29.21A(a); 2011-391, s. 59(a), (b); 2013-382, ss. 5.1, 9.1(c).)

§ 126-7.2: Repealed by Session Laws 2013-382, s. 6.2, effective August 21, 2013, and applicable to grievances filed on or after that date.

§ 126-7.3. Annual compensation surveys.

To guide the Governor and the General Assembly in making decisions regarding the compensation of State employees, the Office of State Human Resources shall conduct annual compensation surveys. The Commission shall present the results of the compensation survey to the Appropriations Committees of the House of Representatives and the Senate no later than two weeks after the convening of the legislature in odd-numbered years and May 1st of even-numbered years. (2013-382, ss. 7.9(b), 9.1(c).)

§ 126-8. Minimum leave granted State employees.

The amount of vacation leave granted to each full-time State employee subject to the provisions of this Chapter shall be determined in accordance with a graduated scale established by the State Human Resources Commission which shall allow the equivalent rate of not less than two weeks' vacation per calendar year, prorated monthly, cumulative to at least 30 days. On December 31 of each year, any State employee who has vacation leave in excess of the allowed accumulation shall have that leave converted to sick leave. Sick leave allowed as needed to such State employees shall be at a rate not less than 10 days for each calendar year, cumulative from year to year. Notwithstanding any other provisions of this section, no full-time State employee subject to the provisions of Chapter 126, as the same appears in the Cumulative Supplement to Volume 3B of the General Statutes, on May 23, 1973, shall be allowed less than the equivalent of three weeks' vacation per calendar year, cumulative to at least 30 days. (1965, c. 640, s. 2; 1973, c. 697, ss. 1, 2; 1975, c. 667, s. 2; 1993, c. 321, s. 73(f); c. 561, s. 18(a); 2013-382, s. 9.1(c).)

§ 126-8.1. Paid leave for certain athletic competition.

(a)   As used in this section, the term "United States team" includes any group leader, coach, official, trainer, or athlete who is a member of an official United States delegation in Pan American, Olympic or international athletic competition.

(b)   Any State employee or public school employee paid by State funds who has been chosen to be a member of a United States team for Pan American, Olympic or international competition shall be granted paid leave, in addition to annual and sick leave that person is otherwise entitled to, for the sole purpose of training for and competing in that competition. The paid leave shall be for the period of the official training camp and competition or 30 days a year, whichever is less.

(c)   The Department of Administration may adopt such rules and regulations as are reasonable and necessary to carry out the provisions of this section, with the approval of the Governor. (1979, c. 708; 1983, c. 717, s. 42; 1985, (Reg. Sess., 1986), c. 955, ss. 44, 45; 2006-203, s. 69.)

§ 126-8.2. Replacement of law-enforcement officer on final sick leave.

When a sworn law-enforcement officer employed by the State is on sick leave, and the head of the department employing the officer has obtained a certification from a physician that the officer will not recover and return to duty, a replacement for the officer may be hired even though the resulting number of employees in the department exceeds the number for which an appropriation was made in the Current Operations Appropriations Act, if sufficient funds are available from appropriations to the department for salaries to pay the salary of both the new employee and the officer on sick leave until the officer's accumulated leave is exhausted or his employment is terminated. (1983 (Reg. Sess., 1984), c. 1034, s. 105.)

§ 126-8.3. Voluntary shared leave.

(a) The State Human Resources Commission, in cooperation with the State Board of Community Colleges and the State Board of Education, shall adopt rules and policies to allow any employee at a State agency to share leave voluntarily with an immediate family member who is an employee of a State agency, community college, or public school; and with a coworker's immediate family member who is an employee of a State agency, community college, or public school. For the purposes of this section, the term "immediate family member" means a spouse, parent, child, brother, sister, grandparent, or grandchild. The term includes the step, half, and in-law relationships. The term "coworker" means that the employee donating the leave is employed by the same agency, department, institution, university, local school administrative unit, or community college as the employee whose immediate family member is receiving the leave.

(b) The State Human Resources Commission shall adopt rules and policies for the voluntary shared leave program to allow an employee at a State agency to donate sick leave to a nonfamily member employee of a State agency. A donor of sick leave to a nonfamily member recipient shall not donate more than five days of sick leave per year to any one nonfamily member recipient. The combined total of sick leave donated to a recipient from nonfamily member donors shall not exceed 20 days per year. Donated sick leave shall not be used for retirement purposes, and employees who donate sick leave shall be notified in writing of the State retirement credit consequences of donating sick leave.

(c) The State Human Resources Commission, the State Board of Education, and the State Board of Community Colleges and all State agencies, departments, and [institutions] shall annually report to the Office of State Human Resources on the voluntary shared leave program. For the prior fiscal year, the report shall include the total number of days or hours of vacation leave and sick leave donated and used by voluntary shared leave recipients and the total cost of the vacation leave and sick leave donated and used. (1999-170, s. 1; 2003-9, s. 1; 2003-284, s. 30.14A(a); 2010-139, ss. 1, 3; 2013-382, ss. 7.8, 9.1(c).)

§ 126-8.4. (See note on condition precedent) No sick leave taken for absences by State employees resulting from adverse reactions to vaccination.

(a)   Absence from work by an employee shall not count against the employee's sick leave, and the employee's salary shall continue during the absence when the employee receives in employment vaccination against smallpox incident to the Administration of Smallpox Countermeasures by Health Professionals, section 304 of the Homeland Security Act, Pub. L. No. 107-296 (Nov. 25, 2002) (to be codified at 42 U.S.C. § 233(p)) and the absence is due to the employee having an adverse medical reaction resulting from the vaccination. The provisions of this subsection shall apply for a maximum of 480 employment hours. The employing department, agency, institution, or entity may require the employee to obtain certification from a health care provider justifying the need for leave after the first 24 hours of leave taken pursuant to this subsection.

(b)   Absence from work by an employee shall not count against the employee's sick leave, and the employee's salary shall continue during the absence when the employee is permanently or temporarily living in the home of a person who receives in employment vaccination against smallpox incident to the Administration of Smallpox Countermeasures by Health Professionals, section 304 of the Homeland Security Act, Pub. L. No. 107-296 (Nov. 25, 2002) (to be codified at 42 U.S.C. § 233(p)) and the absence is due to (i) the employee having an adverse medical reaction resulting from exposure to the vaccinated person, or (ii) the need to care for the vaccinated person who has an adverse medical reaction resulting from the vaccination. The provisions of this subsection shall apply for a maximum of 480 employment hours. The employing department, agency, institution, or entity may require the employee to obtain certification from a health care provider justifying the need for leave after the first 24 hours of leave taken pursuant to this subsection.

(c)   Notwithstanding any other provisions of this Chapter, this section applies to all State employees. (2003-169, s. 4.)

§ 126-8.5. Discontinued service retirement allowance and severance wages for certain State employees.

(a) When the Director of the Budget determines that the closing of a State institution or a reduction in force will accomplish economies in the State Budget, he shall pay either a discontinued service retirement allowance or severance wages to any affected State employee, provided reemployment is not available. As used in this section, "economies in the State Budget" means economies resulting from elimination of a job and its responsibilities or from a lack of funds to support the job. In determining whether to pay a discontinued service retirement allowance or severance wages, the Director of the Budget shall consider the recommendation of the department head involved and any recommendation of the Director of the Office of State Human Resources. Severance wages shall not be paid to an employee who chooses a discontinued service retirement. Severance wages shall not be subject to employer or employee retirement contributions. Severance wages shall be paid according to the policies adopted by the State Human Resources Commission.

Notwithstanding any other provisions of the State's retirement laws, any employee of the State who is a member of the Teachers' and State Employees' Retirement System or the Law-Enforcement Officers' Retirement System and who has his job involuntarily terminated as a result of economies in the State Budget may be entitled to a discontinued service retirement allowance, subject to the approval of the employing agency and the availability of agency funds. An unreduced discontinued service retirement allowance, not otherwise allowed, may be approved for employees with 20 or more years of creditable retirement service who are at least 55 years of age; or a discontinued service retirement allowance, not otherwise allowed, may be approved for employees with 20 or more years of creditable retirement service who are at least 50 years of age, reduced by one-fourth of one percent (1/4 of 1%) for each month that retirement precedes his fifty-fifth birthday. In cases where a discontinued service retirement allowance is approved, the employing agency shall make a lump sum payment to the Administrator of the State Retirement Systems equal to the actuarial present value of the additional liabilities imposed upon the System, to be determined by the System's consulting actuary, as a result of the discontinued service retirement, plus an administrative fee to be determined by the Administrator.

The salary used to determine severance wages under this section is the last annual salary except that if the employee was promoted within the previous 12 months, the last annual salary is that annual salary prior to the promotion. If the annual salary prior to the promotion is used, it shall be adjusted to account for any across-the-board legislative salary increases. Excluded from any calculation are any benefits such as, but not limited to, overtime pay, shift pay, holiday premium, or longevity pay.

(b)　Any employee separated from State government and paid severance wages under this section shall not be employed under a contractual arrangement by any State agency, other than the constituent institutions of The University of North Carolina and the constituent institutions of the North Carolina Community College System, until 12 months have elapsed since the separation. This subsection does not affect any reduction in force rights that the employee may have. (1979, c. 838, s. 22; 1983, c. 761, s. 225; c. 923, s. 217(R); 1983 (Reg. Sess., 1984), c. 1034, s. 251; 1985 (Reg. Sess., 1986), c. 981, s. 1; c. 1024, s. 20; 1987, c. 177, s. 2; 1989 (Reg. Sess., 1990), c. 1066, s. 36(a); 1998-212, s. 28.28(a); 2006-203, s. 6; 2013-382, s. 9.1(c).)

Article 3.

Local Discretion as to Local Government Employees.

§ 126-9. County or municipal employees may be made subject to rules adopted by local governing body.

(a)　When a board of county commissioners adopts rules and regulations governing annual leave, sick leave, hours of work, holidays, and the administration of the pay plan for county employees generally and the county rules and regulations are filed with the Director of the Office of State Human Resources, the county rules will supersede the rules adopted by the State Human Resources Commission as to the county employees otherwise subject to the provisions of this Chapter.

(b)　No county employees otherwise subject to the provisions of this Chapter may be paid a salary less than the minimum nor more than the maximum of the applicable salary range adopted in accordance with this Chapter without approval of the State Human Resources Commission. Provided, however, that subject to the approval of the State Human Resources Commission, a board of county commissioners may adjust the salary ranges applicable to employees who are otherwise subject to the provisions of this Chapter, in order to cause the level of pay to conform to local financial ability and fiscal policy. The State

Human Resources Commission shall adopt policies and regulations to ensure that significant relationships within the schedule of salary ranges are maintained.

(c) When two or more counties are combined into a district for the performance of an activity whose employees are subject to the provisions of this Chapter, the boards of county commissioners of the counties may jointly exercise the authority hereinabove granted in subsections (a) and (b) of this section.

(d) When a municipality is performing an activity by or through employees which are subject to the provisions of this Chapter, the governing body of the municipality may exercise the authority hereinabove granted in subsections (a) and (b) of this section. (1965, c. 640, s. 2; 1975, c. 667, s. 2; 2013-382, s. 9.1(c).)

§ 126-10. Personnel services to local governmental units.

The State Human Resources Commission may make the services and facilities of the Office of State Human Resources available upon request to the political subdivisions of the State. The State Human Resources Commission may establish reasonable charges for the service and facilities so provided, and all funds so derived shall be deposited in the State treasury to the credit of the general fund. (1965, c. 640, s. 2; 1975, c. 667, ss. 2, 12; 2013-382, s. 9.1(c).)

§ 126-11. Local personnel system may be established; approval and monitoring; rules and regulations.

(a) The board of county commissioners of any county may establish and maintain a personnel system for all employees of the county subject to its jurisdiction, which system and any substantial changes to the system, shall be approved by the State Human Resources Commission as substantially equivalent to the standards established under this Chapter for employees of local departments of social services, local health departments, and area mental health programs, local emergency management programs. If approved by the State Human Resources Commission, the employees covered by the county system shall be exempt from all provisions of this Chapter except Article 6.

(a1) With approval of each of the boards of commissioners of the county or counties which comprise the area mental health authority, the area mental health authority may establish and maintain a personnel system for all employees of the area mental health authority, which system and any substantial changes to the system, shall be equivalent to the standards established under this Chapter for employees of area mental health authorities. If approved by the State Human Resources Commission, the employees covered by the area mental health authority system shall be exempt from all provisions of this Chapter except Article 6.

(b) A board of county commissioners may petition the State Human Resources Commission to determine whether any portion of its total personnel system meets the requirements in (a) above. Upon such determination, county employees shall be exempt from the provisions of this Chapter relating to the approved portions of the county personnel system.

(b1) The board of an area mental health authority, with the approval of each of the boards of commissioners of the county or counties which comprise the area mental health authority, may petition the State Human Resources Commission to determine whether any portion of its total personnel system meets the requirements in subsection (a1) above. Upon such determination, area mental health authority employees shall be exempt from the provisions of this Chapter relating to the approved portions of the area mental health authority personnel system except as provided in G.S. 122C-121.

(c) The Office of State Human Resources shall monitor at least annually county or area mental health authority personnel systems approved under this section in order to ensure compliance.

(d) In order to define "substantially equivalent," the State Human Resources Commission is authorized to promulgate rules and regulations to implement the federal merit system standards and these regulations at a minimum shall include: recruitment and selection of employees; position classification; pay administration; training; employee relations; equal employment opportunity; and records and reports. (1965, c. 640, s. 2; 1975, c. 667, s. 2; 1983, c. 674, s. 1; 1991, c. 65, s. 5; c. 564, s. 1; 2013-382, s. 9.1(c).)

Article 4.

Competitive Service.

§ 126-12. Governor and Council of State to determine competitive service.

The Governor, with the approval of the Council of State, shall from time to time determine for which, if any of the positions subject to the provisions of Article 1 of this Chapter, appointments and promotions shall be based on a competitive system of selection. (1965, c. 640, s. 2.)

Article 5.

Political Activity of Employees.

§ 126-13. Appropriate political activity of State employees defined.

(a) As an individual, each State employee retains all the rights and obligations of citizenship provided in the Constitution and laws of the State of North Carolina and the Constitution and laws of the United States of America; however, no State employee subject to the North Carolina Human Resources Act or temporary State employee shall:

(1) Take any active part in managing a campaign, or campaign for political office or otherwise engage in political activity while on duty or within any period of time during which he is expected to perform services for which he receives compensation from the State;

(2) Otherwise use the authority of his position, or utilize State funds, supplies or vehicles to secure support for or oppose any candidate, party, or issue in an election involving candidates for office or party nominations, or affect the results thereof.

(b) No head of any State department, agency, or institution or other State employee exercising supervisory authority shall make, issue, or enforce any rule or policy the effect of which is to interfere with the right of any State employee as an individual to engage in political activity while not on duty or at times during which he is not performing services for which he receives compensation from the State. A State employee who is or may be expected to perform his duties on a twenty-four hour per day basis shall not be prevented from engaging in political activity except during regularly scheduled working hours or at other times when he is actually performing the duties of his office. The willful violation of this subdivision shall be a Class 1 misdemeanor. (1967, c. 821, s. 1; 1985, c. 469, s. 1; c. 617, s. 5; 1993, c. 539, s. 930; 1994, Ex. Sess., c. 24, s. 14(c); 2013-382, s. 9.1(c).)

§ 126-14. Promise or threat to obtain political contribution or support.

(a)   It is unlawful for a State employee or a person appointed to State office, other than elective office or office on a board, commission, committee, or council whose function is advisory only, whether or not subject to the North Carolina Human Resources Act, to coerce:

(1)   a State employee subject to the North Carolina Human Resources Act,

(2)   a probationary State employee,

(3)   a temporary State employee, or

(4)   an applicant for a position subject to the North Carolina Human Resources Act

to support or contribute to a political candidate, political committee as defined in G.S. 163-278.6, or political party or to change the party designation of the individual's voter registration by threatening that change in employment status or discipline or preferential personnel treatment will occur with regard to an individual listed in subdivisions (1) through (4) of this subsection.

(a1)   It is unlawful for an individual as defined in G.S. 138A-3(30)a. to coerce a person as described in G.S. 138A-32(d)(1), (2), or (3) to support or contribute to a political candidate, a political committee as defined in G.S. 163-278.6, or a political party by threatening discipline or promising preferential treatment with regard to that person's business with the individual's State office or that person's activities regulated by the individual's State office.

(b)   Any person violating this section shall be guilty of a Class 2 misdemeanor.

(c) A State employee subject to the North Carolina Human Resources Act, probationary State employee, or temporary State employee who without probable cause falsely accuses a State employee or a person appointed to State office of violating this section shall be subject to discipline or change in employment status in accordance with the provisions of G.S. 126-35, 126-37, and 126-38 and may, as otherwise provided by law, be subject to criminal penalties for perjury or civil liability for libel, slander, or malicious prosecution. (1967, c. 821, s. 1; 1985, c. 469, s. 2; 1991, c. 505, s. 1; 1993, c. 539, s. 931; 1994, Ex. Sess., c. 24, s. 14(c); 2010-169, s. 1(a); 2013-382, s. 9.1(c).)

§ 126-14.1. Threat to obtain political contribution or support.

(a) It is unlawful for any person to coerce:

(1) a State employee subject to the North Carolina Human Resources Act,

(2) a probationary State employee,

(3) a temporary State employee, or

(4) an applicant for a position subject to the North Carolina Human Resources Act

to support or contribute to a political candidate, political committee as defined in G.S. 163-278.6, or political party or to change the party designation of his voter registration by explicitly threatening that change in employment status or discipline or preferential personnel treatment will occur with regard to any person listed in subdivisions (1) through (3) of this subsection.

(b) Any person violating this section shall be guilty of a Class 2 misdemeanor.

(c) A State employee subject to the North Carolina Human Resources Act, probationary State employee, or temporary State employee, who without probable cause falsely accuses a person of violating this section shall be subject to discipline or change in employment status in accordance with the provisions of G.S. 126-34.02 and may, as otherwise provided by law, be subject to criminal penalties for perjury or civil liability for libel, slander, or malicious prosecution. (1985, c. 469, s. 3; 1991, c. 505, s. 2; 1993, c. 539, s. 932; 1994, Ex. Sess., c. 24, s. 14(c); 2013-382, ss. 6.3, 9.1(c).)

§ 126-14.2. Political hirings limited.

(a) It is the policy of this State that State departments, agencies, and institutions select from the pool of the most qualified persons for State government employment based upon job-related qualifications of applicants for employment using fair and valid selection criteria.

(b) All State departments, agencies, and institutions shall select from the pool of the most qualified persons for State government employment without regard to political affiliation or political influence. For the purposes of this section, the "most qualified persons" shall mean each of the State employees or applicants for initial State employment who:

(1) Have timely applied for a position in State government;

(2) Have the essential qualifications for that position; and

(3) Are determined to be substantially more qualified as compared to other applicants for the position, after applying fair and valid job selection criteria, in accordance with G.S. 126-5(e), G.S. 126-7.1, Articles 6 and 13 of this Chapter, and State personnel policies approved by the State Human Resources Commission.

(c) It is a violation of this section giving rise to the remedies set forth in G.S. 126-14.4 if:

(1) The complaining State employee or applicant for initial State employment timely applied for the State government position in question;

(2) The complaining State employee or applicant for initial State employment was not hired into the position;

(3) The complaining State employee or applicant for initial State employment was among the most qualified persons applying for the position as defined in this Chapter;

(4) The successful applicant for the position was not among the most qualified persons applying for the position; and

(5) The hiring decision was based upon political affiliation or political influence.

(d) The provisions of this section shall not apply to positions exempt from this Chapter, except that this section does apply to exempt managerial positions as defined by G.S. 126-5(b)(2). (1997-520, s. 1; 2013-382, s. 9.1(c).)

§ 126-14.3. Open and fair competition.

The State Human Resources Commission shall adopt rules or policies to:

(1) Assure recruitment, selection, and hiring procedures that encourage open and fair competition for positions in State government employment and that encourage the hiring of a diverse State government workforce.

(2) Assure the proper and thorough advertisement of job openings in State government employment and lengthen, as appropriate, the period for submitting applications for State government employment.

(3) Require that a closing date shall be posted for each job opening, unless an exception for critical classifications has been approved by the State Human Resources Commission.

(4) Require that timely written notice shall be provided to each unsuccessful applicant for State employment who is in the pool of the most qualified applicants for a position, as defined by G.S. 126-14.2(b).

(5) Assure that State departments, agencies, and institutions follow similar selection processes when hiring State employees in accordance with this Chapter.

(6) Assure that State supervisory and management personnel, and personnel professionals, receive adequate training and continuing education to carry out the State's policy of hiring from among the most qualified persons.

(7) Establish a monitoring system to measure the effectiveness of State agency personnel procedures to promote fairness and reduce adverse impact on all demographic groups in the State government workforce.

(8) Otherwise implement the State's policy of nonpolitical hiring practices in accordance with this Chapter. (1997-520, s. 1; 2013-382, s. 9.1(c).)

§ 126-14.4: Repealed by Session Laws 2013-382, s. 7.6, effective August 21, 2013.

§ 126-15. Disciplinary action for violation of Article.

Failure to comply with this Article is grounds for disciplinary action which, in case of deliberate or repeated violation, may include dismissal or removal from office. (1967, c. 821, s. 1.)

§ 126-15.1: Repealed by Session Laws 2013-382, s. 3.2, effective August 21, 2013.

Article 6.

Equal Employment and Compensation Opportunity; Assisting in Obtaining State Employment.

§ 126-16. Equal opportunity for employment and compensation by State departments and agencies and local political subdivisions.

All State agencies, departments, and institutions and all local political subdivisions of North Carolina shall give equal opportunity for employment and compensation, without regard to race, religion, color, national origin, sex, age, disability, or genetic information to all persons otherwise qualified. (1971, c.

823; 1975, c. 158; 1977, c. 866, s. 7; 1979, c. 862, s. 3; 1983 (Reg. Sess., 1984), c. 1116, s. 111; 1985, c. 571, s. 2; 1991, c. 65, s. 6; 2013-382, s. 7.1.)

§ 126-16.1. Equal employment opportunity training.

Each State agency, department, and institution and The University of North Carolina shall enroll each newly appointed supervisor or manager within one year of appointment in the Equal Employment Opportunity training offered or approved by the Office of State Human Resources. (1991, c. 416, s. 1; 2013-382, ss. 7.2, 9.1(c).)

§ 126-17. Retaliation by State departments and agencies and local political subdivisions.

No State department, agency, or local political subdivision of North Carolina shall retaliate against an employee for protesting alleged violations of G.S. 126-16. (1977, c. 866, s. 8.)

§ 126-18. Compensation for assisting person in obtaining State employment barred; exception.

It shall be unlawful for any person, firm or corporation to collect, accept or receive any compensation, consideration or thing of value for obtaining on behalf of any other person, or aiding or assisting any other person in obtaining employment with the State of North Carolina; provided, however, any person, firm, or corporation that is duly licensed and supervised by the North Carolina Department of Labor as a private employment service acting in the normal course of business, may collect such regular and customary fees for services rendered pursuant to a written contract when such fees are paid by someone other than the State of North Carolina; however, any person, firm, or corporation collecting fees for this service must have been licensed by the North Carolina Department of Labor for a period of not less than one year.

Any person, firm or corporation collecting fees for this service must make a monthly report to the Department of Labor listing the name of the person, firm or corporation collecting fees and the person for whom a job was found, the nature and purpose of the job obtained, and the fee collected by the person, firm or corporation collecting the fee. Violation of this section shall constitute a Class 1 misdemeanor. (1977, c. 397, s. 1; 1993, c. 539, s. 933; 1994, Ex. Sess., c. 24, s. 14(c).)

§ 126-19. Equal employment opportunity plans; reports; maintenance of services by Director of the Office of State Human Resources.

(a) Each member of the Council of State under G.S. 143A-11, each of the principal departments enumerated in G.S. 143B-6, The University of North Carolina, the judicial branch, and the legislative branch, shall develop and submit on an annual basis an Equal Employment Opportunity plan which shall include goals and programs that provide positive measures to assure equitable and fair representation of North Carolina's citizens. The plans developed by the judicial branch and by the Legislative Services Office on behalf of the legislative branch shall be submitted to the General Assembly on or before June 1 of each year. All other such plans shall be submitted to the Director of the Office of State Human Resources for review and approval on or before March 1, of each year.

(b) Repealed by Session Laws 2013-382, s. 7.3, effective August 21, 2013.

(c) The Director of the Office of State Human Resources will provide services of Equal Employment Opportunity technical assistance, training, oversight, monitoring, evaluation, support programs, and reporting to assure that State government's work force is diverse at all occupational levels. These services shall be provided by qualified personnel. (1991 (Reg. Sess., 1992) c. 919, ss. 2-4; 2013-382, ss. 7.3, 9.1(c).)

§ 126-20. Reserved for future codification purposes.

§ 126-21. Reserved for future codification purposes.

Article 7.

The Privacy of State Employee Personnel Records.

§ 126-22. Personnel files not subject to inspection under § 132-6.

(a) Except as provided in G.S. 126-23 and G.S. 126-24, personnel files of State employees shall not be subject to inspection and examination as authorized by G.S. 132-6.

(b) For purposes of this Article the following definitions apply:

(1) "Employee" means any current State employee, former State employee, or applicant for State employment.

(2) "Employer" means any State department, university, division, bureau, commission, council, or other agency subject to Article 7 of this Chapter.

(3) "Personnel file" means any employment-related or personal information gathered by an employer, the Retirement Systems Division of the Department of State Treasurer, or by the Office of State Human Resources. Employment-related information contained in a personnel file includes information related to an individual's application, selection, promotion, demotion, transfer, leave, salary, contract for employment, benefits, suspension, performance evaluation, disciplinary actions, and termination. Personal information contained in a personnel file includes an individual's home address, social security number, medical history, personal financial data, marital status, dependents, and beneficiaries.

(4) "Record" means the personnel information that each employer is required to maintain in accordance with G.S. 126-23.

(c) Personnel files of former State employees who have been separated from State employment for 10 or more years may be open to inspection and examination except for papers and documents relating to demotions and to disciplinary actions resulting in the dismissal of the employee and personnel files maintained by the Retirement Systems Division of the Department of State Treasurer.

(d) Notwithstanding any provision of this section to the contrary, the Retirement Systems Division of the Department of State Treasurer may disclose the name and mailing address of former State employees to domiciled, nonprofit organizations representing 10,000 or more retired State government, local government, or public school employees. (1975, c. 257, s. 1; 1977, c. 866, s. 9; 2007-508, s. 4.5; 2008-194, s. 11(a); 2013-382, s. 9.1(c).)

§ 126-23. Certain records to be kept by State agencies open to inspection.

(a) Each department, agency, institution, commission and bureau of the State shall maintain a record of each of its employees, showing the following information with respect to each such employee:

(1) Name.

(2) Age.

(3) Date of original employment or appointment to State service.

(4) The terms of any contract by which the employee is employed whether written or oral, past and current, to the extent that the agency has the written contract or a record of the oral contract in its possession.

(5) Current position.

(6) Title.

(7) Current salary.

(8) Date and amount of each increase or decrease in salary with that department, agency, institution, commission, or bureau.

(9) Date and type of each promotion, demotion, transfer, suspension, separation, or other change in position classification with that department, agency, institution, commission, or bureau.

(10) Date and general description of the reasons for each promotion with that department, agency, institution, commission, or bureau.

(11) Date and type of each dismissal, suspension, or demotion for disciplinary reasons taken by the department, agency, institution, commission, or bureau. If the disciplinary action was a dismissal, a copy of the written notice of the final decision of the head of the department setting forth the specific acts or omissions that are the basis of the dismissal.

(12) The office or station to which the employee is currently assigned.

(b)   For the purposes of this section, the term "salary" includes pay, benefits, incentives, bonuses, and deferred and all other forms of compensation paid by the employing entity.

(c)   Subject only to rules and regulations for the safekeeping of the records, adopted by the State Human Resources Commission, every person having custody of such records shall permit them to be inspected and examined and copies thereof made by any person during regular business hours. Except as provided in subsection (d) of this section, any person who is denied access to any such record for the purpose of inspecting, examining or copying the same shall have a right to compel compliance with the provisions of this section by application to a court of competent jurisdiction for a writ of mandamus or other appropriate relief.

(d)   Notwithstanding any other provision of this section, persons in the custody of, or under the supervision of, the Division of Adult Correction and persons in the custody of local confinement facilities are not entitled to access to the records made public under this section and are prohibited from obtaining those records, absent a court order authorizing access to, or custody, or possession.

(e)   An attorney investigating allegations of unlawful misconduct or abuse by a Division of Adult Correction employee may request, and shall be provided with, information sufficient to identify the full name or names of the employee alleged to be involved in the misconduct or abuse in the current position of the employee within the Division; or, the last position held by the employee and the last date of employment by the Division. The attorney may not give the offender copies of departmental records or official documents absent a court order authorizing access to, or custody, or possession. (1975, c. 257, s. 1; c. 667, s. 2; 2007-508, s. 4; 2010-169, s. 18(a); 2011-145, s. 19.1(h); 2011-324, s. 1.1(b); 2013-382, s. 9.1(c).)

§ 126-24. Confidential information in personnel files; access to such information.

All other information contained in a personnel file is confidential and shall not be open for inspection and examination except to the following persons:

(1)   The employee, applicant for employment, former employee, or his properly authorized agent, who may examine his own personnel file in its entirety except for (i) letters of reference solicited prior to employment, or (ii) information concerning a medical disability, mental or physical, that a prudent physician would not divulge to a patient. An employee's medical record may be disclosed to a licensed physician designated in writing by the employee;

(2)   The supervisor of the employee;

(3)   Members of the General Assembly who may inspect and examine personnel records under the authority of G.S. 120-19;

(4)   A party by authority of a proper court order may inspect and examine a particular confidential portion of a State employee's personnel file; and

(5)   An official of an agency of the federal government, State government or any political subdivision thereof. Such an official may inspect any personnel records when such inspection is deemed by the department head of the employee whose record is to be inspected or, in the case of an applicant for employment or a former employee, by the department head of the agency in which the record is maintained as necessary and essential to the pursuance of a proper function of said agency; provided, however, that such information shall not be divulged for purposes of assisting in a criminal prosecution, nor for purposes of assisting in a tax investigation.

Notwithstanding any other provision of this Chapter, any department head may, in his discretion, inform any person or corporation of any promotion, demotion, suspension, reinstatement, transfer, separation, dismissal, employment or nonemployment of any applicant, employee or former employee employed by or assigned to his department or whose personnel file is maintained in his department and the reasons therefor and may allow the personnel file of such person or any portion thereof to be inspected and examined by any person or corporation when such department head shall determine that the release of such information or the inspection and examination of such file or portion thereof is essential to maintaining the integrity of such department or to maintaining the level or quality of services provided by such department; provided that prior to releasing such information or making such file or portion thereof available as provided herein, such department head shall prepare a memorandum setting forth the circumstances which the department head deems to require such disclosure and the information to be disclosed. The memorandum shall be retained in the files of said department head and shall be a public record. (1975, c. 257, s. 1; 1977, c. 866, s. 10; 1977, 2nd Sess., c. 1207.)

§ 126-25. Remedies of employee objecting to material in file.

(a) An employee, former employee, or applicant for employment who objects to material in the employee's file may place in his or her file a written statement relating to the material the employee considers to be inaccurate or misleading.

(b) An employee, former employee, or applicant for employment who objects to material in the employee's file because he or she considers it inaccurate or misleading may seek the removal of such material from the file in accordance with a grievance procedure established by that department. If the agency determines that material in the employee's file is inaccurate or misleading, the agency shall remove or amend the inaccurate material to ensure that the file is accurate. Nothing in this subsection shall be construed to permit an employee to appeal the contents of a performance appraisal or written disciplinary action. (1975, c. 257, s. 1; c. 667, s. 2; 1977, c. 866, s. 11; 1985, c. 638; 2013-382, s. 7.4.)

§ 126-26. Rules and regulations.

The State Human Resources Commission shall prescribe such rules and regulations as it deems necessary to implement the provisions of this Article. (1975, c. 257, s. 1; c. 667, s. 2; 2013-382, s. 9.1(c).)

§ 126-27. Penalty for permitting access to confidential file by unauthorized person.

Any public official or employee who shall knowingly and willfully permit any person to have access to or custody or possession of any portion of a personnel file designated as confidential by this Article, unless such person is one specifically authorized by G.S. 126-24 to have access thereto for inspection and examination, shall be guilty of a Class 3 misdemeanor and upon conviction shall only be fined in the discretion of the court but not in excess of five hundred dollars ($500.00). (1975, c. 257, s. 1; 1993, c. 539, s. 934; 1994, Ex. Sess., c. 24, s. 14(c).)

§ 126-28. Penalty for examining, copying, etc., confidential file without authority.

Any person, not specifically authorized by G.S. 126-24 to have access to a personnel file designated as confidential by this Article, who shall knowingly and willfully examine in its official filing place, remove or copy any portion of a confidential personnel file shall be guilty of a Class 3 misdemeanor and upon conviction shall only be fined in the discretion of the court but not in excess of five hundred dollars ($500.00). (1975, c. 257, s. 1; 1993, c. 539, s. 935; 1994, Ex. Sess., c. 24, s. 14(c).)

§ 126-29. Access to material in file for agency hearing.

A party to a quasi-judicial hearing of a State agency subject to Article 7 of this Chapter, or a State agency subject to Article 7 of this Chapter which is conducting a quasi-judicial hearing, may have access to relevant material in personnel files and may introduce copies of such material or information based on such material as evidence in the hearing either upon consent of the employee, former employee, or applicant for employment or upon subpoena properly issued by the agency either upon request of a party or on its own motion. Nothing in this Article shall impose liability on any agent or officer of the State for compliance with this provision, notwithstanding any other provision of this Article. (1977, c. 866, s. 12; 1987, c. 320, s. 5.)

§ 126-30. Fraudulent disclosure and willful nondisclosure on application for State employment; penalties.

(a) Any employee who knowingly and willfully discloses false or misleading information, or conceals dishonorable military service; or conceals prior employment history or other requested information, either of which are significantly related to job responsibilities on an application for State employment may be subjected to disciplinary action up to and including immediate dismissal from employment. Dismissal shall be mandatory where the applicant discloses false or misleading information in order to meet position qualifications. Application forms for State employment shall include a statement informing applicants of the consequences of such fraudulent disclosure or lack of disclosure.

(b) The employing authority within each department, university, board, or commission, shall verify the status of credentials and the accuracy of statements contained in the application of each new employee within 90 days from the date of the employees employment. Failure to verify the application shall not bar action under subsection (a) above.

(c) The State Human Resources Commission shall issue rules and procedures to implement this section for all departments, agencies and institutions which are not exempted from the North Carolina Human Resources Act under G.S 126-5(c1). Each agency, department and institution which is exempted under G.S. 126-5(c1) shall issue regulations to implement this section pursuant to the rulemaking procedures applicable to it. (1987, c. 666, s. 1; 2013-382, s. 9.1(c).)

§ 126-31. Reserved for future codification purposes.

§ 126-32. Reserved for future codification purposes.

§ 126-33. Reserved for future codification purposes.

Article 8.

Employee Appeals of Grievances and Disciplinary Action.

§ 126-34: Repealed by Session Laws 2013-382, s. 6.1, effective August 21, 2013, and applicable to grievances filed on or after that date.

§ 126-34.01. Grievance; resolution.

Any State employee having a grievance arising out of or due to the employee's employment shall first discuss the problem or grievance with the employee's supervisor, unless the problem or grievance is with the supervisor. Then the employee shall follow the grievance procedure approved by the State Human Resources Commission. The proposed agency final decision shall not be issued nor become final until reviewed and approved by the Office of State Human Resources. The agency grievance procedure and Office of State Human Resources review shall be completed within 90 days from the date the grievance is filed. (2013-382, ss. 6.1, 9.1(c).)

§ 126-34.02. Grievance appeal process; grounds.

(a) Once a final agency decision has been issued in accordance with G.S. 126-34.01, an applicant for State employment, a State employee, or former State employee may file a contested case in the Office of Administrative Hearings under Article 3 of Chapter 150B of the General Statutes. The contested case must be filed within 30 days of receipt of the final agency decision. Except for cases of extraordinary cause shown, the Office of Administrative Hearings shall hear and issue a final decision in accordance with G.S. 150B-34 within 180 days from the commencement of the case. In deciding cases under this section, the Office of Administrative Hearings may grant the following relief:

(1) Reinstate any employee to the position from which the employee has been removed.

(2) Order the employment, promotion, transfer, or salary adjustment of any individual to whom it has been wrongfully denied.

(3) Direct other suitable action to correct the abuse which may include the requirement of payment for any loss of salary which has resulted from the improper action of the appointing authority.

An aggrieved party in a contested case under this section shall be entitled to judicial review of a final decision by appeal to the Court of Appeals as provided in G.S. 7A-29(a). The procedure for the appeal shall be as provided by the rules of appellate procedure. The appeal shall be taken within 30 days of receipt of the written notice of final decision. A notice of appeal shall be filed with the

Office of Administrative Hearings and served on all parties to the contested case hearing.

(b)   The following issues may be heard as contested cases after completion of the agency grievance procedure and the Office of State Human Resources review:

(1)   Discrimination or harassment. - An applicant for State employment, a State employee, or former State employee may allege discrimination or harassment based on race, religion, color, national origin, sex, age, disability, genetic information, or political affiliation if the employee believes that he or she has been discriminated against in his or her application for employment or in the terms and conditions of the employee's employment, or in the termination of his or her employment.

(2)   Retaliation. - An applicant for State employment, a State employee, or former State employee may allege retaliation for protesting discrimination based on race, religion, color, national origin, sex, age, disability, political affiliation, or genetic information if the employee believes that he or she has been retaliated against in his or her application for employment or in the terms and conditions of the employee's employment, or in the termination of the employee's employment.

(3)   Just cause for dismissal, demotion, or suspension. - A career State employee may allege that he or she was dismissed, demoted, or suspended for disciplinary reasons without just cause. A dismissal, demotion, or suspension which is not imposed for disciplinary reasons shall not be considered a disciplinary action within the meaning of this section. However, in contested cases conducted pursuant to this section, an employee may appeal an involuntary nondisciplinary separation due to an employee's unavailability in the same fashion as if it were a disciplinary action, but the agency shall only have the burden to prove that the employee was unavailable. In cases of such disciplinary action the employee shall, before the action is taken, be furnished with a statement in writing setting forth the specific acts or omissions that are the reasons for the disciplinary action and the employee's appeal rights. The employee shall be permitted 15 days from the date the statement is delivered to appeal under the agency grievance procedure. However, an employee may be suspended without warning pending the giving of written reasons in order to avoid undue disruption of work, to protect the safety of persons or property, or for other serious reasons.

(4) Veteran's preference. - An applicant for State employment or a State employee may allege that he or she was denied veteran's preference in violation of the law.

(5) Failure to post or give priority consideration. - An applicant for State employment or a State employee may allege that he or she was denied hiring or promotion because a position was not posted in accordance with this Chapter or because he or she was denied hiring or promotion as a result of a failure to give priority consideration for promotion or reemployment as required by G.S. 126-7.1.

(6) Whistleblower. - A whistleblower grievance as provided for in this Chapter.

(c) Any issue for which an appeal to the Office of Administrative Hearings has not been specifically authorized by this section shall not be grounds for a contested case hearing.

(d) In contested cases conducted pursuant to this section, the burden of showing that a career State employee was discharged, demoted, or suspended for just cause rests with the employer. In all other contested cases, the burden of proof rests on the employee.

(e) The Office of Administrative Hearings may award attorneys' fees to an employee where reinstatement or back pay is ordered or where an employee prevails in a whistleblower grievance. The remedies provided in this subsection in a whistleblower appeal shall be the same as those provided in G.S. 126-87.

(f) The Office of Administrative Hearings shall report to the Office of State Human Resources and the Joint Legislative Administrative Procedure Oversight Committee on the number of cases filed under this section and on the number of days between filing and closing of each case. The report shall be filed on a semiannual basis. (2013-382, ss. 6.1, 9.1(c).)

§ 126-34.1: Repealed by Session Laws 2013-382, s. 6.1, effective August 21, 2013, and applicable to grievances filed on or after that date.

§ 126-34.2. Alternative dispute resolution.

In its discretion, the Commission may adopt alternative dispute resolution procedures for the resolution of matters constituting and not constituting grounds for a grievance under this Article. Any matters not constituting grounds for an appeal under G.S. 126-34.02 shall not be heard by the Office of Administrative Hearings as a contested case. (1995, c. 141, s. 8; 2013-382, s. 6.1.)

§ 126-34.3. Judicial review of fee awards.

With respect to a decision of the Office of Administrative Hearings assessing or refusing to assess reasonable witness fees or a reasonable attorneys' fee, the decision shall be subject to judicial review in accordance with G.S. 126-34.02(a). The reviewing court may reverse or modify the decision of the Office of Administrative Hearings if the decision is unreasonable or the award is inadequate. An employee who obtains a reversal or modification of the Office of Administrative Hearings' decision in an appeal under this section shall be entitled to recover court costs and a reasonable attorneys' fee for representation in connection with the appeal. (2013-382, s. 6.1.)

§ 126-35. Just cause; disciplinary actions for State employees.

(a) No career State employee subject to the North Carolina Human Resources Act shall be discharged, suspended, or demoted for disciplinary reasons, except for just cause. In cases of such disciplinary action, the employee shall, before the action is taken, be furnished with a statement in writing setting forth the specific acts or omissions that are the reasons for the disciplinary action and the employee's appeal rights. The employee shall be permitted 15 days from the date the statement is delivered to appeal to the head of the agency through the agency grievance procedure for a final agency decision. However, an employee may be suspended without warning for causes relating to personal conduct detrimental to State service, pending the giving of written reasons, in order to avoid undue disruption of work or to protect the safety of persons or property or for other serious reasons. If the employee is not satisfied with the final agency decision or is unable, within a reasonable period of time, to obtain a final agency decision, the employee may appeal to the Office of Administrative Hearings. Such appeal shall be filed not later than 30 days after receipt of notice of the final agency decision. The State Human Resources Commission may adopt, subject to the approval of the Governor, rules that define just cause.

(b)   through (d) Repealed by Session Laws 2013-382, s. 6.1, effective August 21, 2013, and applicable to grievances filed on or after that date. (1975, c. 667, s. 10; 1989 (Reg. Sess., 1990), c. 1025, s. 2; 1991, c. 65, s. 7; c. 354, s. 5; c. 722, s. 1; 2000-190, s. 13; 2012-187, s. 8.4; 2013-382, ss. 6.1, 9.1(c).)

§§ 126-36 through 126-41: Repealed by Session Laws 2013-382, s. 6.1, effective August 21, 2013, and applicable to grievances filed on or after that date.

§ 126-42. Reserved for future codification purposes.

Article 9.

The Administrative Procedure Act and Modifications.

§§ 126-43 through 126-44: Repealed by Session Laws 1987, c. 320, s. 9.

§ 126-45: Repealed by Session Laws 1977, c. 866, s. 18.

§§ 126-46 through 126-50. Reserved for future codification purposes.

Article 10.

Interchange of Governmental Employees.

§ 126-51. Short title.

This Article shall be known and may be cited as the "North Carolina Interchange of Governmental Employees Act of 1977." (1977, c. 783, s. 1.)

§ 126-52. Definitions.

For purposes of this Article:

(1) "Assigned employee" means an employee of a sending agency who is assigned or detailed to a receiving agency as part of the employee's regular duties with the sending agency.

(2) "Employee on leave" means an employee on leave of absence without pay from a sending agency who becomes an employee of a receiving agency while on leave from the sending agency.

(3) "Receiving agency" means any division, department, agency, instrumentality, authority, or political subdivision of the federal government or of a state or local government which, under this Article, receives an employee of another governmental division, department, agency, instrumentality, authority, or political subdivision of the federal government or of a state or local government.

(4) "Sending agency" means any division, department, agency, instrumentality, authority, or political subdivision of the federal government or of a state or local government which, under this Article, sends any employee thereof to another governmental division, department, agency, instrumentality, authority, or political subdivision of the federal government or of a state or local government. (1977, c. 783, s. 1.)

§ 126-53. Authority to interchange employees.

(a) Any division, department, agency, instrumentality, authority, or political subdivision of the State of North Carolina is authorized to participate in a program of interchange of employees with divisions, departments, agencies, instrumentalities, authorities, or political subdivisions of the federal government, of another state, or of this State, as a sending agency or a receiving agency.

(b) The period of individual assignment, detail, or leave of absence under an interchange program shall not exceed two years.

(c) The temporary assignment of the employee may be terminated by mutual agreement between the sending agency and the receiving agency.

(d) Elected officials may not participate in a program of interchange under this Article. (1977, c. 783, s. 1.)

§ 126-54. Status of employees of sending agency.

(a) Employees of a sending agency participating in an exchange of personnel authorized by G.S. 126-53 may be considered during such participation to be either assigned employees or employees on leave.

(b) Assigned employees shall be entitled to the same salary and employment benefits to which they would be entitled as employees of the sending agency and shall remain employees of the sending agency for all purposes unless otherwise provided in this Article or in a written agreement between the sending agency and the receiving agency.

(c) Employees on leave shall have the same rights, benefits and obligations other State or local employees subject to this Chapter who are granted leaves of absences, unless otherwise provided in this Article, or in a written agreement between the sending agency and the receiving agency.

(d) When a division, department, agency, instrumentality, authority or political subdivision of the State of North Carolina acts as a sending agency, employees participating in an exchange of personnel authorized by G.S. 126-53, whether considered assigned employees or employees on leave, shall have the same rights, benefits and obligations to participate in and receive benefits, including death benefits, from any retirement system of which they are members as employees of the sending agency, whether they are members of the Teachers' and State Employees' Retirement System, the North Carolina Local Governmental Employees' Retirement System, the Law Enforcement Officers' Benefit and Retirement Fund, or other Retirement System which has been or may be established by the State for public employees; provided, however, that the receiving agency agrees to and makes the employer contributions and deducts from the salary of the employee the employee contributions for continued membership in such Retirement System. Provided, further, that if no contributions are paid into the appropriate Retirement System during the period that the employee participates in the exchange of personnel authorized by this Article, such employee shall remain entitled to death benefits resulting from his death during the period of the exchange. Provided, that where duplicate benefits would otherwise be payable on account of disability or death, the employee or his estate shall elect, within one year of the date of disability or death, which benefits to receive. (1977, c. 783, s. 1.)

§ 126-55. Travel expenses of employees from this State.

A sending agency in this State shall not pay the travel expenses of its assigned or on leave employees and shall not pay the travel expenses of such employees incurred in the course of performing work for the receiving agency. Such expenses shall be borne by the receiving agency. (1977, c. 783, s. 1.)

§ 126-56. Status of employees of other governments.

(a) When a division, department, agency, instrumentality, authority or political subdivision of the State of North Carolina acts as a receiving agency, assigned employees of the sending agency remain the employees of the sending agency and continue to receive the employment benefits of the sending agency unless otherwise specified in a written agreement between the sending agency and the receiving agency.

(b) When a division, department, agency, instrumentality, authority or political subdivision of this State acts as a receiving agency, employees on leave from the sending agency will receive appointments as employees with the receiving agency and will be entitled to the same employment benefits as other employees of the receiving agency unless otherwise specified in a written agreement between the sending agency and the receiving agency. Such appointments may be made without regard to any rules or regulations of the receiving agency regarding the selection of employees; but all rules of the North Carolina Human Resources Act shall apply to State employees. (1977, c. 783, s. 1; 2013-382, s. 9.1(c).)

§ 126-57. Travel expenses of employees of other governments.

A receiving agency in the State of North Carolina may, in accordance with its travel regulations and travel regulations by law, pay the travel expenses incurred in the course of an assigned employee's duties or incurred in the course of the duties of an employee on leave with the receiving agency on the same basis as the travel expenses of regular employees are paid. (1977, c. 783, s. 1.)

§ 126-58. Administration.

The State Human Resources Commission and any State division, department, agency, instrumentality, authority or political subdivision participating in an interchange of employees program may promulgate rules or regulations necessary for the administration of such program, so long as such rules or regulations do not conflict with the provisions of this Article or any other provision of law. (1977, c. 783, s. 1; 2013-382, s. 9.1(c).)

§§ 126-59 through 126-63. Reserved for future codification purposes.

Article 11.

Governor's Commission on Governmental Productivity.

§§ 126-64 through 126-73: Repealed by Session Laws 1985, c. 479, s. 153(a).

Article 12.

Work Options Program for State Employees.

§ 126-74. Work Options Program established.

There is established a Work Options Program for State employees in the Office of State Human Resources to be administered by the State Human Resources Commission. The Director of the Office of State Human Resources shall assign an employee within the Office of State Human Resources, to be known as the

State Work Options Coordinator, to direct the Work Options Program as established in this Article. (1981, c. 917, s. 1; 1991, c. 65, s. 8; 2013-382, s. 9.1(c).)

§ 126-75. Work options for State employees.

(a) The following work options allowed State employees are to be included in the program administered under this Article:

(1) Flexible work hours as established by the State Human Resources Commission;

(2) Job sharing as permitted by the State Human Resources Commission;

(3) Permanent part-time positions as established under the North Carolina Human Resources Act.

(b) The State Human Resources Commission shall examine the present options listed in subsection (a) of this section available to State employees and other options the State Human Resources Commission may make available for a comprehensive program of work options for State employees. The State Human Resources Commission shall, with the concurrence of the agency, determine the need for additional permanent part-time positions within State Government and how increased use of these positions could benefit employee morale and productivity as well as increase the use of the available labor force. None of the provisions of this Article shall be administered to reduce the total number of hours per day a State office normally is open to serve the public. (1981, c. 917, s. 1; 2013-382, s. 9.1(c).)

§ 126-76. Promoting Work Options Program.

The State Human Resources Commission shall develop a program to expand the use of work options. This program shall include training sessions for agency personnel to instruct them in the use of work options available to State employees. The State Human Resources Commission shall also provide technical assistance to agency personnel in developing a Work Options Program for each agency or expanding existing programs in each agency. The

Work Options Coordinator shall also identify personnel positions within the State Personnel System [State Human Resources System] which can effectively be structured in job sharing or permanent part-time employment positions. (1981, c. 917, s. 1; 2013-382, s. 9.1(c).)

§ 126-77. Authority of agencies to participate.

The State Human Resources Commission shall request from each agency assistance in formulating the Work Options Program. Any division, department, agency, instrumentality or authority shall participate in the program of work options as established in this Article. (1981, c. 917, s. 1; 2013-382, s. 9.1(c).)

§ 126-78. Administration.

The State Human Resources Commission and any State division, department, agency, instrumentality or authority participating in the State Work Options Program shall promulgate rules necessary for the administration of the program. (1981, c. 917, s. 1; 1987, c. 827, s. 57; 2013-382, s. 9.1(c).)

§ 126-79: Repealed by Session Laws 2013-382, s. 7.7, effective August 21, 2013.

Article 13.

Veteran's Preference.

§ 126-80. Declaration of policy.

It shall be the policy of the State of North Carolina that, in appreciation for their service to this State and this country during a period of war, and in recognition of the time and advantage lost toward the pursuit of a civilian career, veterans shall be granted preference in employment for positions subject to the provisions of this Chapter with every State department, agency, and institution. (1987 (Reg. Sess., 1988), c. 1064, s. 1.)

§ 126-81. Definitions.

As used in this Article:

(1)   "A period of war" includes World War I (April 16, 1917, through November 11, 1918), World War II (December 7, 1941, through December 31, 1946), the Korean Conflict (June 27, 1950, through January 31, 1955), the period of time between January 31, 1955, and the end of the hostilities in Vietnam (May 7, 1975), or any other campaign, expedition, or engagement for which a campaign badge or medal is authorized by the United States Department of Defense.

(2)   "Veteran" means a person who served in the Armed Forces of the United States on active duty, for reasons other than training, and has been discharged under other than dishonorable conditions.

(3)   "Eligible veteran" means:

a.   A veteran who served during a period of war; or

b.   The spouse of a disabled veteran; or

c.   The surviving spouse or dependent of a veteran who dies on active duty during a period of war either directly or indirectly as a result of such service; or

d.   A veteran who suffered a service-connected disability during peacetime; or

e.   The spouse of a veteran described in subdivision d. of this subsection; or

f.   The surviving spouse or dependent of a person who served in the Armed Forces of the United States on active duty, for reasons other than training, who died for service-related reasons during peacetime. (1987 (Reg. Sess., 1988), c. 1064, s. 1.)

§ 126-82. State Human Resources Commission to provide for preference.

(a)   The State Human Resources Commission shall provide that in evaluating the qualifications of an eligible veteran against the minimum requirements for obtaining a position, credit shall be given for all military service training or schooling and experience that bears a reasonable and functional relationship to the knowledge, skills, and abilities required for the position. This preference applies to initial employment with the State and extends to other employment events including subsequent hirings, promotions, reassignments, and horizontal transfers.

(b)   The State Human Resources Commission shall provide that if an eligible veteran has met the minimum requirements for the position, after receiving experience credit under subsection (a) of this section, he shall receive experience credit as determined by the Commission for additional related and unrelated military service. This preference applies to initial employment with the State and extends to other employment events including subsequent hirings, promotions, reassignments, and horizontal transfers.

(c)   The State Human Resources Commission may provide that in reduction in force situations where seniority or years of service is one of the considerations for retention, an eligible veteran shall be accorded credit for military service.

(d)   Any eligible veteran who has reason to believe that he or she did not receive a veteran's preference in accordance with the provisions of this Article or rules adopted under it may appeal directly to the State Human Resources Commission.

(e)   The willful failure of any employee subject to the provisions of Article 8 of this Chapter to comply with the provisions of this Article or rules adopted under it constitutes personal misconduct in accordance with the provisions and promulgated rules of this Chapter, including those for suspension, demotion, or dismissal. (1987 (Reg. Sess., 1988), c. 1064, s. 1; 2007-286, s. 2; 2013-382, s. 9.1(c).)

§ 126-83. Exceptions.

Notwithstanding G.S. 126-5, and notwithstanding provisions in that section that only certain Articles of this Chapter apply to some employees, this Article applies to all persons covered by this Chapter except those exempted by G.S. 126-5(c)(2), G.S. 126-5(c)(3), G.S. 126-5(c)(4), G.S. 126-5(c1), G.S. 126-5(c2), or G.S. 126-5(c3), but this Article does not apply to those persons covered by G.S. 126-5(a)(2). G.S. 128-15 shall apply to those persons exempted from coverage of this Article, but shall not apply to any person covered by this Article. (1987 (Reg. Sess., 1988), c. 1064, s. 1; 1991, c. 65, s. 9.)

Article 14.

Protection for Reporting Improper Government Activities.

§ 126-84. Statement of policy.

(a) It is the policy of this State that State employees shall be encouraged to report verbally or in writing to their supervisor, department head, or other appropriate authority, evidence of activity by a State agency or State employee constituting:

(1) A violation of State or federal law, rule or regulation;

(2) Fraud;

(3) Misappropriation of State resources;

(4) Substantial and specific danger to the public health and safety; or

(5) Gross mismanagement, a gross waste of monies, or gross abuse of authority.

(b) Further, it is the policy of this State that State employees be free of intimidation or harassment when reporting to public bodies about matters of public concern, including offering testimony to or testifying before appropriate legislative panels. (1989, c. 236, s. 1; 1997-520, s. 5.)

§ 126-85. Protection from retaliation.

(a)   No head of any State department, agency or institution or other State employee exercising supervisory authority shall discharge, threaten or otherwise discriminate against a State employee regarding the State employee's compensation, terms, conditions, location, or privileges of employment because the State employee, or a person acting on behalf of the employee, reports or is about to report, verbally or in writing, any activity described in G.S. 126-84, unless the State employee knows or has reason to believe that the report is inaccurate.

(a1)   No State employee shall retaliate against another State employee because the employee, or a person acting on behalf of the employee, reports or is about to report, verbally or in writing, any activity described in G.S. 126-84.

(b)   No head of any State department, agency or institution or other State employee exercising supervisory authority shall discharge, threaten or otherwise discriminate against a State employee regarding the employee's compensation, terms, conditions, location or privileges of employment because the State employee has refused to carry out a directive which in fact constitutes a violation of State or federal law, rule or regulation or poses a substantial and specific danger to the public health and safety.

(b1)   No State employee shall retaliate against another State employee because the employee has refused to carry out a directive which may constitute a violation of State or federal law, rule or regulation, or poses a substantial and specific danger to the public health and safety.

(c)   The protections of this Article shall include State employees who report any activity described in G.S. 126-84 to the State Auditor as authorized by G.S. 147-64.6B or to the Program Evaluation Division as authorized by G.S. 120-36.12(10). (1989, c. 236, s. 1; 1997-520, s. 6; 2008-196, s. 2(b); 2008-215, s. 8.)

§ 126-86. Civil actions for injunctive relief or other remedies.

Any State employee injured by a violation of G.S. 126-85 who is not subject to Article 8 of this Chapter may maintain an action in superior court for damages, an injunction, or other remedies provided in this Article against the person or agency who committed the violation within one year after the occurrence of the alleged violation of this Article; provided, however, any claim arising under Article 21 of Chapter 95 of the General Statutes may be maintained pursuant to the provisions of that Article only and may be redressed only by the remedies and relief available under that Article. (1989, c. 236, s. 1; 1991 (Reg. Sess., 1992), c. 1021, s. 6; 2013-382, s. 7.10.)

§ 126-87. Remedies.

A court, in rendering a judgment in an action brought pursuant to this Article, may order an injunction, damages, reinstatement of the employee, the payment of back wages, full reinstatement of fringe benefits and seniority rights, costs, reasonable attorney's fees or any combination of these. If an application for a permanent injunction is granted, the employee shall be awarded costs and reasonable attorney's fees. If in an action for damages the court finds that the employee was injured by a willful violation of G.S. 126-85, the court shall award as damages three times the amount of actual damages plus costs and reasonable attorney's fees against the individual or individuals found to be in violation of G.S. 126-84. (1989, c. 236, s.1)

§ 126-88. Notice of employee protections and obligations.

It shall be the duty of an employer of a State employee to post notice in accordance with G.S. 95-9 or use other appropriate means to keep his employees informed of their protections and obligations under this Article. (1989, c. 236, s. 1.)

§ 126-89: Reserved for future codification purposes.

Article 15.

Communications With Members of the General Assembly.

§ 126-90. Communications with members of the General Assembly.

A State employee's right to speak to a member of the General Assembly at the member's request shall not be directly or indirectly limited by the employee's supervisor or by any policy of the department, agency, or institution that employs that State employee. (1997-443, s. 22.2(a).)

§ 126-91: Reserved for future codification purposes.

§ 126-92: Reserved for future codification purposes.

§ 126-93: Reserved for future codification purposes.

§ 126-94: Reserved for future codification purposes.

Article 16.

Flexible Compensation Plan.

§ 126-95. Flexible compensation plan.

(a) The Director of the Budget may provide eligible officers and employees of State departments, institutions, and agencies not covered by the provisions of G.S. 116-17.2 a program of dependent care assistance as available under section 129 and related sections of the Internal Revenue Code of 1986, as amended. The Director of the Budget may authorize State departments, institutions, and agencies to enter into annual agreements with employees who elect to participate in the program to provide for a reduction in salary. With the approval of the Director of the Budget, savings in the employer's share of contributions under the Federal Insurance Contributions Act on account of the reduction in salary may be used to pay some or all of the administrative expenses of the program. Should the Director of the Budget decide to contract with a third party to administer the terms and conditions of a program of dependent care assistance, the Director of the Budget may select a contractor only upon a thorough and completely competitive procurement process.

(b) Notwithstanding any other provisions of law relating to the salaries of officers and employees of departments, institutions, and agencies of State government, the Director of the Budget may provide a plan of flexible compensation to eligible officers and employees of State departments, institutions, and agencies not covered by the provisions of G.S. 116-17.2 for benefits available under section 125 and related sections of the Internal Revenue Code of 1986, as amended. This plan shall not replace, substitute for, or duplicate any benefits provided to employees and officers under Article 1A of Chapter 120 of the General Statutes and Articles 1, 3B, 4, and 6 of Chapter 135 of the General Statutes. The plan may, however, include offerings for products and benefits that are supplemental or additional to these statutory benefits. If a plan of flexible compensation is offered, then a TRICARE supplement shall be offered. In providing a plan of flexible compensation, the Director of the Budget may authorize State departments, institutions, and agencies to enter into agreements with their employees for reductions in the salaries of employees electing to participate in the plan of flexible compensation provided by this section. With the approval of the Director of the Budget, savings in the employer's share of contributions under the Federal Insurance Contributions Act on account of the reduction in salary may be used to pay some or all of the administrative expenses of the program. Should the Director of the Budget decide to contract with a third party to administer the terms and conditions of a plan of flexible compensation as provided by this section, it may select such a contractor only upon a thorough and completely advertised competitive procurement process.

(c) As used in this section, the term "eligible officers and employees" means any officer or employee authorized to participate in the Teachers' and State Employees' Retirement System and the State Health Plan. (2007-117, s. 3; 2013-292, s. 4; 2013-382, s. 1.4.)

§ 126-96: Reserved for future codification purposes.

§ 126-97: Reserved for future codification purposes.

§ 126-98: Reserved for future codification purposes.

§ 126-99: Reserved for future codification purposes.

Chapter 127.

Militia.

§§ 127-1 through 127-127. Repealed by Session Laws 1975, c. 604, s. 1.

Chapter 127A.

Militia.

Article 1.

Classification of Militia.

§ 127A-1. Composition of militia.

The militia of the State shall consist of all able-bodied citizens of the State and of the United States and all other able-bodied persons who have or shall declare their intention to become citizens of the United States, subject to the qualifications prescribed in this Chapter, who shall be drafted into the militia or shall voluntarily accept commission, appointment, or assignment to duty therein. (1917, c. 200, s. 1; C.S., s. 6791; 1949, c. 1130, s. 1; 1957, c. 1043, s. 1; 1963, c. 1016, s. 2; 1967, c. 563, s. 1; 1975, c. 604, s. 2; 2011-195, s. 1(a).)

§ 127A-2. Classification of militia.

The militia shall be divided into the organized and unorganized militia. The organized militia shall consist of four classes: the North Carolina National Guard, the naval militia, the State defense militia and historic military commands. (1975, c. 604, s. 2; 2009-281, s. 1.)

§ 127A-3. Organized militia; National Guard.

The North Carolina National Guard, both Army and Air, shall consist of regularly commissioned, warrant and enlisted personnel within the age limits established by regulations promulgated by the secretary of the appropriate service and shall be organized, governed, armed, equipped and have the duties and responsibilities provided in this Chapter. (1917, c. 200, s. 2; C.S., s. 6792; 1949, c. 1130, s. 1; 1957, c. 136, s. 1; 1961, c. 192, s. 1; 1963, c. 1016, s. 2; 1975, c. 604, s. 2; 2009-281, s. 1; 2011-195, s. 1(a).)

§ 127A-4. Organized militia; naval militia.

The naval militia shall consist of regularly commissioned, warrant and enlisted personnel within the age limits established by regulations promulgated by the secretary of the appropriate service and shall be organized, governed, armed, equipped and have the duties and responsibilities provided in this Chapter. (1917, c. 200, s. 3; C.S., s. 6793; 1949, c. 1130, s. 1; 1975, c. 604, s. 2; 2011-195, s. 1(a).)

§ 127A-5. Organized militia; State defense militia.

The State defense militia shall consist of commissioned, warrant and enlisted personnel called, ordered, appointed or enlisted therein by the Governor under the provisions of Article 5 of this Chapter and shall be organized, governed, armed, equipped and have the duties and responsibilities provided in this Chapter. (1963, c. 1016, s. 2; 1975, c. 604, s. 2; 2011-195, s. 1(a).)

§ 127A-6. Organized militia; historic military commands.

Historic military commands are those historic groups which remain active by meeting at least once a month and which follow military procedures. Only groups designated by the Governor shall fall within this branch of the militia. Any maximum age limits prescribed by this Chapter do not apply to members of historic military commands. (1957, c. 1043, s. 2; 1967, c. 563, s. 2; 1975, c. 604, s. 2; 2011-195, s. 1(a).)

§ 127A-7. Composition of unorganized militia.

The unorganized militia shall consist of all other able-bodied citizens of the State and of the United States and all other able-bodied persons who have or shall declare their intention to become citizens of the United States, who shall be at least 17 years of age, except those who have been convicted of a felony or discharged from any component of the military under other than honorable conditions. (1917, c. 200, s. 4; C.S., s. 6794; 1949, c. 1130, s. 1; 1963, c. 1016, s. 2; 1975, c. 604, s. 2; 1983, c. 314, s. 1; 2011-195, s. 1(a).)

§ 127A-8. Exemptions from duty with the militia.

The officers, judicial and executive, of the government of the United States and the State of North Carolina, persons in the military or naval service of the United States, customhouse clerks, persons employed by the United States in the transmission of mail, artificers and personnel employed in the armories, arsenals and navy yards of the United States, pilots, and mariners actually employed in the sea service of any citizen or merchant within the United States shall be exempt from duty with the militia without regard to age, and all persons who, because of religious beliefs, claim exemption from duty with the militia, if the conscientious holding of the belief by that person is established under the regulations prescribed for exemption from service with the Armed Forces of the United States, shall be exempted from militia service in a combatant capacity; but no person so exempted shall be exempt from militia service in any capacity that shall be declared noncombatant for the Armed Forces of the United States. (1917, c. 200, s. 5; C.S., s. 6795; 1975, c. 604, s. 2; 2011-195, s. 1(a).)

§ 127A-9. Number of troops authorized.

In time of peace the State shall maintain only those troops that are authorized by the President of the United States; but nothing contained in this Chapter shall be construed as limiting the rights of the State in the use of the North Carolina National Guard or the State defense militia or both within its borders in time of peace. Nothing contained in this Chapter shall prevent the organization and maintenance of State police or constabulary. (1917, c. 200, s. 8; C.S., s. 6797; 1963, c. 1016, s. 2; 1975, c. 604, s. 2; 2009-281, s. 1; 2011-195, s. 1(a).)

§ 127A-10. Corps entitled to retain privileges.

Any corps of artillery, cavalry, or infantry existing in the State on the passage of the act of Congress of May 8, 1792, which by the laws, customs, or usages of the State has been in continuous existence since the passage of that act, under its provisions and under the provisions of section 232 and sections 1625 to 1660, both inclusive, of Title 16 of the revised statutes of 1873 and the act of Congress of January 21, 1903, relating to the militia, shall be allowed to retain its ancient privileges, subject, nevertheless, to all duties required by law of the militia; but these organizations may be a part of the North Carolina National Guard, and entitled to all the privileges of this Chapter, and shall conform in all respects to the organization, discipline, and training of the North Carolina National Guard in time of war. For purposes of training and when on active duty in the service of the United States they may be assigned to higher units, as the President may direct, and shall be subject to the orders of officers under whom they shall be serving. (1917, c. 200, s. 87; C.S., s. 6798; 1975, c. 604, s. 2; 2009-281, s. 1; 2011-195, s. 1(a).)

§§ 127A-11 through 127A-15. Reserved for future codification purposes.

Article 2.

General Administrative Officers.

§ 127A-16. Governor as commander in chief.

(a) The Governor shall be commander in chief of the militia and shall have power to call out the militia to execute the laws, secure the safety of persons and property, suppress riots or insurrections, repel invasions and provide disaster relief.

(b) The Governor shall have the additional power, subject to the availability of funding, to place individuals, units, or parts of units of the North Carolina National Guard in a State Active Duty status to assist with the planning, support, and execution of activities connected with the swearing in and installation of the Governor and other members of the Council of State. (1917, c. 200, s. 11; C.S., s. 6799; 1975, c. 604, s. 2; 1999-442, s. 1.)

§ 127A-17. Commander in chief to prescribe regulations.

The commander in chief shall have the power and the duty, from time to time, to issue orders and to prescribe regulations relating to the organized and unorganized militia that are necessary for the militia at all times to conform to the federal requirements of the United States government relating thereto. (1917, c. 200, s. 36; C.S., s. 6800; 1963, c. 1016, s. 2; 1975, c. 604, s. 2; 2011-195, s. 1(a).)

§ 127A-17.1. Confidentiality of National Guard records.

Notwithstanding any provision of Chapter 143B of the General Statutes, no records of the North Carolina National Guard in the Department of Public Safety shall be disclosed or used for any purpose except for official purposes, and no records shall be disclosed, destroyed or used in any manner which is in violation of any existing federal law or regulation. Nothing in this Chapter shall convert records which are the property of the federal government into State property. (1977, c. 70, s. 3; 2009-281, s. 1; 2011-145, s. 19.1(g); 2011-195, s. 1(a).)

§ 127A-18. Personal staff of Governor.

The Governor may detail not more than 10 active North Carolina National Guard members and two active naval militia members who shall in addition to their regular duties, perform the duties of aides-de-camp on the personal staff of the Governor. (1917, c. 200, s. 12; C.S., s. 6801; 1959, c. 218, s. 1; 1975, c. 604, s. 2; 2009-281, s. 1; 2011-195, s. 1(a).)

§ 127A-19. Adjutant General.

The military head of the militia shall be the Adjutant General who shall hold the rank of major general. The Adjutant General shall be appointed by the Governor in the Governor's capacity as commander in chief of the militia, in consultation with the Secretary of Public Safety, and shall serve at the pleasure of the Governor. No person shall be appointed as Adjutant General who has less than five years' commissioned service in an active status in any component of the

Armed Forces of the United States. The Adjutant General, while holding this office, may be a member of the active North Carolina National Guard or naval militia.

Subject to the approval of the Governor and in consultation with the Secretary of Public Safety, the Adjutant General may appoint (i) a deputy adjutant general who may hold the rank of major general, and (ii) an assistant adjutant general for Army National Guard, and an assistant adjutant general for Air National Guard, each of whom may hold the rank of brigadier general and who shall serve at the pleasure of the Governor. The Adjutant General may also employ staff members and other personnel as authorized by the Secretary and funded. (1917, c. 200, s. 14; C.S., s. 6802; 1925, c. 54; 1939, c. 14; 1949, c. 1225; 1959, c. 218, s. 2; 1973, c. 620, s. 9; 1975, c. 604, s. 2; 1977, c. 70, s. 2; 1979, c. 481; 1995, c. 122, s. 1; 2005-314, s. 1; 2008-162, s. 3; 2009-281, s. 1; 2011-145, s. 19.1(g); 2011-195, s. 1(a).)

§ 127A-20. Administrative and operational relationships of the Adjutant General.

In all administrative and operational matters affecting the militia while under State control, the Adjutant General shall be responsible to and subject to the direction and supervision of the Secretary of Public Safety. (1973, c. 620, s. 9; 1975, c. 604, s. 2; 1977, c. 70, s. 2; 2011-145, s. 19.1(g).)

§ 127A-21. United States property and fiscal officer.

(a) The Governor of the State, in consultation with the Secretary of Public Safety, shall appoint, designate, or detail, subject to the approval of the Secretary of the Army and the Secretary of the Air Force, a qualified commissioned officer of the North Carolina National Guard who is also a commissioned officer of the Army National Guard of the United States or the Air National Guard of the United States, as the case may be, to be the United States property and fiscal officer for North Carolina. If the officer is not on active duty, the President may order the officer to active duty, with the officer's consent, to serve as a property and fiscal officer.

(b) The status of the United States property and fiscal officer is that of a reserve commissioned officer of the United States Army or Air Force, as appropriate, on extended active duty and detailed for duty with the National Guard Bureau for administrative purposes. In the officer's capacity as United States property and fiscal officer, the officer will function under the direction of and cooperate fully with the State Adjutant General.

(c) The assumption and performance of duties and responsibilities, pay and allowances, and other personnel actions to include retention and retirement of an officer appointed and serving as the United States property and fiscal officer will be governed by regulations promulgated by the National Guard Bureau or pursuant to regulations promulgated by the secretary of the appropriate service. (1975, c. 604, s. 2; 1977, c. 70, s. 2; 2009-281, s. 1; 2011-145, s. 19.1(g); 2011-195, s. 1(a).)

§ 127A-22. North Carolina property and fiscal officer.

(a) Upon full mobilization of the North Carolina National Guard into federal service to the extent that the functions of a United States property and fiscal officer no longer exist or are authorized under federal statutes, the Governor of the State, in consultation with the Secretary of Public Safety, may appoint, designate or detail a qualified individual to serve at the pleasure of the Governor as the North Carolina property and fiscal officer for any composition of a nonfederally recognized State National Guard or State defense militia organized under the provisions of this Chapter.

(b) In consideration of the North Carolina property and fiscal officer's services for the responsibility, care, utilization, and issue of State or federal facilities and property, under the jurisdiction of the State of North Carolina, the officer shall receive from the State a just and proper salary as authorized by the Governor; the salary to constitute a charge upon appropriations made to the Department of Public Safety.

(c) The North Carolina property and fiscal officer shall be an employee of the Department of Public Safety. The officer shall be required to give good and sufficient bond to the State, the amount thereof to be determined by the Governor, for the faithful performance of duties and for the safekeeping and proper distribution of the funds and property entrusted to the officer's care. The officer shall receipt for and account for all funds and property allotted to the officer's custody from the appropriation for military purposes by State and federal agencies, and shall make returns and reports through the Secretary of Public Safety concerning the property and funds as required by the Governor or State laws. (1917, c. 200, ss. 24, 25; C.S., ss. 6804, 6805; 1929, c. 317, s. 1; 1957, c. 136, s. 3; 1963, c. 1016, s. 2; 1973, c. 620, s. 9; 1975, c. 604, s. 2; 1977, c. 70, s. 2; 2009-281, s. 1; 2011-145, s. 19.1(g); 2011-195, s. 1(a).)

§ 127A-23. Commissions for commandants and officers at qualified educational institutions.

The Governor of North Carolina is authorized to appoint and commission, as staff officers of the North Carolina unorganized militia, the officers of any university, college, academy or other educational institution which qualifies as provided in this section. Any university, college, academy or other educational institution shall be qualified under this section when the institution has been regularly incorporated under and by virtue of the laws of North Carolina; the institution, as a part of its courses of study, regularly teaches military science and tactics; the Department of Defense at Washington, D.C., has detailed an officer of the Armed Forces of the United States as professor or assistant professor of military science and tactics; the institution has been designated as qualified by the secretary of the appropriate service and has been made a unit of the Senior or Junior Reserve Officers' Training Corps, or the institution, not having a unit of the Reserve Officers' Training Corps, has been approved and authorized by the Secretary of Defense to participate in the National Defense Cadet Corps Training Program or other military training programs under Title 10, United States Code, sections 3540 and 4651.

Any qualified institution desiring the appointment of officers in the North Carolina unorganized militia shall make application to the Governor setting forth all requisite facts as to its qualifications, the names of the persons to be commissioned, the rank desired for each, and the person's position at the institution. The application shall be signed by the chancellor, president, superintendent or other presiding official, under the seal of the institution. Upon receipt of the application, the Governor may appoint and commission the officers of a qualified institution as follows: the chancellor, president, superintendent or other presiding official, as colonel; the vice-president, principal or other officer second in authority, as major; the professors and members of the faculty, as captains. The persons so commissioned shall have no connection with the North Carolina National Guard or other military forces of the State, nor shall they exercise any military authority other than in the discharge of their duties at their respective institutions. The commissions issued under this section may be terminated at the will of the Governor. (1919, c. 265, ss. 1, 2, 3; C.S., s. 6812; 1929, c. 61, s. 1; 1963, c. 1095; 1973, c. 476, s. 128; 1975, c. 604, s. 2; 2009-281, s. 1; 2011-195, s. 1(a).)

§§ 127A-24 through 127A-28. Reserved for future codification purposes.

Article 3.

National Guard.

§ 127A-29. National Guard.

The North Carolina National Guard class of the four classes of the organized militia as established under G.S. 127A-2 is hereby designated the "North Carolina National Guard." Those elements of the North Carolina National Guard which receive federal recognition by the United States government shall hold a dual status both as State troops and as a reserve component of the Armed Forces of the United States. In its federal status, the North Carolina National Guard shall be subject to federal laws and regulations pertaining thereto. The Adjutant General shall insure compliance with those federal laws and regulations and with all State laws and orders of the Governor not inconsistent with them. (1975, c. 604, s. 2; 2009-281, s. 1; 2011-195, s. 1(a).)

§ 127A-30. Organization of National Guard units.

Except as otherwise specifically provided by the laws of the United States, the organization of the North Carolina National Guard, including the composition of all its units, shall be the same as that which is or may hereafter be prescribed for the regular United States Army or Air Force subject in time of peace to general exceptions authorized by the Secretary of Defense. (1917, c. 200, s. 7; C.S., s. 6808; 1959, c. 218, s. 4; 1975, c. 604, s. 2; 2009-281, s. 1; 2011-195, s. 1(a).)

§ 127A-31. Location of units.

The Governor shall determine and fix the location of the units and headquarters of the North Carolina National Guard within the State; but no organization of the North Carolina National Guard, members of which shall be entitled to and shall have received compensation under the provisions of the act of Congress approved June 3, 1916, as amended, shall be disbanded without the consent of the President, nor without that consent shall the commissioned or enlisted strength of any such organization be reduced below the minimum that is now or shall be hereafter prescribed therefor by the President. (1917, c. 200, s. 9; C.S., s. 6809; 1921, c. 120, s. 2; 1975, c. 604, s. 2; 2009-281, s. 1; 2011-195, s. 1(a).)

§ 127A-32. Officers appointed and commissioned; oath of office.

All officers of the North Carolina National Guard shall be appointed and commissioned by the Governor as follows, viz.:

(1)   Except as otherwise specifically provided by the laws of the United States, the qualifications for appointment as an officer in the North Carolina National Guard shall be the same as those prescribed for the regular establishment, subject to general exceptions authorized by the Secretary of Defense.

(2)   Candidates for appointment shall make written application therefor on forms prescribed by the secretary of the appropriate service, to the Adjutant General, State of North Carolina, through command channels for comment by endorsements thereon.

(3)   No person shall hereafter be appointed an officer of the North Carolina National Guard unless the person has established to the satisfaction of a board of officers that person's physical, moral, and professional qualifications to perform the duties of the grade and position for which examined, subject to general exceptions authorized by the Secretary of Defense. The board shall consist of three or more commissioned officers of the appropriate service, appointed under regulations promulgated by the secretary of the appropriate service.

(4)   Candidates appointed as officers of the North Carolina National Guard shall take and subscribe to the following oath of office:

"I, (First Name - Middle Name - Last Name), do solemnly swear that I will support and defend the Constitution of the United States and the Constitution of the State of North Carolina against all enemies, foreign and domestic; that I will bear true faith and allegiance to the same; that I will obey orders of the President of the United States and of the Governor of the State of North Carolina; that I make this obligation freely, without any mental reservation or purpose of evasion, and that I will well and faithfully discharge the duties of the office of (Grade) (Branch) in the National Guard of the State of North Carolina upon which I am about to enter, so help me God." (1917, c. 200, s. 15; C.S., s. 6811; 1921, c. 120, s. 3; 1959, c. 218, s. 5; 1973, c. 620, s. 9; 1975, c. 604, s. 2; 2009-281, s. 1; 2011-195, s. 1(a).)

§ 127A-33. Promotion of officers by seniority and in accordance with regulations.

The promotion of all officers shall be by seniority as far as practicable and in the best interest of the service within the organization, and in accordance with regulations promulgated by the secretary of the appropriate service. (1917, c. 200, s. 17; C.S., s. 6814; 1921, c. 120, s. 4; 1959, c. 218, s. 7; 1975, c. 604, s. 2; 2011-195, s. 1(a).)

§ 127A-34. Relative rank among officers of same grade.

Officers of the North Carolina National Guard in the same grade rank among themselves according to the date of rank established by regulations promulgated by the secretary of the appropriate service and the Adjutant General of the State of North Carolina. (1917, c. 200, s. 19; C.S., s. 6816; 1921, c. 120, s. 5; 1927, c. 227, s. 1; 1959, c. 218, s. 8; 1961, c. 192, s. 2; 1963, c. 1016, s. 2; 1975, c. 604, s. 2; 2009-281, s. 1.)

§ 127A-35. Elimination and disposition of officers; efficiency board; transfer to inactive status.

(a) Whenever the efficiency or general fitness, including physical fitness, of a North Carolina National Guard officer is in question, the Adjutant General, State of North Carolina, may order the officer to appear before an efficiency board to determine whether or not the appointment of the officer should be withdrawn. The efficiency board will be composed of not less than three commissioned officers, all senior in rank to the officer undergoing investigation. A member of the board serving in a legal or medical advisory capacity may be junior to any person, other than a judge advocate, law specialist, or medical officer being considered. The findings of an efficiency board are not final until reviewed and approved by the Secretary of Public Safety and the Governor of the State of North Carolina.

(b) Commissions of officers of the North Carolina National Guard may be vacated upon resignation, absence without leave for 30 days, pursuant to sentence of a court martial, or pursuant to regulations promulgated by the secretary of the appropriate service.

(c) Officers of the North Carolina National Guard may, upon their own request, be transferred to the inactive North Carolina National Guard, subject to exceptions authorized by the Adjutant General, State of North Carolina, or the Secretary of Defense. (1917, c. 200, s. 28; C.S., s. 6818; 1959, c. 218, s. 9; 1975, c. 604, s. 2; 1977, c. 70, s. 2; 2009-281, s. 1; 2011-145, s. 19.1(g); 2011-195, s. 1(a).)

§ 127A-36. Retirement of officers.

Retirement of officers shall be regulated so as to conform to federal laws and regulations of the United States relating to retirement of National Guard officers. (1917, c. 200, s. 29; C.S., s. 6819; 1949, c. 1130, s. 2; 1975, c. 604, s. 2; 2009-281, s. 1.)

§ 127A-37. Enlistments in National Guard; oath of enlistment.

(a) Enlistments in the North Carolina National Guard shall be for the periods and subject to the qualifications as prescribed by the secretary of the appropriate service.

(b)   Enlisted persons shall not be recognized as members of the North Carolina National Guard until they shall have subscribed to the following oath of enlistment:

"I do hereby acknowledge to have voluntarily enlisted this ____ day of _____, ____, in the (Army) (Air) National Guard of the State of North Carolina and as a Reserve of the (Army) (Air Force) with membership in the (Army National Guard of the United States) (Air National Guard of the United States) for a period of (Years - Months - Days) under the conditions prescribed by law, unless sooner discharged by proper authority.

"I, (First Name - Middle Name - Last Name), do solemnly swear (or affirm) that I will support and defend the Constitution of the United States and of the State of North Carolina against all enemies, foreign and domestic; that I will bear true faith and allegiance to them; and that I will obey the orders of the President of the United States and the Governor of North Carolina and the orders of the officers appointed over me, according to law, regulations, and the Uniform Code of Military Justice, so help me God." (1917, c. 200, s. 30; C.S., s. 6820; 1921, c. 120, s. 6; 1957, c. 136, s. 6; 1959, c. 218, s. 10; 1975, c. 604, s. 2; 1999, c. 456, s. 59; 2009-281, s. 1; 2011-195, s. 1(a).)

§ 127A-38. Discharge of enlisted personnel.

(a)   Enlisted personnel discharged from service in the North Carolina National Guard shall receive a discharge in writing in the form and with the classification that is or shall be prescribed under regulations promulgated by the appropriate service.

(b)   Discharges may be given prior to the expiration of terms of enlistment under regulations prescribed by the Adjutant General, State of North Carolina, or pursuant to regulations promulgated by the secretary of the appropriate service. (1917, c. 200, s. 32; C.S., s. 6822; 1959, c. 218, s. 12; 1975, c. 604, s. 2; 2009-281, s. 1; 2011-195, s. 1(a).)

§ 127A-39. Membership continued in the National Guard.

When called or ordered into federal service and discharged therefrom, members shall continue their membership in the North Carolina National Guard until the expiration of their enlistment or appointment, unless sooner terminated by proper authority. (1921, c. 120, s. 8; C.S., s. 6822(a); 1959, c. 218, s. 13; 1975, c. 604, s. 2; 2009-281, s. 1; 2011-195, s. 1(a).)

§ 127A-40. Pensions for the members of the North Carolina National Guard.

(a) Every member and former member of the North Carolina National Guard who meets the requirements of this section shall receive, commencing at age 60, a pension of ninety-five dollars ($95.00) per month for 20 years' creditable military service with an additional nine dollars fifty cents ($9.50) per month for each additional year of such service; provided, however, that the total pension shall not exceed one hundred ninety dollars ($190.00) per month. The requirements for a pension are that each member shall:

(1) Have served and qualified for at least 20 years' creditable military service, including National Guard, reserve and active duty, under the same requirement specified for entitlement to retired pay for nonregular service under Chapter 67, Title 10, United States Code.

(2) Have at least 15 years of the aforementioned service as a member of the North Carolina National Guard.

(3) Have received an honorable discharge from the North Carolina National Guard.

(b) Payment to a retired member of the North Carolina National Guard under the provisions of this section will cease at the death of the individual and no payment will be made to beneficiaries or to the decedent's estate, except that the legal representative of a retired member who dies shall be entitled to a full check for the month in which the death occurred.

(c) No individual receiving retired pay as a result of length of service, age or physical disability retirement from any of the regular components of the Armed Forces of the United States will be eligible for benefits under this section.

(d) Nothing contained in this section shall preclude or in any way affect the benefits that an individual may be entitled to from State, federal or private retirement systems.

(e) Repealed by Session Laws 1989, c. 792, s. 2.3.

(f) The Board of Trustees of the Teachers' and State Employees' Retirement System shall administer the provisions of this section. The Secretary of Public Safety shall determine the eligibility of North Carolina National Guard members for the benefits provided in this section and shall certify those eligible to the Board of Trustees. In addition, the Department of Public Safety shall, on and after July 1, 1983, provide the Board of Trustees with an annual census population, by age and the number of years of creditable service, for all former members of the North Carolina National Guard in receipt of a pension as well as for all active members of the North Carolina National Guard who are not in receipt of a pension and who have seven and more years of creditable service. The Department of Public Safety shall also provide the Board of Trustees an annual census population of all former members of the North Carolina National Guard who are not in receipt of a pension and who have 15 and more years of creditable service. The Department of State Treasurer shall make pension payments to those persons certified from the North Carolina National Guard Pension Fund, which shall include general fund appropriations made to the Department of State Treasurer. The Board of Trustees shall have performed an annual actuarial valuation of the fund and shall have the financial responsibility for maintaining the fund on a generally accepted actuarial basis. The Department of Public Safety shall provide the Department of State Treasurer with whatever assistance is required by the State Treasurer in carrying out the State Treasurer's and the Board of Trustees' financial responsibilities.

(g) The provisions of this section shall apply to any member or former member of the North Carolina National Guard who is qualified for the above retirements with eligibility commencing at age 60 or July 1, 1974, whichever is the later date.

(h) If, for any reason, the North Carolina National Guard Pension Fund shall be insufficient to pay in full any pension benefits, or other charges, then all benefits or payments shall be reduced pro rata, for as long as the deficiency in amount exists. No claim shall accrue with respect to any amount by which a pension or benefit payment shall have been reduced.

(h1) Any member or former member of the North Carolina National Guard who is qualified for benefits under this section and who is a member of a domiciled employees' or retirees' association that has at least 2,000 members, the majority of whom are active or retired employees of the State or public school employees, may authorize, in writing, the periodic deduction from the member's retirement benefits a designated lump sum to be paid to the employees' or retirees' association. The authorization shall remain in effect until revoked by the member. A plan of deductions pursuant to this subsection shall become void if the employees' or retirees' association engages in collective bargaining with the State, any political subdivision of the State, or any local school administrative unit.

(i) Pensions for members of the North Carolina National Guard shall be subject to future legislative change or revision. (1973, c. 625, s. 1; c. 1241, ss. 1-3; 1975, c. 604, s. 2; 1977, c. 70, s. 2; 1979, c. 870; 1983, c. 761, ss. 250, 251; 1989, c. 792, s. 2.3; 2002-126, s. 6.4(g); 2005-276, s. 29.27; 2006-66, s. 22.20; 2007-323, s. 28.21A; 2009-66, s. 10; 2009-281, s. 1; 2009-451, s. 26.21; 2011-145, s. 19.1(g); 2011-195, s. 1(a); 2013-287, s. 3.)

§ 127A-41. Uniforms, arms and equipment.

The North Carolina National Guard shall, as far as practicable, be uniformed, armed, and equipped with the same type of uniforms, arms and equipment as is or shall be provided for the appropriate regular service. (1917, c. 200, s. 37; C.S., s. 6824; 1959, c. 218, s. 15; 1975, c. 604, s. 2; 2009-281, s. 1; 2011-195, s. 1(a).)

§ 127A-41.1. Stay of legal and court proceedings because of State military service.

At any stage of any legal proceeding in any court in which a person called into service of the State by the Governor is involved, either as plaintiff or defendant, during the period of service or within 60 days after the conclusion of the period of active service, all actions and proceedings:

(1) May be stayed by the court on its own motion; or

(2) Shall be stayed on application by the member or by a person acting on behalf of the member, unless, in the opinion of the court, the ability of the plaintiff to prosecute the action or the defendant to conduct a defense is not materially affected by reason of the military service. (1997-153, s. 5; 2011-195, s. 1(a).)

§ 127A-41.2. Operation of post exchanges.

(a) The North Carolina National Guard is authorized to operate post exchanges.

(b) The North Carolina National Guard is authorized to enter into agreements with the Army & Air Force Exchange Service to operate post exchanges. (2007-60, s. 2; 2009-281, s. 1.)

§ 127A-42. Distinguished Service Medal by Governor of North Carolina.

There is hereby created the North Carolina Distinguished Service Medal which shall be of appropriate design, and a ribbon, together with a rosette or other device to be worn in lieu thereof. This medal and appurtenances thereto shall be of a design approved by the Governor. Upon the recommendation of the Secretary of Public Safety and a board consisting of the Adjutant General and all other general officers and officers assigned to authorized general-officer-grade vacancies of the North Carolina National Guard, the Governor is authorized to present the medal to any member or former member of the Armed Forces of the United States discharged under honorable conditions, who has distinguished himself or herself by exceptionally meritorious conduct in the performance of outstanding service to the North Carolina National Guard. The Governor, on the Governor's own authority, may award the medal to the Secretary of Public Safety, the Adjutant General, or any other active or inactive general officer or flag officer of the Armed Forces of the United States who has distinguished himself or herself by especially meritorious conduct in the performance of his or her duties. (1955, c. 255, s. 2; 1963, c. 1016, s. 2; 1973, c. 1124; 1975, c. 604, s. 2; 1977, c. 230, s. 1; 2009-281, s. 1; 2011-145, s. 19.1(g); 2011-195, s. 1(a).)

§ 127A-43. North Carolina National Guard Meritorious Service Medal.

There is hereby created the North Carolina National Guard Meritorious Service Medal which shall be of appropriate design, and a ribbon, together with a rosette or other device to be worn in lieu thereof. This medal and appurtenances thereto shall be of a design approved by the Governor or the Governor's designee. The Governor or the Governor's designee is authorized to award this medal upon the recommendation of the Secretary of Public Safety in consultation with the Adjutant General and a board of officers appointed by the Adjutant General. Any member or former member of the Armed Forces of the United States discharged under honorable conditions, who has distinguished himself or herself by heroism, meritorious achievement, or meritorious service to the North Carolina National Guard, is eligible for this award. The Governor, on the Governor's own authority, may award the medal to the Secretary of Public Safety, the Adjutant General or any other active or inactive general officer or flag officer of the Armed Forces of the United States who has distinguished himself or herself by heroism, meritorious achievement, or meritorious service to the North Carolina National Guard. The required heroism, achievement, or service, while of a lesser degree than that required for awarding of the North Carolina Distinguished Service Medal, must nevertheless be accomplished with distinction. (1973, c. 966, s. 1; 1975, c. 604, s. 2; 1977, c. 230, s. 2; 2009-281, s. 1; 2011-145, s. 19.1(g); 2011-195, s. 1(a).)

§ 127A-44. North Carolina National Guard Commendation Medal.

There is hereby created the North Carolina National Guard Commendation Medal which shall be of appropriate design, and a ribbon, together with a rosette or other device to be worn in lieu thereof. This medal and appurtenances thereto shall be of a design approved by the Governor or the Governor's designee. The Adjutant General of North Carolina or the Adjutant General's designee, who shall not be below the rank of colonel (O-6), may award this medal. Any member or former member of the Armed Forces of the United States discharged under honorable conditions, who distinguishes himself or herself by example or the performance of a specific act in behalf of the North Carolina National Guard, is eligible for this award. (1975, c. 604, s. 2; 1977, c. 230, s. 3; 1991, c. 367, s. 2; 2011-195, s. 1(a).)

§ 127A-44.1. North Carolina National Guard Achievement Medal.

There is hereby created the North Carolina National Guard Achievement Medal which shall be of appropriate design, and a ribbon, together with a rosette or other device to be worn in lieu thereof. This medal and appurtenances thereto shall be of a design approved by the Governor or the Governor's designee. The Adjutant General of North Carolina or the Adjutant General's designee, who shall not be below the rank of lieutenant colonel (O-5), may award this medal. Any member or former member of the Armed Forces of the United States discharged under honorable conditions, who distinguishes himself or herself by example or the performance of a specific act in behalf of the North Carolina National Guard, is eligible for this award. (1991, c. 367, s. 3; 2011-195, s. 1(a).)

§ 127A-45. North Carolina National Guard State Active Duty Award.

There is hereby created the North Carolina National Guard State Active Duty Award which shall be a ribbon of appropriate design. This ribbon and appurtenances thereto shall be of a design approved by the Governor or the Governor's designee. The Adjutant General of North Carolina may present this ribbon to members of the North Carolina National Guard who, by order of the Governor, satisfactorily serve a tour of State active duty. To be worthy of this award, the nature of the tour of State active duty must have been a distinct and notable service to the State or to a community, as determined by the Adjutant General of North Carolina. On or after July 1, 1991, this award may also be presented to active guard personnel and reserve personnel who satisfactorily participate in tours of State active duty. (1973, c. 966, s. 2; 1975, c. 604, s. 2; 1991, c. 367, s. 1; 2011-195, s. 1(a).)

§ 127A-45.1. North Carolina National Guard Governor's Unit Citation.

There is hereby created the North Carolina National Guard Governor's Unit Citation which shall be a streamer, a unit emblem, and a certificate, all of appropriate design as approved by the Governor or the Governor's designee. The Governor or the Governor's designee is authorized to present the unit citation, upon recommendation of the Adjutant General, subject to the approval of the Secretary, to any unit of North Carolina National Guard distinguishing itself by extraordinary heroism or meritorious service while in a State active duty status. The unit must display such gallantry, determination, and esprit de corps in accomplishing its mission under conditions which set it apart and above other units. (1977, c. 229, s. 1; 2009-281, s. 1; 2011-195, s. 1(a).)

§ 127A-45.2. North Carolina National Guard Meritorious Unit Citation.

There is hereby created the North Carolina National Guard Meritorious Unit Citation which shall be a streamer, a unit emblem, and a certificate, all of appropriate design as approved by the Governor or the Governor's designee. The Adjutant General is authorized to present this citation to any unit of the North Carolina National Guard distinguishing itself through heroism or meritorious service to the State of North Carolina. The required heroism or meritorious service, while of a lesser degree than that required for the award of the North Carolina National Guard Governor's Unit Citation, must nevertheless have been accomplished with distinction. (1977, c. 229, s. 2; 2009-281, s. 1; 2011-195, s. 1(a).)

§ 127A-45.2A. North Carolina National Guard Outstanding Unit Award.

There is hereby created the North Carolina National Guard Outstanding Unit Award which shall be a streamer, a unit emblem, and a certificate, all of appropriate design as approved by the Governor or the Governor's designee. The Adjutant General may present this citation to any unit of the North Carolina National Guard distinguishing itself through meritorious achievement or service to the State of North Carolina. The required meritorious service, while of a lesser degree than that required for the award of the North Carolina National Guard Meritorious Unit Citation, must nevertheless have been accomplished with distinction. (1991, c. 367, s. 4; 2011-195, s. 1(a).)

§ 127A-45.3. North Carolina National Guard Distinguished Civilian Service Medal.

There is hereby created the North Carolina National Guard Distinguished Civilian Service Medal which shall be of appropriate design, rosette or other device to be worn in lieu thereof, and citation certificate, of a design approved by the Governor or the Governor's designee. The Governor or the Governor's designee is authorized to award this medal upon the recommendation of the Adjutant General of North Carolina and a board of officers and noncommissioned officers appointed by the Adjutant General, to United States citizens and governmental officials at the policy development level who render distinguished service to the North Carolina National Guard. (1977, c. 796; 2009-281, s. 1; 2011-195, s. 1(a).)

§ 127A-45.4. North Carolina National Guard Outstanding Civilian Service Medal.

There is hereby created the North Carolina National Guard Outstanding Civilian Service Medal which shall be of appropriate design, rosette or other device to be worn in lieu thereof, and citation certificate, of a design approved by the Governor or the Governor's designee. The Adjutant General of North Carolina is authorized to award this medal upon the recommendation of a board of officers and noncommissioned officers, appointed by the Adjutant General, to United States citizens and governmental officials who render outstanding service to the North Carolina National Guard. (1977, c. 796; 2009-281, s. 1; 2011-195, s. 1(a).)

§ 127A-45.5. North Carolina National Guard Meritorious Civilian Service Award.

There is hereby created the North Carolina National Guard Meritorious Civilian Service Award which shall consist of a certificate of a design approved by the Governor or the Governor's designee. The Adjutant General of North Carolina or the Adjutant General's designee, who shall not be below the grade of general officer, is authorized to confer this award. This award may be granted to individuals, organizations, corporations, associations and other groups, making a substantial contribution to the North Carolina National Guard. (1977, c. 796; 2009-281, s. 1; 2011-195, s. 1(a).)

§ 127A-45.5A. Other awards.

The Adjutant General may, from time to time, create other awards and medals to recognize meritorious service or outstanding achievement. The creation of the awards and medals shall be approved by the Governor. The Governor or the Governor's designee shall approve the design of the awards and medals. (1991, c. 367, s. 5; 2011-195, s. 1(a).)

§ 127A-46. Authority to wear medals, ribbons and other awards.

The Adjutant General may prescribe those medals, ribbons and other awards and decorations that may be worn by members of the militia, not inconsistent with regulations of the respective Armed Forces of the United States. (1939, c. 344; 1959, c. 218, s. 16; 1967, c. 563, s. 4; 1975, c. 604, s. 2; 2011-195, s. 1(a).)

§ 127A-47. Courts-martial for National Guard.

Courts-martial for military personnel of the North Carolina National Guard not in the service of the United States shall be of three kinds, namely, general courts-martial, special courts-martial, and summary courts-martial. They shall be constituted, have cognizance of the same subjects, and possess like powers as similar courts provided for by the Uniform Code of Military Justice and Manual for Courts-Martial, United States. The proceedings of courts-martial of the North Carolina National Guard shall follow the forms and modes of procedure prescribed for such similar courts. (1917, c. 200, s. 55; C.S., s. 6825; 1963, c. 1018, s. 1; 1975, c. 604, s. 2; 2009-281, s. 1; 2010-193, s. 1; 2011-195, s. 1(a).)

§ 127A-48. General courts-martial.

General courts-martial for military personnel of the North Carolina National Guard not in the service of the United States may be convened by orders of the Governor of the State or of the Adjutant General, and these courts shall have the power to impose punishments in like manner and to the extent prescribed by the Uniform Code of Military Justice and Manual for Courts-Martial, United States, as shall be in use by the Armed Forces of the United States at the time of the offense, except that (i) no court shall have the authority to impose confinement as part of the sentence unless the court consisted of a military judge and not less than five members, except that a defendant who requests a military judge alone may be sentenced to confinement, and (ii) no court shall have the authority to impose confinement in excess of one year and one day as part of a sentence. (1917, c. 200, s. 56; C.S., s. 6826; 1957, c. 136, s. 7; 1963, c. 1018, s. 2; 1975, c. 604, s. 2; 2009-281, s. 1; 2010-193, s. 2; 2011-195, s. 1(a).)

§ 127A-49. Special courts-martial; appointments, power and authority.

In the North Carolina National Guard, not in the service of the United States, special courts-martial may be appointed by any of the following:

(1)   The commander of a brigade, regiment, comparable or higher command of the North Carolina Army National Guard, provided that the commander is a general officer.

(2)   The commander of a wing, group, separate squadron, comparable or higher command of the North Carolina Air National Guard, provided that the commander is a general officer.

(3)   The commander or officer in charge of any North Carolina National Guard command when empowered by the Governor or the Adjutant General of North Carolina, provided that the commander or officer is a general officer.

Except as to commissioned officers, special courts-martial shall have the power and authority to try any person subject to military law for any crimes or offenses within the jurisdiction of a general military court. Special courts-martial shall have the power to impose punishments in like manner and to the extent prescribed by the Uniform Code of Military Justice and Manual for Courts-Martial, United States, as shall be in use by the Armed Forces of the United States at the time of the offense, except that (i) no court shall have the authority to impose confinement as part of the sentence unless the court consisted of a military judge and not less than three members except that a defendant who requests a military judge alone may be sentenced to confinement, and (ii) no court shall have the authority to impose confinement in excess of six months as part of a sentence. (1917, c. 200, s. 57; C.S., s. 6827; 1957, c. 136, s. 8; 1963, c. 1018, s. 3; 1973, c. 1123; 1975, c. 604, s. 2; 2009-281, s. 1; 2010-193, s. 3; 2011-195, s. 1(a).)

§ 127A-50. Summary courts-martial.

In the North Carolina National Guard, not in the service of the United States, summary courts-martial may be appointed by any of the following:

(1) Any person who may convene a general or special court-martial.

(2) The commander of a battalion, comparable or higher command of the North Carolina Army National Guard, provided that the commander is an officer of the grade of major or above.

(3) The commander of a detached squadron, comparable or higher command of the North Carolina Air National Guard, provided that the commander is an officer of the grade of major or above.

The court shall consist of one officer who shall have the power to administer oaths and try enlisted personnel of each respective command for breaches of discipline and violations of laws governing those organizations. These courts shall also have the power to impose punishments in like manner and to the extent prescribed by the Uniform Code of Military Justice and Manual for Courts-Martial, United States, as shall be in use by the Armed Forces of the United States at the time of the offense, except that no court shall have the authority to impose confinement as part of a sentence. There shall be no right to demand trial by court-martial. (1917, c. 200, s. 58; C.S., s. 6828; 1957, c. 136, s. 9; 1963, c. 1018, s. 4; 1975, c. 604, s. 2; 1983, c. 315, s. 1; 2009-281, s. 1; 2010-193, s. 4; 2011-195, s. 1(a).)

§ 127A-50.1. Military judges.

The Adjutant General shall appoint military judges to preside over courts-martial of the North Carolina National Guard not in federal service. Minimum requirements for appointment as a military judge are:

(1) Certification as a military judge by the Judge Advocate General of the United States Army, Air Force, Navy, Marines, or Coast Guard.

(2) Designation as a judge advocate by the Judge Advocate General of the United States Army, Navy, Air Force, Marines, or Coast Guard.

(3) Membership in the North Carolina National Guard, the National Guard of another state, or the active or reserve components of the Armed Forces of the United States. (1987, c. 649, s. 1; 2010-193, s. 5; 2011-195, s. 1(a).)

§ 127A-51. Nonjudicial punishment.

Any commander of the North Carolina National Guard, not in the service of the United States, may, in addition to or in lieu of admonition or reprimand, impose nonjudicial punishment in like manner and to the extent prescribed by Article 15 of the Uniform Code of Military Justice and Manual for Courts-Martial, United States, as shall be currently in use by the Armed Forces of the United States except that there shall be no right to demand trial by court-martial. (1957, c. 136, s. 10; 1975, c. 604, s. 2; 1983, c. 315, s. 2; c. 316, s. 1; 2009-281, s. 1; 2010-193, s. 6; 2011-195, s. 1(a).)

§ 127A-52. Jurisdiction of courts-martial.

The jurisdiction of courts-martial of the North Carolina National Guard, not in the service of the United States, shall be as prescribed by the Manual for Courts-Martial, United States, as shall be currently in use by the Armed Forces of the United States. Such courts-martial shall have jurisdiction to try accused persons for offenses committed while serving without the State and while going to and returning from service without the State in like manner and to the same extent as while serving within the State. (1957, c. 136, s. 10; 1975, c. 604, s. 2; 1983, c. 316, s. 2; 2009-281, s. 1; 2010-193, s. 7; 2011-195, s. 1(a).)

§ 127A-53. Manual for Courts-Martial.

Trials and proceedings by all courts and boards shall be in accordance with the Manual for Courts-Martial, United States, as shall be currently in use by the Armed Forces of the United States, except as modified by this Chapter. (1917, c. 200, s. 64; C.S., s. 6831; 1957, c. 136, s. 14; 1975, c. 604, s. 2; 1983, c. 316, s. 3; 2010-193, s. 8; 2011-195, s. 1(a).)

§ 127A-54. Pretrial confinement; sentences; where executed.

(a) A defendant may be arrested and placed under pretrial confinement in a local government confinement facility, but a determination shall be made under subsection (b) of this section whether he or she shall remain confined pending the court-martial. If the defendant is not released from confinement, he or she shall be transferred into the custody of the Sheriff of Wake County and confined in the Wake County confinement facility pending trial. All costs of transportation and confinement are to be paid from funds appropriated to the Department of Public Safety as reimbursements to the local government or agency providing the transportation and confinement.

(b) The provisions of Article 26 of Chapter 15A of the General Statutes shall apply to any defendant who has been placed into pretrial confinement, in the same manner as if the defendant had been placed into confinement for an alleged violation of the criminal laws of this State. Nothing in this section is intended to abridge the right of habeas corpus.

(c) Any defendant whose sentence by a military court includes confinement shall be placed into the custody of the Division of Adult Correction of the Department of Public Safety. The Division of Adult Correction of the Department of Public Safety is authorized to transfer physical custody of the defendant to a local confinement facility. (1917, c. 200, s. 61; C.S., s. 6832; 1975, c. 604, s. 2; 2010-193, s. 9; 2011-145, s. 19.1(g), (h).)

§ 127A-55. Forms for courts-martial procedure.

In the North Carolina National Guard, not in the service of the United States, forms for courts-martial procedure shall be substantially as those set forth in the Appendices, Manual for Courts-Martial, United States, as shall be currently in use by the Armed Forces of the United States, with any modifications required by this Chapter. (1957, c. 136, s. 13; 1975, c. 604, s. 2; 1983, c. 316, s. 4; 2009-281, s. 1; 2010-193, s. 10; 2011-195, s. 1(a).)

§ 127A-56. Powers of courts-martial.

In the North Carolina National Guard, not in the service of the United States, presidents of courts-martial and summary court officers shall have power to issue warrants to arrest an accused person and to bring the person before a court for trial whenever the person has disobeyed an order in writing from the convening authority to appear before the court, a copy of the charge or charges having been delivered to the accused with the order, and to issue subpoenas and subpoenas duces tecum, and to enforce by attachment attendance of witnesses and the production of books, papers, records and other articles subject to a subpoena duces tecum, and to sentence for a refusal to be sworn or to answer as provided in actions before civil courts. The presiding officer shall also have power to punish for contempt occurring in the presence of the court. (1917, c. 200, s. 60; C.S., s. 6830; 1957, c. 136, s. 12; 1975, c. 604, s. 2; 1983, c. 316, s. 5; 2009-281, s. 1; 2010-193, s. 11; 2011-195, s. 1(a).)

§ 127A-57. Execution of processes and sentences.

All warrants and other processes authorized by this Chapter and sentences of any of the military courts of this State shall be executed by any sheriff, deputy sheriff, or State or local law enforcement officer into whose hands they may be placed for service or execution, and the officer shall make return thereof to the officer issuing or imposing the same. The service or execution of process or sentence shall be made by the officer without tender or advancement of fee therefor; but all costs in these cases shall be paid from funds appropriated to the Department of Public Safety. (1917, c. 200, s. 62; C.S., s. 6833; 1973, c. 108, s. 80; 1975, c. 604, s. 2; 2010-193, s. 12; 2011-145, s. 19.1(g); 2011-195, s. 1(a).)

§ 127A-58: Repealed by Session Laws 2010-193, s. 13, effective December 1, 2010.

§ 127A-59. (See note for contingency) Sentences.

When any sentence to fine or imprisonment is imposed by any military court of this State, it shall be the duty of the military judge, president of the court, or summary court officer, upon the approval of the court's findings and sentence, to make out and sign a certificate entitling the case, giving the name of the accused, the date and place of trial, the date of approval of sentence, and the terms of the sentence. The trial counsel shall deliver the certificate to the Clerk of the Superior Court of Wake County, and it shall thereupon be the duty of the clerk to take the actions necessary to carry the sentence into execution in the same manner as prescribed by law for the collection of fines, or commitment to service of terms of imprisonment, in criminal cases determined in the courts of this State. The Administrative Office of the Courts shall ensure that the State's criminal history records include pertinent information relating to a court-martial under this Chapter in a like manner as a comparable offense under the State's criminal laws would be recorded. (1917, c. 200, s. 63; C.S., s. 6834; 1973, c. 108, s. 81; 1975, c. 604, s. 2; 2010-193, s. 14; 2011-195, s. 1(a).)

§ 127A-60. Approval of sentence.

No sentence imposed by a special or general court-martial of the North Carolina National Guard, not in the service of the United States, shall be executed until approved by the Governor. Any officer convicted by a general court-martial and dismissed from the service shall be forever disqualified from holding a commission in the militia. (1917, c. 200, s. 65; C.S., s. 6835; 1975, c. 604, s. 2; 2009-281, s. 1; 2010-193, s. 15; 2011-195, s. 1(a).)

§ 127A-61. Disposition of fines.

Fines imposed by courts-martial under this Chapter shall be disposed of as prescribed in Article IX, Sec. 7, of the Constitution of North Carolina. (1975, c. 604, s. 2.)

§ 127A-62. Appeals; discretionary review.

(a) Jurisdiction. - Court-martial judgments which include a sentence to confinement shall have a right of appeal to the Wake County Superior Court. The provisions of G.S. 15A-1451 shall apply to appeals under this section.

(b) Filing and Service. - An appeal under this section must be made in writing and filed with the Clerk of Superior Court of Wake County within 10 days after the approval of the sentence by the Governor. A copy of the petition shall be filed with the military court and the military trial counsel of record. For the purposes of a filing fee, the appeal shall be treated as an administrative appeal to the Superior Court.

(c) Assertion of Errors. - All errors, including, but not limited to, the following, must be asserted or shall be deemed waived:

(1) Any error of law, including the following:

a. The court erroneously failed to dismiss the charge prior to the court-martial.

b. The court's ruling was contrary to law with regard to motions made before or during the trial or with regard to the admission or exclusion of evidence.

c. The evidence, at the close of all the evidence, was insufficient to justify submission of the case to the court-martial panel, whether or not a motion so asserting was made before verdict.

d. The court erroneously instructed the court-martial panel.

(2) The verdict is contrary to the weight of the evidence.

(3) For any other cause, the defendant did not receive a fair and impartial trial.

(d) Appointment of Superior Court Judge. - The appeal shall be heard by a judge assigned by the Chief Justice of the North Carolina Supreme Court, to be heard at a session of the Wake County Superior Court designated by the Chief Justice.

(e) Applicable Law. - The presiding judge, in determining whether there were errors, shall apply the law as provided for trial by courts-martial under this Article.

(f) Setting Aside of Findings or Sentence. - The findings or sentence, or both, may be modified or set aside, in whole or in part, by the court on the ground of newly discovered evidence, fraud on the court, lack of jurisdiction over the accused or the offense, or error prejudicial to the substantial rights of the accused.

(g)   Hearings and Rehearings. - The court may remand the matter to the court-martial for evidentiary hearings or other proceedings, to be conducted by a military judge alone, that it deems necessary prior to the court's final disposition of the case. If the court sets aside the findings or sentence, the court may, except when the setting aside is based on lack of sufficient evidence in the record to support the findings, order a rehearing. If the court sets aside the findings and sentence and does not order a rehearing, the court shall dismiss the charges. If the court orders a rehearing, but the convening authority finds a rehearing impractical, the convening authority shall dismiss the charges.

(h)   Counsel. -

(1)   The Staff Judge Advocate of the North Carolina National Guard shall:

a.   Designate a judge advocate who is qualified and certified under Article 27(b) of the Uniform Code of Military Justice, and who is a member of the North Carolina Bar, to represent the defendant.

b.   Designate a judge advocate who is qualified and certified under Article 27(b) of the Uniform Code of Military Justice, and who is a member of the North Carolina Bar, to represent the State.

(2)   The counsel designated to represent the defendant under sub-subdivision a. of subdivision (1) of this subsection shall not be the counsel who represented the defendant at the court-martial.

(3)   Where a defendant alleges ineffective assistance of prior counsel as a ground for relief, the defendant shall be deemed to waive the attorney-client privilege with respect to both oral and written communications between the defendant and the prior counsel to the extent the defendant's prior counsel reasonably believes the communications are necessary to defend against the allegations of ineffectiveness. This waiver of the attorney-client privilege shall be automatic upon the filing of the pleadings alleging ineffective assistance of prior counsel, and the Wake County Superior Court need not enter an order waiving the privilege.

(4)   The Adjutant General, upon the recommendation of the Staff Judge Advocate, shall place the designated judge advocates described in this subsection onto State active duty for the periods of time necessary for either counsel to provide adequate representation to the respective parties, if regularly scheduled unit training periods are insufficient. The Staff Judge Advocate shall verify to the Adjutant General whether any such additional periods of time are necessary.

(i)   Discretionary Review. - Review of decisions by the Wake County Superior Court shall be pursuant to G.S. 7A-31.1.

(j)   The rules for practice and procedure for review of courts-martial by the Wake County Superior Court shall be consistent with those prescribed for review of administrative appeals by the Superior Court, except as modified by this section. (2010-193, s. 16; 2011-195, s. 1(a).)

§ 127A-63. Reserved for future codification purposes.

§ 127A-64. Availability of resources for National Guard Family Assistance Centers; report.

(a)   To the extent feasible and practicable, State and local agencies who provide services directed at individuals who have served in the active or reserve components of the Armed Forces of the United States and their families shall make personnel and other resources available to the National Guard Family Assistance Centers.

(b)   The Department of Public Safety shall report annually to the Chairs of the House of Representatives and Senate Appropriations Subcommittees on Justice and Public Safety and to the House of Representatives Committee on Homeland Security, Military, and Veterans Affairs on the activities of the National Guard Family Assistance Centers. This report shall include information on services provided as well as on the number and type of members of the active or reserve components of the Armed Forces of the United States, veterans, and family members served. (2011-145, s. 19.1(g); 2011-185, s. 1.)

§ 127A-65. Reserved for future codification purposes.

§ 127A-66. Reserved for future codification purposes.

Article 4.

Naval Militia.

§ 127A-67. Organization and equipment.

The organization of the naval militia shall be units of convenient size, in each of which the number and rank of officers and the distribution of the total enlisted strength among the several ratings of petty officers and other enlisted personnel shall be such as are prescribed by the Secretary of the Navy, who may also prescribe the number of officers and the number of petty officers and other enlisted personnel required for the organization of the units into larger bodies for administrative and other purposes, and the arms and equipment of the naval militia shall be those which are now or may hereafter be prescribed by the Secretary of the Navy. (1917, c. 200, s. 66; C.S., s. 6836; 1975, c. 604, s. 2; 2011-195, s. 1(a).)

§ 127A-68. Officers appointed to naval militia.

Officers of the United States Navy and Marine Corps may, with the approval of the Secretary of the Navy, be appointed by the Governor and commissioned as officers of the naval militia. (1917, c. 200, s. 67; C.S., s. 6837; 1975, c. 604, s. 2; 2011-195, s. 1(a).)

§ 127A-69. Officers assigned to duty.

Line officers of the naval militia may be for line duties only, for engineering duties only, or for aeronautic duties only. (1917, c. 200, s. 68; C.S., s. 6838; 1975, c. 604, s. 2.)

§ 127A-70. Discipline in naval militia.

The naval militia shall be subject to the system of discipline prescribed for the United States Navy and Marine Corps, and the commanding officer of a naval militia unit or a naval militia officer in command of naval militia forces on shore or on any vessel of the United States Navy loaned to the State, or on any vessel on which such forces are training, whether within or without the State, or wherever, either within or without the State, naval militia forces of the State shall be assembled pursuant to orders, shall have power without trial by courts-martial to impose upon members of the naval militia the punishments which the commanding officer of a vessel of the United States Navy is authorized by law to impose. (1917, c. 200, s. 69; C.S., s. 6839; 1975, c. 604, s. 2; 2011-195, s. 1(a).)

§ 127A-71. Disbursing and accounting officer.

The Governor shall appoint a disbursing officer, approved by and of a rank prescribed by the Secretary of the Navy, to perform the duties the Secretary of the Navy may prescribe. The Governor shall also appoint the disbursing officer, or another officer of the appropriate finance office of the naval militia that the Governor may elect, as accounting officer for each unit thereof, or at the Governor's option for each larger unit or combination of units, who shall be responsible for the proper accounting for all public property issued to and for the use of the unit or larger unit or combination of units. (1917, c. 200, s. 70; C.S., s. 6840; 1975, c. 604, s. 2; 2011-195, s. 1(a).)

§ 127A-72. Rendition of accounts.

Accounting officers shall render accounts as prescribed by the Governor or by the Secretary of the Navy, and shall be required to give good and sufficient bond to the State and to the United States, in the sums that the Governor or the Secretary of the Navy directs, and conditioned upon the faithful accounting for all public property and for the safekeeping of the part thereof in the personal custody of the officer. Accounting officers may issue any or all such property to other officers or enlisted personnel of the naval militia under applicable rules and regulations. (1917, c. 200, s. 71; C.S., s. 6841; 1975, c. 604, s. 2; 2011-195, s. 1(a).)

§ 127A-73. Disbandment of naval militia.

No part of the naval militia which is entitled to compensation under the provisions of an act of Congress approved August 29, 1916, shall be disbanded without the consent of the President. (1917, c. 200, s. 86; C.S., s. 6842; 1975, c. 604, s. 2.)

§ 127A-74. Courts-martial for naval militia.

Courts-martial for the naval militia, not in the service of the United States, shall be organized, have the same powers, functions and authorities, and follow the same procedures as courts-martial for the North Carolina National Guard as set forth in G.S. 127A-47 through 127A-62. (1975, c. 604, s. 2; 2009-281, s. 1; 2011-195, s. 1(a).)

§§ 127A-75 through 127A-79. Reserved for future codification purposes.

Article 5.

State Defense Militia.

§ 127A-80. Authority to organize and maintain North Carolina State Defense Militia.

(a) The Governor is authorized to organize any part of the unorganized militia as a State force for discipline and training, into companies, battalions, regiments, brigades or similar organizations, as deemed necessary for the defense of the State; to maintain, uniform and equip this military force within the appropriations available; to exercise discipline in the same manner as is now or may hereafter be provided by the laws of the State for the North Carolina National Guard. The military force shall be subject to the call or the order of the Governor to execute the law and secure the safety of persons and property, suppress riots or insurrections, repel invasions or provide disaster relief, as may now or hereafter be provided by law for the North Carolina National Guard or for the State militia.

(b) The military force shall be designated as the "North Carolina State Defense Militia" and shall be composed of personnel of the unorganized militia as may volunteer for service therein or be drafted as provided by law. To be eligible for service in an enlisted status, a person must be at least 17 years of age. To be eligible for service as an officer, a person must be at least 18 years of age. The force and its personnel shall be additional to and distinct from the North Carolina National Guard organized under existing law. A person may not become a member of the defense militia established under this section, if a member of a reserve component of the Armed Forces of the United States.

(c) The Governor is hereby authorized: to prescribe rules and regulations governing the appointment of officers, the enlistment of other personnel, the organization, administration, equipment, discipline and discharge of the personnel of the military force; to requisition from the Secretary of Defense arms and equipment that are in possession of and can be spared by the Department of Defense; and to furnish the facilities of available armories, equipment, State premises and property, for the purpose of drill and instruction.

(d) The force shall not be called, ordered, or in any manner drafted, as such, into the military service of the United States, but no person shall by reason of membership therein, be exempt from military service under any federal law.

(e) The Governor is hereby authorized to transfer to the benefit of the State defense militia any available and unexpended funds which the Governor finds necessary for its use from any appropriations to the North Carolina National Guard by the General Assembly, and for the same purpose to allot monies from the Contingency and Emergency Fund with the concurrence of the Council of State. Upon disbandment of the State defense militia any monies or balance to the credit of any unit of this organization shall be paid into the State treasury for the benefit of the North Carolina National Guard, and all property, clothing, and equipment belonging to the State shall be transferred to the account of the North Carolina National Guard for disposition in accordance with the best interests of the State and as deemed advisable by the Governor. Upon disbandment of any unit of the State defense militia prior to the disbandment of the entire organization, the Governor is authorized to direct the transfer of any State property or balance of funds of the disbanded unit to any other unit, including any new unit or units organized to fill vacancies, or otherwise, as the Governor may direct.

(f)   The State defense militia shall be subject to the military laws of the State not inconsistent with or contrary to the provisions contained in this Article with the following exceptions:

The provisions of G.S. 127A-117, 127A-118, and 127A-139 as amended, shall not be applicable to the personnel and units of the State defense militia.

(g)   There shall be allowed annually to each unit or company of the State defense militia the funds necessary for armory rent, heat, light, stationery, printing, and other expenses.

(h)   All payments are to be made by the Secretary of Public Safety in accordance with State laws in semiannual installments on the first day of July and the first day of January of each year, but no payment shall be made unless all assemblies and duties required by law are duly performed by all organizations named.

(i)   The commander of each organization participating in the appropriation herein named shall render an itemized statement of all funds received from any source whatsoever for the support of the organization in the manner and on the forms prescribed by the Secretary of Public Safety. Failure on the part of any commander to submit promptly when due the financial statement of the organization will be sufficient cause to withhold all appropriations for the organization. (1941, c. 43; 1943, c. 166; 1945, c. 209, s. 1; c. 835; 1957, c. 1083; 1963, c. 1016, s. 1; 1975, c. 604, s. 2; 1977, c. 70, s. 2; c. 553; 1983, c. 314, ss. 2, 3; 2009-281, s. 1; 2011-145, s. 19.1(g); 2011-195, s. 1(a).)

§ 127A-81. State defense militia cadre.

(a)   The Governor is authorized: to organize and regulate part of the unorganized militia as a State defense militia cadre in units or commands which the Governor may deem necessary to provide a cadre for an active State defense militia; to prescribe regulations for the maintenance of the property and equipment of the cadre, for the exercise of its discipline, and for its training and duties.

(b)   The cadre shall be designated the "North Carolina State Defense Militia Cadre" and shall be composed of a force of officers and enlisted personnel raised by appointment of the Governor, or otherwise, as may be provided by law. The Secretary of Public Safety may reimburse cadre members for expenses actually incurred, not to exceed the amount appropriated and authorized for the purpose by the General Assembly.

(c) The Governor's authority under this Article shall not be subject to regulations prescribed by the Secretary of Defense. Age and membership requirements for the State defense militia generally, as set forth in G.S. 127A-80, shall apply. The training of the cadre need not be in accordance with training regulations issued by the Department of Defense. The provisions of G.S. 127A-80(c), (d), (g), (h) and (i) shall also apply to cadres.

(d) The total authorized strength of the cadre, its authorized officer and enlisted strength, the composition of each of its units or commands, and the allocation of cadre units or commands among the counties, cities, and towns of the State, shall be as prescribed by the Governor in suitable regulations enforced through the Adjutant General, or as otherwise provided by law.

(e) The duties of the State defense militia cadre shall be as ordered and directed by the Governor from time to time, or in regulations, and may include authority to take charge of armories and other military installations and real properties used by the North Carolina National Guard, together with any other property that the regulations may provide, when and if the North Carolina National Guard, or any part thereof, is inducted into the service of the United States, or, for any extended period of time, is absent on any duty from its home station. In addition, the cadre shall have duties appropriate to the organization, maintenance, and training of a military cadre to act as a nucleus for the organization of an active State defense militia whenever the necessity may arise. (1963, c. 1016, s. 1; 1975, c. 604, s. 2; 1977, c. 70, s. 2; 1983, c. 314, s. 4; 1991 (Reg. Sess., 1992), c. 1030, s. 35; 2009-281, s. 1; 2011-145, s. 19.1(g); 2011-195, s. 1(a).)

§§ 127A-82 through 127A-86. Reserved for future codification purposes.

Article 6.

Unorganized Militia.

§ 127A-87. Unorganized militia ordered out for service.

The commander in chief may at any time, in order to execute the law, secure the safety of persons and property, suppress riots or insurrections, repel invasions or provide disaster relief, in addition to the North Carolina National Guard, the State defense militia and the naval militia, order out the whole or any part of the unorganized militia. When the militia of this State or a part thereof is called forth under the Constitution and laws of the United States, the Governor shall first order out for service the North Carolina National Guard, the State defense militia or naval militia, or any part thereof that may be necessary, and if the number available is insufficient, the Governor shall then order out any part of the unorganized militia that the Governor may deem necessary. During the absence or organizations of the North Carolina National Guard or naval militia in the service of the United States, their state designations shall not be given to new organizations. (1917, c. 200, s. 46; C.S., s. 6860; 1963, c. 1016, s. 2; 1975, c. 604, s. 2; 2009-281, s. 1; 2011-195, s. 1(a).)

§ 127A-88. Manner of ordering out unorganized militia.

The Governor shall, when ordering out the unorganized militia, designate the number. The Governor may order them out either by calling for volunteers or by draft. The Governor may attach them to the several organizations of the North Carolina National Guard, the State defense militia or naval militia, as may be best for the service. (1917, c. 200, s. 47; C.S., s. 6861; 1963, c. 1016, s. 2; 1975, c. 604, s. 2; 2009-281, s. 1; 2011-195, s. 1(a).)

§ 127A-89. Draft of unorganized militia.

If the unorganized militia is ordered out by draft, the Governor shall designate the persons in each county to make the draft, and prescribe rules and regulations for conducting it. (1917, c. 200, s. 48; C.S., s. 6862; 1975, c. 604, s. 2; 2011-195, s. 1(a).)

§ 127A-90. Punishment for failure to appear.

Every member of the militia ordered out for duty, or who shall volunteer or be drafted, who does not appear at the time and place ordered, shall be liable to punishment as determined by a court-martial. (1917, c. 200, s. 49; C.S., s. 6863; 1975, c. 604, s. 2; 2011-195, s. 1(a).)

§ 127A-91. Promotion of marksmanship.

The Adjutant General is authorized to detail a commissioned officer of the North Carolina National Guard or member of the State defense militia to promote rifle marksmanship among the State defense militia and the unorganized militia of the State. The officer or member so detailed shall serve without pay and it shall be the duty of the officer or member to organize and supervise rifle clubs in schools, colleges, universities, clubs and other groups, under rules and regulations prescribed by the Adjutant General and in a manner that will make them, when duly organized, acceptable for membership in the National Rifle Association. Provided, that these duties and efforts shall in nowise interfere or conflict with clubs of schools or units operating in Reserve Officers' Training Corps or similar schools under the supervision of instructors of the Armed Forces of the United States. (1937, c. 449; 1963, c. 1016, s. 2; 1975, c. 604, s. 2; 2009-281, s. 1; 2011-195, s. 1(a).)

§§ 127A-92 through 127A-96. Reserved for future codification purposes.

Article 7.

Regulations as to Active Service.

§ 127A-97. National Guard and naval militia first ordered out.

In all cases the North Carolina National Guard and naval militia as provided for in this Chapter shall be first ordered into service. (1917, c. 200, s. 44; C.S., s. 6857; 1975, c. 604, s. 2; 2009-281, s. 1; 2011-195, s. 1(a).)

§ 127A-98. Regulations enforced on active State service.

Whenever any portion of the militia is called into active State service to execute the law, secure the safety of persons and property, suppress riots or insurrections, repel invasions or provide disaster relief, the provisions of the Uniform Code of Military Justice of the United States, governing the Armed Forces of the United States, and the regulations prescribed for the Armed Forces of the United States, and the regulations issued thereunder, shall be enforced and regarded as part of this Chapter until this portion of the militia is relieved from the duty. As to offenses committed when the provisions of the Uniform Code of Military Justice of the United States are so enforced, courts-martial shall possess, in addition to the jurisdiction and power of sentence and punishment herein vested in them, all additional jurisdiction and power of sentence and punishment exercisable by like courts under the provisions of the Uniform Code of Military Justice of the United States or regulations or laws governing the Armed Forces of the United States or the customs and usages thereof; but no punishment under the Code that extends to the taking of life shall in any case be inflicted except in case of war, invasion, or insurrection, declared by a proclamation of the Governor to exist and then only after approval by the Governor of the sentence inflicting that punishment. Imprisonment other than in guardhouse shall be executed in county jails or other prisons designated by the Governor for that purpose. (1917, c. 200, s. 45; C.S., s. 6858; 1963, c. 1018, s. 6; 1975, c. 604, s. 2; 2011-195, s. 1(a).)

§ 127A-99. Regulations governing unorganized militia.

Whenever any part of the unorganized militia is ordered out, it shall be governed by the same rules and regulations and be subject to the same penalties as the North Carolina National Guard or naval militia. (1917, c. 200, s. 35; C.S., s. 6859; 1975, c. 604, s. 2; 2009-281, s. 1; 2011-195, s. 1(a).)

§§ 127A-100 through 127A-104. Reserved for future codification purposes.

Article 8.

Pay of Militia.

§ 127A-105. Rations and pay on State service.

The militia of the State, both officers and enlisted personnel, when called into the service of the State by the Governor shall receive the same pay as when called or ordered into the service of the United States, and shall be rationed or paid the equivalent thereof, provided that no officer or enlisted personnel shall receive less than 18 times the minimum hourly wage per day as provided for in G.S. 95-25.3(a). (1813, c. 850, s. 5, P.R.; R.C., c. 70, s. 84; Code, s. 3248; Rev., s. 4856; 1907, c. 316; 1917, c. 200, s. 50; C.S., s. 6864; 1935, c. 452; 1959, c. 218, s. 17; 1975, c. 604, s. 2; 1997-153, s. 2; 1997-443, s. 7.12(c).)

§ 127A-106. Paid by the State.

When the militia or any portion thereof is ordered by the Governor into State service, the pay (including payment for any leave earned as a result of more than 30 days of continuous service), subsistence, transportation and other necessary expenses incident thereto shall be paid by the State Treasurer, upon the approval of the Governor. (1917, c. 200, s. 52; C.S., s. 6866; 1975, c. 604, s. 2; 1993, c. 257, s. 12; 1997-153, s. 6; 1997-443, s. 7.12(c); 2011-195, s. 1(a).)

§ 127A-107. Rate of pay for other service.

The Governor may, whenever the public service requires it, order upon special or regular duty any officer or enlisted member of the North Carolina National Guard or naval militia, and the expenses and compensation therefor of the officer or enlisted member shall be paid out of the appropriations made to the Department of Public Safety. The officers or enlisted members shall receive the same rate of pay as officers and enlisted members of the same grade and like service of the Armed Forces of the United States, provided that no such officer or enlisted member shall receive less than 18 times the minimum hourly wage per day as provided for in G.S. 95-25.3(a). Officers and enlisted members when on duty in connection with examining boards, efficiency boards, advisory boards, courts of inquiry or similar duty shall be allowed per diem and subsistence prescribed for lawful State boards and commissions generally for such duty. Officers and enlisted members serving on general or special courts-martial shall receive the base pay of their rank. No staff officer or enlisted member who receives a salary from the State as such shall be entitled to any additional compensation other than actual and necessary expenses incurred while traveling upon orders issued by the proper authority. (1917, c. 200, s. 51; C.S., s. 6865; 1935, c. 451; 1949, c. 1130, s. 4; 1959, c. 218, s. 18; 1963, c. 1019, s. 1; 1969, c. 986; 1971, c. 204; 1973, c. 620, s. 9; 1975, c. 604, s. 2; 1977, c. 70, s. 2; 1997-153, s. 3; 1997-443, s. 7.12(c); 2009-281, s. 1; 2011-145, s. 19.1(g); 2011-195, s. 1(a).)

§ 127A-108. Pay and care of soldiers, airmen and sailors disabled in service.

A member of the North Carolina National Guard, the State defense militia, or the naval militia who without fault or negligence on the member's part is disabled through illness, injury, or disease contracted or incurred while on duty or by reason of duty in the service of the State or while reasonably proceeding to or returning from duty shall receive the actual necessary expenses for care and medicine and medical attention at the expense of the State and if the disability temporarily incapacitates the member from pursuing the member's usual business or occupation the member shall receive during his or her incapacity the pay and allowances that are provided for the same grade and rating in like circumstances in the active Armed Forces of the United States. If the member is permanently disabled, the member shall receive the pensions and benefits that persons under similar circumstances in the Armed Forces of the United States receive from the United States. In case a member dies as a result of such an injury, illness or disease within one year after it has been incurred or contracted, the surviving spouse, minor children, or dependent parents of the member shall receive the pension and benefits as persons under similar circumstances receive from the United States.

The cost incurred by reason of this section shall be paid out of the Contingency and Emergency Fund, or another fund designated by law.

The Adjutant General, with the approval of the Governor, shall make and publish regulations pursuant to this section that are necessary for its implementation. Before the name of any person is placed on the disability or pension rolls of the State under this section, proof shall be made in accordance with these regulations that the applicant is entitled to the care, pension, or benefit.

Nothing in this section shall in any way limit or condition any other payment to a member that the law allows, except that any payments made under the provisions of Chapter 97 of the General Statutes or under federal statutes as now or hereafter amended shall be deducted from the payments made under this section. (1917, c. 200, s. 54; C.S., s. 6868; 1959, c. 218, s. 19; c. 763; 1965, c. 1058; 1975, c. 604, s. 2; 2009-281, s. 1; 2011-195, s. 1(a).)

§ 127A-109. Pay of general and field officers.

General and field officers when away from their home stations visiting the organizations of their commands, for inspection and instruction under orders from proper authority, shall receive actual necessary expenses and the pay of their rank. (1917, c. 200, s. 53; C.S., s. 6867; 1975, c. 604, s. 2.)

§ 127A-110. Proceedings against third party injuring or killing organized militia personnel.

(a) The right of a member of the North Carolina National Guard, the State defense militia, or the naval militia to compensation and other benefits under G.S. 127A-108 shall not be affected by the fact that the injury or death was caused under circumstances creating a liability in some person other than the State, or "third party," to pay damages therefor. The respective rights and interests of the member under this Article, and the State, if any, in respect of the common-law cause of action against a third party and the damages recovered shall be as set forth in this section.

(b) The member or personal representative if the member be dead, shall have the exclusive right to proceed to enforce the liability of the third party by appropriate proceedings if the proceedings are instituted not later than 12 months after the date of injury or death, whichever is later. During this 12-month period, and at any time thereafter if summons is issued against the third party during the 12-month period, the member or personal representative shall have the right to settle with the third party and to give a valid and complete release of all claims to the third party by reason of the injury or death, subject to the provisions of subsection (h) of this section.

(c) If settlement is not made and summons is not issued within the 12-month period described in subsection (b) of this section, then all rights of the member, or personal representative if the member be dead, against the third party shall pass by operation of the period fixed by the statute of limitations applicable to these rights and if the State has not settled with or instituted proceedings against the third party within this time, then all such rights shall revert to the member or personal representative 60 days before the expiration of the applicable statute of limitations.

(d) The person in whom the right to bring a proceeding or make settlement is vested shall, during the continuation thereof, also have the exclusive right to make settlement with the third party and the release of the person having the right shall fully acquit and discharge the third party except as provided by subsection (h) of this section. A proceeding so instituted by the person having the right shall be brought in the name of the member or personal representative and the State shall not be a necessary or proper party thereto. If the member or personal representative refuses to cooperate with the State by being the party plaintiff, then the action shall be brought in the name of the State and the member or personal representative shall be made a party plaintiff or party defendant by order of court.

(e) The amount of compensation and other benefits paid or payable on account of the injury or death shall not be admissible in evidence in any proceeding against the third party. If the third party defending the proceeding, by answer duly served on the State, sufficiently alleges that actionable negligence of the State joined and concurred with the negligence of the third party in producing the injury or death, then an issue shall be submitted to the jury in the case as to whether actionable negligence of the State joined and concurred with the negligence of the third party in producing the injury or death. The State shall have the right to appear, to be represented, to introduce evidence, to cross-examine adverse witnesses, and to argue to the jury as to this issue as fully as though it were a party although not named or joined as a party to the proceeding. The issue as to the State's negligence shall be the last of the issues submitted to the jury. If the verdict is that actionable negligence of the State did join and concur with that of the third party in producing the injury or death, then the court shall reduce the damages awarded by the jury against the third party by the amount which the State would otherwise be entitled to receive therefrom by way of subrogation hereunder and the entire amount recovered, after such reduction, shall belong to the member or personal representative free of any claim by the State and the third party shall have no further right by way of contribution or otherwise against the State, except any right which may exist by reason of an express contract of indemnity between the State and the third party, which was entered into prior to the injury to the member.

(f) (1) Any amount obtained by any person by settlement with, judgment against, or otherwise from the third party by reason of the injury or death shall be disbursed by order of the court for the following purposes and in the following order of priority:

a. First to the payment of actual court costs taxed by judgment.

b. Second to the payment of the fee of the attorney representing the person making settlement or obtaining judgment, and this fee shall not exceed one third of the amount obtained or recovered of the third party.

c. Third to the reimbursement of the State for all benefits by way of compensation or medical treatment expense paid or to be paid by the State pursuant to G.S. 127A-108.

d. Fourth to the payment of any amount remaining to the member or personal representative.

(2) The attorney fee paid under subdivision (1) of this subsection shall be paid by the member and the State in direct proportion to the amount each shall receive under sub-subdivisions (1)c. and d. of this subsection and shall be deducted from the payments when distribution is made.

(g) In any proceeding against or settlement with the third party, every party to the claim for compensation shall have a lien to the extent of the party's interest under subsection (f) of this section upon any payment made by the third party by reason of the injury or death, whether paid in settlement, in satisfaction of judgment, as consideration for covenant not to sue, or otherwise and the lien may be enforced against any person receiving the funds. Neither the member or personal representative nor the State shall make any settlement with or accept any payment from the third party without the written consent of the other and no release to or agreement with the third party shall be valid or enforceable for any purpose unless both State and member or personal representative join therein; provided, that this sentence shall not apply if the State is made whole for all benefits paid or to be paid by the member or personal representative under this Chapter less attorney's fees as provided by subsection (f) of this section and the release to or agreement with the third party is executed by the member. The

Attorney General shall have the right on behalf of the State to reduce by compromise its claim.

(h)   Institution of proceedings against or settlement with the third party, or acceptance of benefits under this Chapter, shall not in any way or manner affect any other remedy which any party to the claim for compensation may have except as otherwise specifically provided in this Chapter, and the exercise of one remedy shall not in any way or manner be held to constitute an election of remedies so as to bar the other. (1967, c. 1081, s. 1; 1975, c. 604, s. 2; 2011-195, s. 1(a); 2012-194, s. 26.)

§ 127A-111. Civilian leave option.

(a)   A member of the North Carolina National Guard called into service of the State by the Governor shall have the right to take leave without pay from his or her civilian employment. No member of the North Carolina National Guard shall be forced to use or exhaust his or her vacation or other accrued leaves from his or her civilian employment for a period of active service. The choice of leave shall be solely within the discretion of the member.

(b)   The Commissioner of Labor shall enforce the provisions of this section pursuant to Chapter 95 of the General Statutes. (1997-153, s. 4.)

§§ 127A-112 through 127A-115. Reserved for future codification purposes.

Article 9.

Privilege of Organized State Militia and Reserve Components of the Armed Forces of the United States.

§ 127A-116. Leaves of absence for State officers and employees.

The Governor or the Governor's designee shall promulgate appropriate policy and regulations relating to leaves of absence for short periods of military training and for State or federal military duty or special emergency management service of all officers and employees of the State and its political subdivisions, including officers and employees of public educational facilities under the sponsorship of the State, without loss of pay, time or efficiency rating. (1917, c. 200, s. 88; C.S., s. 6869; 1937, c. 224, s. 1; 1949, c. 1274; 1975, c. 604, s. 2; 2001-513, s. 23(b).)

§ 127A-117. Contributing members.

Each organization of the North Carolina National Guard and naval militia may, besides its regular and active members, enroll contributing members on payment in advance by each person desiring to become a contributing member of not less than ten dollars ($10.00) per annum, which money shall be paid into the unit fund. Each contributing member shall be entitled to receive from the commanding officer thereof a certificate of membership. (1917, c. 200, s. 90; C.S., s. 6871; 1967, c. 218, s. 3; 1975, c. 604, s. 2; 2009-281, s. 1; 2011-195, s. 1(a).)

§ 127A-118. Organizations may own property; actions.

Organizations of the North Carolina National Guard and naval militia shall have the right to own and keep real and personal property, which shall belong to the organization; and the commanding officer of any organization may recover for its use debts or effects belonging to it, or damages for injury to the property. An action for recovery of debts, effects, or damages must be brought in the name of the commanding officer of the organization before any court of justice within the State having jurisdiction; and no suit or complaint pending in his or her name shall be abated by his or her ceasing to be commanding officer of the organization; but upon motion of the commander succeeding him or her the new commander shall be admitted to prosecute the suit or complaint in like manner and with like effect as if it had been originally commenced by him or her. (1917, c. 200, s. 92; C.S., s. 6872; 1975, c. 604, s. 2; 2009-281, s. 1; 2011-195, s. 1(a).)

§ 127A-119. When families of soldiers, airmen and sailors supported by county.

When any citizen of the State is absent on duty as a member of the North Carolina National Guard, State defense militia or naval militia, and the member's family members are unable to support themselves during the member's absence, the board of commissioners of the member's county, on application, shall make a reasonable allowance towards their maintenance. (1917, c. 200, s. 93; C.S., s. 6873; 1963, c. 1019, s. 2; 1975, c. 604, s. 2; 2009-281, s. 1; 2011-195, s. 1(a).)

§§ 127A-120 through 127A-124. Reserved for future codification purposes.

Article 10.

Care of Military Property.

§ 127A-125. Custody of military property.

All public military property, except when used in the performance of military duty, shall be kept in armories, or other properly designated places of deposit; and it shall be unlawful for any person charged with the care and safety of public military property to allow it out of his or her custody, except as specified in this section. (1917, c. 200, s. 38; C.S., s. 6874; 1975, c. 604, s. 2; 2011-195, s. 1(a).)

§ 127A-126. Other suitable storage facilities.

All public military property of every description which may not be distributed among the units of the North Carolina National Guard or State defense militia according to law shall be stored and kept at suitable storage facilities as determined by the Adjutant General. (1917, c. 200, s. 39; C.S., s. 6875; 1959, c. 218, s. 20; 1963, c. 1019, s. 3; 1975, c. 604, s. 2; 2009-281, s. 1; 2011-195, s. 1(a).)

§ 127A-127. Property kept in good order.

Every officer and enlisted member belonging to any unit equipped with public military property shall keep and preserve the property in good order; and for neglect to do so may be punished as a court-martial may direct. (1917, c. 200, s. 40; C.S., s. 6877; 1959, c. 218, s. 22; 1975, c. 604, s. 2; 2011-195, s. 1(a).)

§ 127A-128. Equipment and vehicles.

Equipment and vehicles issued by the Department of Defense to the North Carolina National Guard or State defense militia shall be used solely for military purposes, except in those specific cases where nonmilitary use is authorized by the Department of Defense or the Governor. Necessary expense in maintaining equipment and vehicles, not provided for by the federal government, shall be a proper charge against State funds appropriated for the North Carolina National Guard: Provided, the expense shall be specifically authorized by the Governor and certified by the Adjutant General. (1917, c. 200, s. 41; C.S., s. 6878; 1921, c. 120, s. 9; 1959, c. 218, s. 23; 1963, c. 1019, s. 4; 1967, c. 563, s. 5; 1975, c. 604, s. 2; 2009-281, s. 1; 2011-195, s. 1(a).)

§ 127A-129. Transfer of property.

All officers accountable or responsible for public funds, property, or books, before being relieved from the duty, shall turn them over according to the regulations prescribed by the Governor. (1917, c. 200, s. 42; C.S., s. 6879; 1975, c. 604, s. 2; 2011-195, s. 1(a).)

§ 127A-130. Replacement of lost or damaged property.

Whenever any military property issued to the North Carolina National Guard or State defense militia shall have been lost, damaged, or destroyed, and upon report of a disinterested surveying officer it shall appear that the loss, damage, or destruction of property was due to carelessness or neglect, or that its loss, damage or destruction could have been avoided by exercise of able care, the money value of the property shall be charged to the responsible officer or enlisted member, and the pay of the officers and enlisted members from both federal and State funds at any time accruing may be stopped and applied to the payment of any such indebtedness until it is discharged. (1917, c. 200, s. 43; C.S., s. 6880; 1959, c. 218, s. 24; 1963, c. 1019, s. 5; 1975, c. 604, s. 2; 2009-281, s. 1; 2011-195, s. 1(a).)

§ 127A-131. Unlawful conversion or willful destruction of military property.

(a)   If any person shall willfully or wantonly destroy or injure, willfully retain after demand made or otherwise convert to the person's own use any property of the State or of the United States issued for the purpose of arming or equipping the militia of the State or if any person shall purchase any property of the State or of the United States knowing it to be unlawfully obtained, the person shall be guilty of a Class 1 misdemeanor.

(b)   Any person, firm or corporation receiving in pledge or buying from any other person, firm or corporation for the purpose of resale any goods, to include arms, ammunition, explosives, equipment, clothing, supplies and materials, which may reasonably be thought to be the property of the Armed Forces of the United States and their reserve components or of the militia of the State of North Carolina, shall keep a register and shall enter therein a true and accurate record of each purchase, showing the name, social security number and address of the person from whom purchased, the name and address of the firm or corporation from whom purchased, together with the amount paid for each item or lot of small items, the date of purchase, the serial numbers of all items bearing serial numbers, and any other marks, brands or descriptions which will serve to identify the items purchased. The register shall be at all times open to the inspection of the public. Any person, firm or corporation failing to comply with this provision shall be guilty of a Class 1 misdemeanor; and any person, firm or corporation making a false entry in such register shall be guilty of a Class 1 misdemeanor. (1876-7, c. 272, s. 19; Code, s. 3274; Rev., ss. 3536, 3537; C.S., ss. 6881, 6882; 1959, c. 218, s. 25; 1963, c. 1019, s. 6; 1975, c. 604, s. 2; 1993, c. 539, s. 936; 1994, Ex. Sess., c. 24, s. 14(c); 2011-195, s. 1(a).)

§§ 127A-132 through 127A-136. Reserved for future codification purposes.

Article 11.

Support of Militia.

§ 127A-137. Requisition for federal funds.

The Governor shall make requisition upon the secretary of the appropriate service for the State allotment from federal funds as may be appropriate for the support of the militia. (1917, c. 200, s. 23; C.S., s. 6887; 1921, c. 120, s. 10; 1963, c. 1019, s. 8; 1975, c. 604, s. 2; 2011-195, s. 1(a).)

§ 127A-138. Local appropriations; unit funds.

(a) Every municipality and county within the State is hereby authorized and empowered to appropriate for the benefit of any unit or units of the militia the amounts of public funds from year to year as the governing body of the municipality or county may deem wise, patriotic and expedient; and is further authorized, either alone or in connection with others, to provide heat, electricity, water, telephone service and other costs of operation and maintenance of any armory. These appropriations may be funded by the levy of property taxes pursuant to G.S. 153A-149 and G.S. 160A-209 or by the allocation of other revenues whose use is not otherwise restricted by law.

(b) Any funds donated to any unit or units of the militia by local governments, civic organizations or private sources, short-term rental of their armory buildings, or funds earned through vending machine commissions and items of similar nature shall remain at the unit or units to be expended in accordance with rules and regulations prescribed by the Secretary. (1947, c. 1010, s. 8; 1975, c. 604, s. 2; 1979, c. 701, s. 1; 2011-195, s. 1(a).)

§ 127A-139. Allowances made to different organizations and personnel.

(a) There may be allowed each year to the following officers, under rules and regulations prescribed by the Secretary of Public Safety, as follows: to general officers, and commanders of divisions, corps, groups, brigades, regiments, separate battalions, squadrons or similar organizations, not to exceed two hundred and twenty-five dollars ($225.00); to commanding officers of companies, batteries, troops, detachments and similar units not to exceed two hundred dollars ($200.00); to executive officers, adjutants, plans and training officers, logistical officers and commissioned officers in comparable assignments in divisions, corps, groups, brigades, regiments, battalions, squadrons and similar organizations, not to exceed two hundred dollars ($200.00). No officer shall be entitled to receive any part of the amounts named in this subsection unless the officer has performed satisfactorily all duties required of the officer by law and regulations and has pursued any course of instruction that may from time to time be required.

(b)   There may be allowed annually to the supply sergeant of each company, battery, troop, detachment, and similar organizations, a sum of money not to exceed one hundred dollars ($100.00) for services satisfactorily performed.

(c)   There shall be allowed annually sufficient funds to be allocated by the Secretary of Public Safety among the federally recognized units of the North Carolina National Guard and their headquarters, a pistol team, a rifle team, aviation support facilities, and aviation flight activities for administrative and operating expenses, including heat, electricity, telephone, postage, office supplies and equipment, minor repairs and replacement of equipment, and any other expenses and special items of equipment not otherwise provided that may be authorized in accordance with North Carolina National Guard rules and regulations.

(d)   Repealed by Session Laws 1979, c. 701, s. 2.

(e)   The commanding officers of all organizations participating in the appropriations herein made shall render an itemized statement of all funds received from any source whatever for the support of their respective organizations in the manner and on the forms prescribed by the Secretary through the Adjutant General. Failure on the part of any officer to submit promptly when due the financial statement of the officer's organization will be sufficient cause to withhold all appropriations for the organization. (1917, c. 200, s. 97; 1919, c. 311; C.S., s. 6889; 1921, c. 120, s. 11; 1923, c. 24; 1924, c. 6; 1927, c. 227, s. 2; 1949, c. 1130, s. 5; 1951, c. 1144, s. 1; 1953, c. 1246; 1959, c. 421; 1963, c. 1020; 1967, c. 563, s. 6; 1973, c. 1460; 1975, c. 604, s. 2; 1977, c. 70, s. 2; 1979, c. 701, s. 2; 2009-281, s. 1; 2011-145, s. 19.1(g); 2011-195, s. 1(a).)

§§ 127A-140 through 127A-144. Reserved for future codification purposes.

Article 12.

General Provisions.

§ 127A-145. Reports of officers.

All officers of the North Carolina National Guard, the State defense militia, and the naval militia shall make returns and reports to the Governor, the Secretary of Defense, or to officers designated by them, at the times and in the form from time to time prescribed. (1917, c. 200, s. 21; C.S., s. 6890; 1963, c. 1019, s. 10; 1975, c. 604, s. 2; 2009-281, s. 1; 2011-195, s. 1(a).)

§ 127A-146. Officer to give notice of absence.

When any officer shall have occasion to be absent from the officer's usual residence one week or more, the officer shall notify the officer next in command, and also the officer's next superior officer in command, of the officer's intended absence, and shall arrange for the officer next in command to handle and attend to all official communications. (1917, c. 200, s. 22; C.S., s. 6891; 1975, c. 604, s. 2; 2011-195, s. 1(a).)

§ 127A-147. Orders, rules, regulations and Uniform Code of Military Justice applicable to militia when not in service of United States.

The North Carolina National Guard, State defense militia and naval militia, when not in the service of the United States, shall be governed by State law, the orders, rules and regulations of the Adjutant General, regulations promulgated by the secretary of the appropriate service of the Armed Forces of the United States, and the Uniform Code of Military Justice, as amended from time to time. (1917, c. 200, s. 34; C.S., s. 6892; 1963, c. 1018, s. 7; 1975, c. 604, s. 2; 2009-281, s. 1; 2010-193, s. 21; 2011-195, s. 1(a).)

§ 127A-148. Commander may prevent trespass and disorder.

The commander upon any occasion of duty may place in arrest during the continuance thereof any person who shall trespass upon the campground, parade ground, armory, or other place devoted to that duty, or who shall in any way or manner interrupt or molest the orderly discharge of duty by those under arms, or shall disturb or prevent the passage of troops going to or returning from any duty. The commander may prohibit and prevent the sale or use of all spirituous liquors, wine, ale, beer, or cider, the holding of huckster or auction sales, and all gambling within the limits of the post, campground or place of encampment, parade or drill under his or her command, or within any limits not exceeding one mile therefrom that the commander may prescribe. The commander may in the commander's discretion abate as common nuisance all such sales. (1917, c. 200, s. 94; C.S., s. 6893; 1975, c. 604, s. 2; 2011-195, s. 1(a).)

§ 127A-149. Power of arrest in certain emergencies.

In the event members of the North Carolina National Guard or State defense militia are called out by the Governor pursuant to the authority vested in the Governor by the Constitution, they shall have the power of arrest reasonably necessary to accomplish the purpose for which they have been called out. (1959, c. 453; 1963, c. 1019, s. 11; 1975, c. 604, s. 2; 2009-281, s. 1; 2011-195, s. 1(a).)

§ 127A-150. Immunity of guardsmen from civil and criminal liability.

(a) A member of the North Carolina National Guard or State defense militia, while acting in aid of civil authorities and in the line of duty, shall have the immunities of a law-enforcement officer.

(b) Members of the North Carolina National Guard or State defense militia shall have the immunities of a law-enforcement officer whenever they are called upon to execute the laws; engage in disaster relief; suppress or prevent actual or threatened riot or insurrection; repel invasion; or apprehend or disperse any sniper, rioters, mob or unlawful assembly.

(c) Any civil claim against a member of the North Carolina National Guard or State defense militia allegedly arising from the action or inaction of the member of the North Carolina National Guard or State defense militia while in line of duty shall be filed within two years of the date of the occurrence or forever barred. (1969, c. 969; 1975, c. 604, s. 2; 2009-281, s. 1; 2011-195, s. 1(a).)

§ 127A-151. Organizing company without authority.

If any person shall organize a military company, or drill or parade under arms as a military body, except under the militia laws and regulations of the State, or shall exercise or attempt to exercise the power or authority of a military officer in this State, without holding a commission from the Governor, the person shall be guilty of a Class 1 misdemeanor. (1893, c. 374, s. 38; Rev., s. 3538; C.S., s. 6894; 1975, c. 604, s. 2; 1993, c. 539, s. 937; 1994, Ex. Sess., c. 24, s. 14(c); 2011-195, s. 1(a).)

§ 127A-152. Placing name on muster roll wrongfully.

If any officer of the militia of the State shall knowingly or willfully place, or cause to be placed, on any muster roll the name of any person not regularly or lawfully enlisted, or the name of any enlisted member who is dead or who has been discharged, transferred, or has lost membership for any cause whatsoever, or who has been convicted of any infamous crime, the officer shall be guilty of a Class 1 misdemeanor. (1893, c. 374, s. 33; Rev., s. 3539; C.S., s. 6895; 1975, c. 604, s. 2; 1993, c. 539, s. 938; 1994, Ex. Sess., c. 24, s. 14(c); 2011-195, s. 1(a).)

§ 127A-153. Protection of uniform.

(a) The wearing of any military uniform of the United States by members of the militia shall be pursuant to applicable regulations promulgated by the respective branches of the Armed Forces of the United States and regulations of the Adjutant General of North Carolina not inconsistent with federal uniform regulations.

(b) The wearing of any military uniform of the State by members of the militia shall be pursuant to applicable regulations promulgated by the Adjutant General of North Carolina.

(c) Members of the militia who violate the regulations referred to in subsections (a) and (b) of this section shall, upon conviction by a court-martial, be punished in like manner and to the extent prescribed by Article 134 of the Uniform Code of Military Justice and Manual for Courts-Martial, United States, as shall be in use by the Armed Forces of the United States at the time of the offense.

(d) Persons not subject to courts-martial who violate the regulations referred to in subsections (a) and (b) of this section may be charged and tried in the State courts and upon conviction shall be punished as provided in subsection (c) of this section. (1921, c. 120, s. 12; C.S., s. 6895(a); 1963, c. 1017; 1975, c. 604, s. 2; 2010-193, s. 22; 2011-195, s. 1(a).)

§ 127A-154. Upkeep of properties.

There shall be paid from the appropriations for the North Carolina National Guard the amounts necessary for the maintenance, upkeep, and improvement of State military properties and facilities. Provided, these expenditures shall be approved and authorized by the Governor. (1921, c. 120, s. 13; C.S., s. 6895(b); 1975, c. 604, s. 2; 2009-281, s. 1; 2011-195, s. 1(a).)

§ 127A-155. When officers authorized to administer oaths.

Officers of the North Carolina National Guard are authorized to administer oaths in all circumstances pertaining to any military matter whenever an oath is required. (1949, c. 1130, s. 6; 1975, c. 604, s. 2; 2009-281, s. 1; 2011-195, s. 1(a).)

§§ 127A-156 through 127A-160. Reserved for future codification purposes.

Article 13.

Armories.

§ 127A-161. Definitions.

As used in this Article, the following terms mean:

(1) Armory. - Any building or building complex and related facilities, including the lands for them, which are intended to be utilized by the militia for training, administration, storage, and the maintenance and servicing of equipment.

(2) Armory site. - That land, meeting federal and State specifications, upon which an armory may be constructed.

(3) Department. - The North Carolina Department of Public Safety.

(4) Facilities. - Those adjuncts to an armory, including but not limited to yards, storage buildings, sheds, ramps, racks, target ranges, furniture, fixtures and other equipment and installations.

(5) Funds. - Any monies appropriated by any municipality, county, the State or the United States government and made available for the purpose of acquiring armory sites or constructing or repairing any armory, warehouse, or other facility for the use of any unit or for any other purpose in connection with the housing, training, instruction or promotion of the interest of any unit.

(6) Municipality. - Any incorporated city, town or village.

(7) Unit. - Any organizational entity of the militia. (1947, c. 1010, s. 1; 1973, c. 620, s. 9; 1975, c. 604, s. 2; 1977, c. 70, s. 2; 2011-145, s. 19.1(g); 2011-195, s. 1(a).)

§ 127A-162. Authority to foster development of armories and facilities.

The Department of Public Safety is authorized and empowered to foster the development in North Carolina of adequate armories and other necessary facilities for the proper housing, instruction, training and administration of all units and facilities necessary for the proper protection, care, maintenance, repair, issue and upkeep of public and military property issued to or for the use of any unit. (1947, c. 1010, s. 4; 1973, c. 620, s. 9; 1975, c. 604, s. 2; 1977, c. 70, s. 2; 2011-145, s. 19.1(g).)

§ 127A-163. Powers of Department specified.

The Department of Public Safety is further authorized and empowered:

(1)   To act as an agency of the State of North Carolina for the purpose of setting up and administering any statewide plan for the acquisition of armories and armory sites, for the construction and maintenance of armories and for providing facilities which are now or may be necessary in order to comply with any federal law and in order to receive, administer and disburse any funds which may be provided by act of Congress for such purpose;

(2)   When acting as an agency of the State of North Carolina under subdivision (1) of this section, to promulgate statewide plans for the acquisition of armories and armory sites, for the construction and maintenance of armories and other facilities that are desirable or necessary to meet the requirements and receive the benefits of any federal legislation with respect thereto;

(3)   To receive and administer any funds which may be appropriated by any act of Congress or otherwise for the acquisition of armories and armory sites, for the construction and maintenance of armories, and for providing facilities that may at any time become available for those purposes;

(4)   To receive and administer any other funds which may be available in furtherance of any activity in which the Department of Public Safety is authorized and empowered to engage under the provisions of this Article; and

(5)   To adopt rules to carry out the intent and purpose of this Article. (1947, c. 1010, s. 5; 1973, c. 620, s. 9; 1975, c. 604, s. 2; 1977, c. 70, s. 2; 2011-145, s. 19.1(g); 2011-195, s. 1(a).)

§ 127A-164. Power to acquire land, make contracts, etc.

In furtherance of the duties, power, and authority given herein, the Department of Public Safety is authorized and empowered within the limitations of G.S. 143-341 to accept and hold title to real property in the name of the State of North Carolina, and to enter in contracts and do any and all things necessary to carry out any statewide programs for the acquisition of armories and armory sites, the construction and maintenance of armories, and to provide facilities which may be considered by it as necessary for any unit and which may be authorized by act of Congress or otherwise. (1947, c. 1010, s. 6; 1973, c. 620, s. 9; 1975, c. 604, s. 2; 1977, c. 70, s. 2; 2011-145, s. 19.1(g).)

§ 127A-165. Counties and municipalities may lease, convey or acquire property for use as armory.

Every municipality and county of the State of North Carolina is hereby authorized and empowered to lease or convey by deed to the State of North Carolina:

(1)   Any existing armory and the land adjacent thereto;

(2)   Any real property suitable for the construction of an armory, warehouse or other facility; and

(3)   Any real property suitable for use in the administration, instruction and training of any unit.

Every municipality and county is further authorized and empowered to acquire any real property which may be suitable for use as an armory or for the construction of an armory thereon, or for any other purpose of a unit. The contracting of an indebtedness and the expenditure of public funds by any municipality or county to comply with the provisions of this Article are hereby declared to be a necessary expense and for a public purpose. (1947, c. 1010, s. 7; 1949, c. 1066, s. 1; 1975, c. 604, s. 2.)

§ 127A-166. Prior conveyances validated.

All conveyances of real property made before April 20, 1949, by any municipality or county of the State of North Carolina to the State of North

Carolina for armory purposes are hereby validated and ratified in every respect. (1949, c. 1066, s. 2; 1975, c. 604, s. 2.)

§ 127A-167. Appropriations to supplement available funds authorized.

Any city or town and any county in the State, separately or jointly, may make appropriations to supplement available federal or State funds to be used for the construction of armory facilities for the North Carolina National Guard. Appropriations made under authority of this Article shall be in the amounts and in the proportions deemed adequate and necessary by the governing body of the county and/or municipality desiring to participate in the armory construction program. (1955, c. 1181, s. 1; 1975, c. 604, s. 2; 2009-281, s. 1; 2011-195, s. 1(a).)

§ 127A-168. Local financial support.

Each county and city in this State is authorized to make appropriations for the purposes of this Article and to fund them by levy of property taxes pursuant to G.S. 153A-149 and G.S. 160A-209 and by the allocation of other revenues whose use is not otherwise restricted by law. (1955, c. 1181, s. 2; 1961, c. 1042; 1973, c. 803, s. 12; 1975, c. 604, s. 2; 2011-195, s. 1(a).)

§ 127A-169. Unexpended portion of State appropriation.

The unexpended portion of any appropriation from the General Fund of the State for the purposes set out in this Article, or in Article 17 of this Chapter, remaining at the end of any biennium, shall not revert to the General Fund of the State, but shall constitute part of a permanent fund to be expended from time to time in the manner and for the purposes set out in this Article. (1949, c. 1202, s. 2; 1975, c. 604, s. 2; 2011-195, s. 1(a); 2013-360, s. 36.11(f).)

§§ 127A-170 through 127A-174. Reserved for future codification purposes.

Article 14.

National Guard Mutual Assistance Compact.

§ 127A-175. Purposes.

(a) Provide for mutual aid among the party states in the utilization of the National Guard to cope with emergencies.

(b) Permit and encourage a high degree of flexibility in the deployment of National Guard forces in the interest of efficiency.

(c) Maximize the effectiveness of the National Guard in those situations which call for its utilization under this Compact.

(d) Provide protection for the rights of National Guard personnel when serving in other states on emergency duty. (1969, c. 674, s. 1; 1975, c. 604, s. 2; 2009-281, s. 1.)

§ 127A-176. Entry into force and withdrawal.

(a) This Compact shall enter into force when enacted into law by any two states. Thereafter, this Compact shall become effective as to any other state upon its enactment thereof.

(b) Any party state may withdraw from this Compact by enacting a statute repealing the same, but no such withdrawal shall take effect until one year after the governor of the withdrawing state has given notice in writing of such withdrawal to the governors of all other party states. (1969, c. 674, s. 1; 1975, c. 604, s. 2.)

§ 127A-177. Definitions; mutual aid.

(a) As used in this Article:

(1) "Emergency" means an occurrence or condition, temporary in nature, in which police and other public safety officials and locally available National

Guard forces are, or may reasonably be expected to be, unable to cope with substantial and imminent danger to the public safety.

(2) "Requesting state" means the state whose governor requests assistance in coping with an emergency.

(3) "Responding state" means the state furnishing aid, or requested to furnish aid.

(b) Upon request of the governor of a party state for assistance in an emergency, the governor of a responding state shall have authority under this Compact to send without the borders of the responding state and place under the temporary command of the appropriate National Guard or other military authorities of the requesting state all or any part of the National Guard forces of the responding state as the governor of the responding state may deem necessary, and the exercise of the governor's discretion in this regard shall be conclusive.

(c) The governor of a party state may withhold the National Guard forces of that governor's state from such use and recall any forces or part or member thereof previously deployed in a requesting state.

(d) Whenever National Guard forces of any party state are engaged in another state in carrying out the purposes of this Compact, the members thereof so engaged shall have the same powers, duties, rights, privileges and immunities as members of National Guard forces in such other state. The requesting state shall save members of the National Guard forces of responding states harmless from civil liability for acts or omissions in good faith which occur in the performance of their duty while engaged in carrying out the purposes of this Compact, whether the responding forces are serving the requesting state within its borders or are in transit to or from such service.

(e) Subject to the provisions of subsections (f), (g) and (h) of this section, all liability that may arise under the laws of the requesting state, the responding state, or a third state on account of or in connection with a request for aid, shall be assumed and borne by the requesting state.

(f) Any responding state rendering aid pursuant to this Compact shall be reimbursed by the requesting state for any loss or damage to, or expense incurred in the operation of any equipment answering a request for aid, and for the cost of the materials, transportation and maintenance of National Guard personnel and equipment incurred in connection with such request: Provided, that nothing herein contained shall prevent any responding state from assuming such loss, damage, expense or other cost.

(g) Each party state shall provide, in the same amounts and manner as if they were on duty within their state, for the pay and allowances of the personnel of its National Guard units while engaged without the state pursuant to this Compact and while going to and returning from such duty pursuant to this Compact. Such pay and allowances shall be deemed items of expense reimbursable under subsection (f) of this section by the requesting state.

(h) Each party state providing for the payment of compensation and death benefits to injured members and the representatives of deceased members of its National Guard forces in case such members sustain injuries or are killed within their own state, shall provide for the payment of compensation and death benefits in the same manner and on the same terms in case such members sustain injury or are killed while rendering aid pursuant to this Compact. Such compensation and death benefits shall be deemed items of expense reimbursable pursuant to subsection (f) of this section. (1969, c. 674, s. 1; 1975, c. 604, s. 2; 2009-281, s. 1; 2011-195, s. 1(a).)

§ 127A-178. Delegation.

Nothing in this Compact shall be construed to prevent the governor of a party state from delegating any of the governor's responsibilities or authority respecting the National Guard, provided that such delegation is otherwise in accordance with law. For purposes of this Compact, however, the governor shall not delegate the power to request assistance from another state. (1969, c. 674, s. 1; 1975, c. 604, s. 2; 2009-281, s. 1; 2011-195, s. 1(a).)

§ 127A-179. Limitations.

Nothing in this Compact shall:

(1) Expand or add to the functions of the National Guard, except with respect to the jurisdictions within which such functions may be performed;

(2) Authorize or permit National Guard units to be placed under the field command of any person not having the military or National Guard rank or status required by law for the field command position in question. (1969, c. 674, s. 1; 1975, c. 604, s. 2; 2009-281, s. 1; 2011-195, s. 1(a).)

§ 127A-180. Construction and severability.

This Compact shall be liberally construed so as to effectuate the purposes thereof. The provisions of this Compact shall be severable and if any phrase, clause, sentence or provision of this Compact is declared to be contrary to the constitution of any state or of the United States or the applicability thereof to any government, agency, person or circumstance is held invalid, the validity of the remainder of this Compact and the applicability thereof to any government, agency, person or circumstance shall not be affected thereby. If this Compact shall be held contrary to the constitution of any state participating herein, the Compact shall remain in full force and effect as to the remaining party states and in full force and effect as to the state affected as to all severable matters. (1969, c. 674, s. 1; 1975, c. 604, s. 2.)

§ 127A-181. Payment of liability to responding state.

Upon presentation of a claim therefor by an appropriate authority of a state whose National Guard forces have aided this State pursuant to the Compact, any liability of this State pursuant to G.S. 127A-177(f) shall be paid out of the general fund. (1969, c. 674, s. 1; 1975, c. 604, s. 2; 2009-281, s. 1; 2011-195, s. 1(a).)

§ 127A-182. Status, rights and benefits of forces engaged pursuant to Compact.

In accordance with G.S. 127A-177(h), members of the National Guard forces of this State shall be deemed to be in State service at all times when engaged pursuant to this Compact, and shall be entitled to all rights and benefits provided pursuant to the laws of this State. (1969, c. 674, s. 1; 1975, c. 604, s. 2; 2009-281, s. 1; 2011-195, s. 1(a).)

§ 127A-183. Injury or death while going to or returning from duty.

All benefits to be paid under G.S. 127A-177(h) shall include any injury or death sustained while going to or returning from such duty. (1969, c. 674, s. 1; 1975, c. 604, s. 2; 2011-195, s. 1(a).)

§ 127A-184. Authority of responding state required to relieve from assignment or reassign officers.

Nothing in this Compact shall authorize or permit state officials or military officers of the requesting state to relieve from assignment or reassign officers or noncommissioned officers of National Guard units of the responding state without authorization by the appropriate authorities of the responding state. (1969, c. 674, s. 1; 1975, c. 604, s. 2; 2009-281, s. 1; 2011-195, s. 1(a).)

§§ 127A-185 through 127A-189. Reserved for future codification purposes.

Article 15.

North Carolina National Guard Tuition Assistance Act of 1975.

§ 127A-190: Recodified as Part 2 of Article 23 of Chapter 116, G.S. 116-209.50 through 116-209.55, by Session Laws 2010-31, s. 17.3(b), effective July 1, 2010.

§ 127A-191: Recodified as Part 2 of Article 23 of Chapter 116, G.S. 116-209.50 through 116-209.55, by Session Laws 2010-31, s. 17.3(b), effective July 1, 2010.

§ 127A-192: Recodified as Part 2 of Article 23 of Chapter 116, G.S. 116-209.50 through 116-209.55, by Session Laws 2010-31, s. 17.3(b), effective July 1, 2010.

§ 127A-193: Recodified as Part 2 of Article 23 of Chapter 116, G.S. 116-209.50 through 116-209.55, by Session Laws 2010-31, s. 17.3(b), effective July 1, 2010.

§ 127A-194: Recodified as Part 2 of Article 23 of Chapter 116, G.S. 116-209.50 through 116-209.55, by Session Laws 2010-31, s. 17.3(b), effective July 1, 2010.

§ 127A-195: Recodified as Part 2 of Article 23 of Chapter 116, G.S. 116-209.50 through 116-209.55, by Session Laws 2010-31, s. 17.3(b), effective July 1, 2010.

§ 127A-196: Recodified as Part 2 of Article 23 of Chapter 116, G.S. 116-209.50 through 116-209.55, by Session Laws 2010-31, s. 17.3(b), effective July 1, 2010.

§ 127A-197: Recodified as Part 2 of Article 23 of Chapter 116, G.S. 116-209.50 through 116-209.55, by Session Laws 2010-31, s. 17.3(b), effective July 1, 2010.

§ 127A-198: Recodified as Part 2 of Article 23 of Chapter 116, G.S. 116-209.50 through 116-209.55, by Session Laws 2010-31, s. 17.3(b), effective July 1, 2010.

§ 127A-199: Recodified as Part 2 of Article 23 of Chapter 116, G.S. 116-209.50 through 116-209.55, by Session Laws 2010-31, s. 17.3(b), effective July 1, 2010.

§ 127A-200: Recodified as Part 2 of Article 23 of Chapter 116, G.S. 116-209.50 through 116-209.55, by Session Laws 2010-31, s. 17.3(b), effective July 1, 2010.

Article 16.

National Guard Reemployment Rights.

§ 127A-201. Entitlement.

Any member of the North Carolina National Guard who, at the direction of the Governor, enters State duty, is entitled, upon honorable release from State duty, to all the reemployment rights provided for in this Article. (1979, c. 155, s. 1.)

§ 127A-202. Rights.

Upon release from State duty, the employee shall make written application to the employee's previous employer for reemployment within five days of the employee's release from duty or from hospitalization continuing after release. If the employee is still qualified for the employee's previous employment, the employee shall be restored to his previous position or to a position of like seniority, status and salary, unless the employer's circumstances now make the restoration unreasonable. If the employee is no longer qualified for the employee's previous employment, the employee shall be placed in another position, for which the employee is qualified, and which will give the employee appropriate seniority, status and salary, unless the employer's circumstances now make the placement unreasonable. (1979, c. 155, s. 1; 2011-195, s. 1(a).)

§ 127A-202.1. Discrimination against persons who serve in the North Carolina National Guard and acts of reprisal prohibited.

(a)   It is the policy of this State that all individuals shall be afforded the right to perform, apply to perform, or have an obligation to perform service in the North Carolina National Guard without fear of discrimination or retaliatory action from their employer or prospective employer on the basis of that membership, application for membership, performance of service, application for service, or obligation.

(b)   An individual who is a member of the North Carolina National Guard who performs, has performed, applies to perform, or has an obligation to perform service in the North Carolina National Guard shall not be denied initial employment, reemployment, retention in employment, promotion, or any benefit of employment by an employer on the basis of that membership, application for membership, performance of service, application for service, or obligation.

(c)   A person shall be considered to have denied a member of the North Carolina National Guard initial employment, reemployment, retention in employment, promotion, or a benefit of employment in violation of this section if the member's membership, application for membership, performance of service, application for service, or obligation for service in the North Carolina National Guard is a motivating factor in that person's action, unless the person can prove by the greater weight of the evidence that the same unfavorable action would have taken place in the absence of the member's membership, application for membership, performance of service, application for service, or obligation.

(d) Nothing in this section shall be construed to require a person to pay salary or wages to a member of the North Carolina National Guard during the member's period of active service.

(e) The Commissioner of Labor shall enforce the provisions of this section according to Article 21 of Chapter 95 of the General Statutes, including the rules and regulations issued pursuant to that Article.

(f) This section shall also apply when a member of the North Carolina National Guard is called into active duty at the direction of the President, the Governor, or by any other competent authority. (1997-153, s. 1; 2004-130, s. 3.)

§ 127A-203. Penalties for denial.

If any employer, public or private, fails or refuses to comply with G.S. 127A-202, the superior court for the district of the employer's place of business may, upon the filing of a motion, petition, or other appropriate pleading by the employee, require the employer to comply with G.S. 127A-202 and to compensate the employee for any loss of wages or benefits suffered by reason of the employer's unlawful failure or refusal. (1979, c. 155, s. 1.)

§ 127A-204: Reserved for future codification purposes.

§ 127A-205: Reserved for future codification purposes.

§ 127A-206: Reserved for future codification purposes.

§ 127A-207: Reserved for future codification purposes.

§ 127A-208: Reserved for future codification purposes.

§ 127A-209: Reserved for future codification purposes.

Article 17.

Armory and Facility Development Projects and Plan.

§ 127A-210. Armory and facility development project plan.

(a) Plan Prepared. - No later than July 1 of each year, the Department of Public Safety shall prepare a statewide plan for armories for a period of seven years into the future. The plan shall be known as the Armory and Facilities Development Plan. If the plan differs from the Armory and Facilities Development Plan adopted for the preceding calendar year, the Department shall indicate the changes and the reasons for such changes. The Department shall submit the plan to the Director of the Budget for review.

(b) Projects Listed. - The plan shall list the following armory and facilities projects based on their status as of May 1 of the year in which the plan is prepared:

(1) Projects approved by the Congress of the United States but for which federal funds have not been appropriated.

(2) Projects for which the Congress of the United States has appropriated funds.

(c) Project Priorities and Funding Recommendations. - The Department shall assign a priority to each project within each of the two categories listed under subsection (b) of this section, either by giving the project a number with "1" assigned to the highest priority, or by recommending no funding. The Department shall state its reasons for recommending the funding, deferral, or elimination of a project. The Department shall determine the priority of a project based on the following criteria: federal requirements, a project's proximity to transportation infrastructure and other critical State and federal assets, and a project's ability to further the mission of the National Guard.

(d) Distribution of the Plan. - The Director of the Budget shall provide copies of the plan to the General Assembly along with the recommended biennial budget and the recommended revised budget for the second year of the biennium.

(e) Budget Recommendations. - The Director of the Budget shall determine which projects, if any, will be included in the recommended biennial budget and in the recommended revised budget for the second year of the biennium. The budget document transmitted to the General Assembly shall identify the projects or types of projects recommended for funding.

(f) Definitions. - For purposes of this section, the terms "armory," "armory site," and "facilities" shall have the same meaning as in G.S. 127A-161. (2013-360, s. 36.11(e).)

Chapter 127B.

Military Affairs.

Article 1.

Military Property Sales Facilities.

§127B-1. Military property sales facility defined.

Any person, partnership, association or corporation who engages in the business of selling, consigning, purchasing, transferring or in any way acquiring military property for resale, is a "military property sales facility". Specifically excluded are facilities operated by the United States Government, the State of North Carolina or any of its agencies and persons, partnerships, associations or corporations selling or purchasing military property pursuant to a contract with the United States Government, the State of North Carolina or any of its agencies. (1985, c. 522, s. 1.)

§ 127B-2. Military property defined.

"Military property" means property originally manufactured for the United States or State of North Carolina which is a type and kind issued for use in, or furnished and intended for, the Armed Forces of the United States or the militia of the State of North Carolina. (1985, c. 522, s. 1; 2011-183, s. 91.)

§ 127B-3. License.

No person, partnership, association or corporation shall engage in the business of selling military property or purchasing military property for resale without first having obtained a license to do so from the local governing body of the city, town, or county in which it is located and by paying the county, State, and municipal tax required by law, and otherwise complying with the requirements made in this and succeeding sections. The license shall be posted in a prominent place, easily visible to the public, on the designated premises. (1985, c. 522, s. 1.)

§ 127B-4. Local governing authorities to grant and control license; bond.

(a) The governing body of any city, town, or county in this State may grant to such person, partnership, association or corporation as who shall produce satisfactory evidence of good character, a license authorizing such person, partnership, association or corporation to carry on the business of a military property sales facility. The license shall designate the building in which the person, partnership, association or corporation shall carry on the business, and no person, partnership, association or corporation shall carry on the business of a military property sales facility without being duly licensed, nor in any other building than the one designated in the license.

(b) Any person or the principal officers of any association or corporation or all the partners of any partnership applying for a license shall furnish the governing body the following information:

(1) Full name, and any other names used by the applicant during the preceding five years, or in the case of a partnership, association or corporation, the applicant shall list any partnership, association, or corporate names used during the preceding five years;

(2) Current address, and all addresses used by the applicant during the preceding five years;

(3) Physical description;

(4) Age;

(5) Driver's license number, if any, and state of issuance;

(6) Recent color photograph;

(7) Record of felony convictions; and

(8) Record of other convictions during the preceding five years.

(c) Every person, partnership, association or corporation so licensed to carry on the business of a military property sales facility shall, at the time of receiving a license, file with the governing body of the city, town, or county granting the license, a bond payable to the city, town, or county in the sum of one thousand dollars ($1,000), to be executed by the person licensed and by two responsible sureties, or a surety company licensed to do business in the State of North Carolina, to be approved of by the governing body. The bond shall be for the faithful performance of the requirements and obligations pertaining to the business licensed. The governing body, may revoke the license and sue for forfeiture of the bond upon a breach of the licensee's duties under the bond. Any person who may obtain a judgment against a military property sales facility and upon which judgment execution is returned unsatisfied may maintain an action in his own name upon the bond of the military property sales facility, in any court having jurisdiction of the amount demanded to satisfy the judgment. (1985, c. 522, s. 1.)

§ 127B-5. Perjury; punishment.

Any person who shall willfully commit perjury in any application for a permit pursuant to this Article shall be guilty of a Class 1 misdemeanor. (1985, c. 522, s. 1; 1993, c. 539, s. 939; 1994, Ex. Sess., c. 24, s. 14(c).)

§ 127B-6. Records to be kept.

(a) Every military property sales facility owner shall keep a book in which shall be legibly written, at the time of each transaction involving the acquisition by any means of used or new military property by the military property sales facility owner, his employee or agent, from any person, partnership, association or corporation, the following information:

(1) An account and description of the used or new military property including if applicable, the manufacturer's name, the model, the model number, the serial number of the property, and any engraved numbers or initials found on the property. Property lacking any identifying mark or characteristic shall be marked by the military property sales facility owner in such a way as to allow clear identification of the property.

(2) The amount of money paid;

(3) The date of the transaction; and

(4) The name and residence of the person selling, consigning or transferring the used or new military property.

(b) The military property sales facility owner, or his employee or agent shall require that the person selling the new or used military property, to present two forms of positive identification to him before the military property sales facility personnel may complete any transaction regarding the buying, consigning or acquiring of new or used military property. The presentation of any one state or federal government issued identification containing a photographic representation imprinted on it shall constitute compliance with the identification requirements of this paragraph. The military property sales facility owner or his employee or agent shall legibly record this identification information next to the person's name and residence in the book required to be kept. Both the military property sales facility owner, his employee or agent and the seller, consignor or transferor of the military property shall sign the record entry.

(c) The book shall be a permanent record to be kept at all times on the premises of the place of business of the military property sales facility and shall be made available, during regular business hours, to any law enforcement officer who requests to inspect the book. A copy of the records required to be kept by this section shall be filed within 48 hours of the transaction in the office of the local law enforcement agency serving the city, town, or county which issued the license to the military. Mailing the required copy to the local law enforcement agency within 48 hours shall constitute compliance with this section. (1985, c. 522, s. 1.)

§ 127B-7. Penalties.

Any dealer who violates the provisions of this Article shall be guilty of a Class 2 misdemeanor. In addition, any dealer convicted of violating this Article shall be ineligible for a dealer's permit for a period of three years from the date of conviction. Each violation shall constitute a separate and distinct offense. (1985, c. 522, s. 1; 1993, c. 539, s. 940; 1994, Ex. Sess., c. 24, s. 14(c).)

§§ 127B-8 through 127B-9. Reserved for future codification purposes.

Article 2.

Discrimination Against Military Personnel.

§ 127B-10. Purpose.

The General Assembly finds and declares that military personnel in North Carolina vitally affect the general economy of this State and that it is in the public interest and public welfare to ensure that no discrimination against military personnel is practiced by any business. (1985, c. 522, s. 1.)

§ 127B-11. Private discrimination prohibited.

No person shall discriminate against any officer, warrant officer or enlisted person of the military forces of the State or of the United States because of their membership therein. No member of these military forces shall be prejudiced or injured by any person, employer, officer or agent of any corporation, company or firm with respect to their employment, position or status or denied or disqualified for employment by virtue of their membership or service in the military forces of this State or of the United States. (1985, c. 522, s. 1; 2011-183, s. 92.)

§ 127B-12. Public discrimination prohibited.

No officer or employee of the State, or of any county, city and county, municipal corporation, school district, water district, or other district shall discriminate against any officer, warrant officer or enlisted person of the military forces of the State or of the United States because of their membership therein. No member of the military forces shall be prejudiced or injured by any officer or employee of the State, or of any county, city and county, municipal corporation, school district, water district, or other district with respect to their employment, appointment, position or status or denied or disqualified for or discharged from their employment or position by virtue of their membership or service in the military forces of this State or of the United States. (1985, c. 522, s. 1; 2011-183, s. 93.)

§ 127B-13. Refusing entrance prohibited.

No person shall prohibit or refuse entrance to any officer, warrant officer or enlisted person of the military forces of this State or of the United States into any public place of entertainment, of amusement, or accommodation because the officer or enlisted person is wearing the uniform of the organization to which they belong or because of their membership or service in the military forces of this State or of the United States. (1985, c. 522, s. 1; 2011-183, s. 94.)

§ 127B-14. Employer discrimination prohibited.

No employer or officer or agent of any corporation, company, or firm, or other person shall discharge any person from employment because of the performance of any emergency military duty by reason of being an officer, warrant officer or enlisted person of the military forces of this State or the United States. (1985, c. 522, s. 1; 2011-183, s. 95.)

§ 127B-15. Penalties.

Any person who violates the provisions of this Article shall be deemed guilty of a Class 2 misdemeanor. Each violation shall constitute a separate and distinct offense. (1985, c. 522, s. 1; 1993, c. 539, s. 941; 1994, Ex. Sess., c. 24, s. 14(c).)

Article 3.

Research Collaboration on Health and Other Problems.

§ 127B-20. Collaboration on research to address health and other problems required; report by UNC General Administration.

(a) The General Administration of The University of North Carolina, in collaboration with Operation Re-Entry North Carolina at East Carolina University, North Carolina Translational and Clinical Sciences Institute, other institutions of higher education in this State, the North Carolina National Guard, and the United States Department of Veterans Affairs, shall, to the extent available resources allow, collaborate on research to address the behavioral health problems and challenges facing military personnel, veterans, and their families.

(b) The research required by this section shall be conducted by collaborative research teams which shall include civilian investigators from institutions of higher learning in this State and private research organizations, health providers in regional and national military health system institutions, and providers and investigators in VISN 6 in the VA system. These teams shall aggressively pursue federal funding to conduct the research required by this section.

(c) At a minimum, the research required by this section shall include the following goals:

(1) To define the behavioral health problems facing service members, veterans, and their families, with a special emphasis on the behavioral health needs of the reserve components of the Armed Forces of the United States, including the National Guard.

(2) To develop, implement, and evaluate innovative pilot programs to improve the quality, accessibility, and delivery of behavioral health services provided to this population.

(3) To evaluate the effectiveness of new programs put into place by the National Guard and other military organizations to address the behavioral health challenges facing military service personnel, veterans, and family members. The National Guard shall cooperate in providing information to assess the effectiveness of behavioral health services provided to it and its members.

(4) To contribute to the knowledge of evidence-based behavioral health screening, diagnosis, treatment, and recovery supports for military service personnel, veterans, and their families.

(5) To study other issues pursuant to requests by the various branches of the active and reserve components of the Armed Forces of the United States and the United States Department of Veterans Affairs, in order to improve behavioral health services for service members, veterans, and their families.

(d) On July 1, 2012, and annually thereafter, the General Administration of The University of North Carolina shall report its findings to the Joint Legislative Health Care Oversight Committee and to the House of Representatives and Senate Appropriations Subcommittees on Health and Human Services. (2011-185, s. 10(a)-(d).)

Chapter 127C.

North Carolina Military Affairs Commission.

§ 127C-1. Commission established; purpose; transaction of business.

(a) Establishment. - There is established the North Carolina Military Affairs Commission. The Commission shall be established within the Office of the Governor. The Department of Commerce is responsible for organizational, budgetary, and administrative purposes.

(b) Purpose. - The Commission shall provide advice, counsel, and recommendations to the Governor, the General Assembly, the Secretary of Commerce, and other State agencies on initiatives, programs, and legislation that will continue and increase the role that North Carolina's military installations, the National Guard, and Reserves play in America's defense strategy and the economic health and vitality of the State. The Commission is authorized to:

(1) Coordinate and provide recommendations to the Governor, General Assembly, and State agencies to protect North Carolina's military installations from encroachment or other initiatives that could result in degradation or restrictions to military operations, training ranges, or low-level routes.

(2) Cooperate with military installations to facilitate the military mission, training, and continued presence of major military installations in the State and notify the commanding military officer of a military installation and the governing body in affected counties and municipalities of any economic development or other projects that may impact military installations.

(3) Identify and support ways to provide a sound infrastructure, adequate housing and education, and transition support into North Carolina's workforce for military members and their families, military retirees, and veterans.

(4) Lead the State's initiative to prepare for the next round of Base Realignment and Closure (BRAC), as defined by the Governor and the General Assembly, with input from local military communities.

(5) Identify and support economic development organizations and initiatives that focus on leveraging the military and other business opportunities to help create jobs and expand defense and homeland security related economic development activity in North Carolina.

(6) Assist military installations located within the State by coordinating with commanders, communities, and State and federal agencies on affairs that affect military installations and may require State coordination and assistance.

(7) Support the long-term goal of a viable and prosperous military presence in the State, which shall include development of comprehensive economic impact studies of military activities in North Carolina, updated every two years with recommendations for initiatives to support this goal.

(8) Support the Army's Compatible Use Buffer Program, the Working Lands Group, and related initiatives.

(9) Adopt processes to ensure that all planning, coordination, and actions are conducted with timely consideration having been given to relevant military readiness or training concerns and with appropriate communications with all potentially affected military entities.

(10) Share information and coordinate efforts with the North Carolina congressional delegation and other federal agencies, as appropriate.

(11) Any other issue or matter that the Commission deems essential to fulfilling its purpose.

(c) Transaction of Business. - The Commission shall meet, at a minimum, at least once during each quarter and shall provide a report on military affairs to the Governor and to the General Assembly at least every six months. Prior to the start of a Regular Session of the General Assembly, the Commission shall report to the General Assembly with recommendations, if any, for legislation. Priority actions or issues may be submitted at any time. (2001-424, s. 12.1; 2013-227, s. 2.)

§ 127C-2. Membership.

(a) The North Carolina Military Affairs Commission shall consist of 21 voting members who are appointed by the Governor, the Speaker of the House of Representatives, and the President Pro Tempore of the Senate, nonvoting members, and nonvoting ex officio members as designated in this section.

(b) The voting members of the Commission shall be appointed as follows:

(1) Eleven members appointed by the Governor, consisting of:

a. One person residing near Camp Lejeune, who is retired from the military and is actively involved in a military affairs organization, or a person who is involved in military issues through civic, commercial, or governmental relationships.

b. One person residing near Marine Corps Air Station Cherry Point, who is retired from the military and is actively involved in a military affairs organization, or a person who is involved in military issues through civic, commercial, or governmental relationships.

c. One person residing near Seymour Johnson Air Force Base, who is retired from the military and is actively involved in a military affairs organization, or a person who is involved in military issues through civic, commercial, or governmental relationships.

d. One person residing near Ft. Bragg, who is retired from the military and is actively involved in a military affairs organization, or a person who is involved in military issues through civic, commercial, or governmental relationships.

e. One person residing near Coast Guard Station Elizabeth City, who is retired from the military and is actively involved in a military affairs organization, or a person who is involved in military issues through civic, commercial, or governmental relationships.

f. Six persons who may reside in any part of the State, who are involved in military issues through civic, commercial, or governmental relationships.

(2) Five members appointed by the Speaker of the House of Representatives, consisting of:

a. One member of the House of Representatives. A House member who has served in the military or has extensive experience in the area of military affairs shall be selected.

b. One person residing near Camp Lejeune, who is retired from the military and is actively involved in a military affairs organization, or a person who is involved in military issues through civic, commercial, or governmental relationships.

c. One person residing near Marine Corps Air Station Cherry Point, who is retired from the military and is actively involved in a military affairs organization, or a person who is involved in military issues through civic, commercial, or governmental relationships.

d. One person residing near Seymour Johnson Air Force Base, who is retired from the military and is actively involved in a military affairs organization, or a person who is involved in military issues through civic, commercial, or governmental relationships.

e. One person residing near Ft. Bragg, who is retired from the military and is actively involved in a military affairs organization, or a person who is involved in military issues through civic, commercial, or governmental relationships.

(3) Five members appointed by the President Pro Tempore of the Senate, consisting of:

a. One member of the Senate. A Senate member who has served in the military or has extensive experience in the area of military affairs shall be selected.

b. One person residing near Camp Lejeune, who is retired from the military and is actively involved in a military affairs organization, or a person who is involved in military issues through civic, commercial, or governmental relationships.

c. One person residing near Marine Corps Air Station Cherry Point, who is retired from the military and is actively involved in a military affairs organization, or a person who is involved in military issues through civic, commercial, or governmental relationships.

d. One person residing near Seymour Johnson Air Force Base, who is retired from the military and is actively involved in a military affairs organization, or a person who is involved in military issues through civic, commercial, or governmental relationships.

e. One person residing near Ft. Bragg, who is retired from the military and is actively involved in a military affairs organization, or a person who is involved in military issues through civic, commercial, or governmental relationships.

(c) The following members of the General Assembly shall serve as nonvoting members of the Commission:

(1) One member of the House of Representatives, appointed by the Speaker of the House of Representatives, who represents a district which contains all or any portion of one of the military installations described in sub-subdivisions b. through e. of subdivision (2) of subsection (b) of this section.

(2) One member of the Senate appointed by the President Pro Tempore of the Senate, who represents a district which contains all or any portion of one of the military installations described in sub-subdivisions b. through e. of subdivision (3) of subsection (b) of this section.

(d) The following office holders or their designee, shall serve as nonvoting ex officio members of the Commission:

(1) The Lieutenant Governor.

(2) Secretary of Public Safety.

(3) Secretary of Commerce.

(4) The Secretary of Transportation.

(5) The Secretary of the Department of Environment and Natural Resources.

(6) The Commissioner of Agriculture.

(7) Adjutant General of the North Carolina National Guard.

(8) The Mayor of Elizabeth City, or designee.

(9) The Mayor of Fayetteville, or designee.

(10) The Mayor of Goldsboro, or designee.

(11) The Mayor of Havelock, or designee.

(12) The Mayor of Jacksonville, or designee.

(13) The Assistant Secretary for Veterans Affairs, Department of Administration.

(14) The President of The University of North Carolina.

(15) The President of the North Carolina Community College System.

(16) The Superintendent of Public Instruction.

(e) The following officers, or their designee, shall be invited to serve as nonvoting ex officio members of the Commission:

(1) Commanding General, 18th Airborne Corps, Ft. Bragg.

(2) Commanding General, Marine Corps Installations East.

(3) Commanding Officer, Marine Corps Air Station, Cherry Point.

(4) Commanding Officer, 4th Fighter Wing, Seymour Johnson Air Force Base.

(5) Commanding Officer, U.S. Army Corps of Engineers, Wilmington District.

(6) Commanding Officer, U.S. Coast Guard Base, Elizabeth City.

(7) Commanding Officer, Marine Corps Air Station, New River.

(8) Commanding Officer, Camp Lejeune Marine Corps Base.

(9) Commanding Officer, Fleet Readiness Center East.

(10) Commanding Officer, Military Ocean Terminal, Sunny Point.

(11) Commanding Officer, Coast Guard Sector North Carolina.

(12) Commanding Officer, Naval Support Activity Hampton Roads.

(f) The Chair of the Commission shall be appointed by the Governor from the voting members of the Commission.

(g) The voting members of the Commission shall serve for two-year terms, with no prohibition against being reappointed, except initial appointments shall be for terms as follows:

(1) The Governor shall initially appoint seven members for a term of two years and four members for a term of three years.

(2) The President Pro Tempore of the Senate shall initially appoint the member of the Senate and two members for a term of two years and two members for a term of three years.

(3) The Speaker of the House of Representatives shall initially appoint the member from the House of Representatives and two members for a term of two years and two members for a term of three years.

Initial terms shall commence on August 1, 2013.

(h) The initial meeting of the Commission shall be within 30 days of the effective date of this act at a time and place to be determined by the Secretary of Commerce. The first order of business at the initial meeting of the Commission shall be the adoption of bylaws and establishment of committees, after which the Commission shall meet upon the call of the Chairman or the Military Advisor within the Office of the Governor. The members shall receive no compensation for attendance at meetings, except a per diem expense reimbursement. Members of the Commission who are not officers or employees of the State shall receive reimbursement for subsistence and travel expenses at rates set out in G.S. 138-5 from funds made available to the Commission. Members of the Commission who are officers or employees of the State shall be reimbursed for travel and subsistence at the rates set out in G.S. 138-6 from funds made available to the Commission. The Department of Commerce shall use funds within its budget for the per diem, subsistence, and travel expenses authorized by this subsection. (2001-424, s. 12.1; 2001-486, s. 2.9(a), (b); 2004-49, s. 1; 2011-145, ss. 9.6A, 19.1(g); 2013-227, s. 2.)

§ 127C-3. Military Advisor.

The Military Advisor within the Office of the Governor shall serve as the administrative head of the Commission and be responsible for the operations and normal business activities of the Commission, with oversight by the Commission. (2001-424, s. 12.1; 2013-227, s. 2.)

§ 127C-4: Repealed by Session Laws 2013-227, s. 2, effective August 1, 2013.

Chapter 128.

Offices and Public Officers.

Article 1.

General Provisions.

§ 128-1. No person shall hold more than one office; exception.

No person who shall hold any office or place of trust or profit under the United States, or any department thereof or under this State, or under any other state or government, shall hold or exercise any other office or place of trust or profit under the authority of this State, or be eligible to a seat in either house of the

General Assembly except as provided in G.S. 128-1.1, or by other General Statute. (Const., art. 14, s. 7; Rev., s. 2364; C.S., s. 3200; 1967, c. 24, s. 24; 1969, c. 1070; 1971, c. 697, s. 1; 1983, c. 609, s. 9.)

§ 128-1.1. Dual-office holding allowed.

(a) Any person who holds an appointive office, place of trust or profit in State or local government is hereby authorized by the General Assembly, pursuant to Article VI, Sec. 9 of the North Carolina Constitution, to hold concurrently one other appointive office, place of trust or profit, or an elective office in either State or local government.

(b) Any person who holds an elective office in State or local government is hereby authorized by the General Assembly, pursuant to Article VI, Sec. 9 of the North Carolina Constitution to hold concurrently one other appointive office, place of trust or profit, in either State or local government.

(c) Any person who holds an office or position in the federal postal system or is commissioned as a special officer or deputy special officer of the United States Bureau of Indian Affairs is hereby authorized to hold concurrently therewith one position in State or local government.

(c1) Where authorized by federal law, any State or local law enforcement agency may authorize its law enforcement officers to also perform the functions of an officer under 8 U.S.C. § 1357(g) if the agency has a Memorandum of Agreement or Memorandum of Understanding for that purpose with a federal agency. State and local law enforcement officers authorized under this provision are authorized to hold any office or position with the applicable federal agency required to perform the described functions.

(d) The term "elective office," as used herein, shall mean any office filled by election by the people when the election is conducted by a county board of elections under the supervision of the State Board of Elections. (1971, c. 697, s. 2; 1975, c. 174; 1987, c. 427, s. 10; 2006-259, s. 24(a); 2011-31, s. 13.)

§ 128-1.2. Ex officio service by county and city representatives and officials.

Except when the resolution of appointment provides otherwise, whenever the governing body of a county or city appoints one of its own members or officials to another board or commission, the individual so appointed is considered to be serving on the other board or commission as a part of the individual's duties of office and shall not be considered to be serving in a separate office.

As used in this section, the term "official" means (i) in the case of a county, the county manager, acting county manager, interim county manager, county attorney, finance officer, or clerk to the board and (ii) in the case of a city, the city manager, acting city manager, interim city manager, city attorney, finance officer, city clerk, or deputy clerk. As used in this section, the term "city" has the meaning provided in G.S. 160A-1. (1983, c. 651, s. 1; 1991, c. 508, s. 5.)

§ 128-2. Holding office contrary to the Constitution; penalty.

If any person presumes to hold any office, or place of trust or profit, or is elected to a seat in either house of the General Assembly, contrary to Article VI, Sec. 9 of the North Carolina Constitution, he shall forfeit all rights and emoluments incident thereto. (1790, c. 319, P.R.; 1792, c. 366, P.R.; 1793, c. 393, P.R.; 1796, c. 450, P.R.; 1811, c. 811, P.R.; R.C., c. 77, s. 1; Code, s. 1870; Rev., s. 2365; C.S., s. 3201; Ex. Sess., 1924, c. 110; 1971, c. 697, s. 3.)

§ 128-3. Bargains for office void.

All bargains, bonds and assurances made or given for the purchase or sale of any office whatsoever, the sale of which is contrary to law, shall be void. (5 and 6 Edw. VI, c. 16, s. 3; R.C., c. 77, s. 2; Code, s. 1871; Rev., s. 2366; C.S., s. 3202.)

§ 128-4. Receiving compensation of subordinates for appointment or retention; removal.

Any official or employee of this State or any political subdivision thereof, in whose office or under whose supervision are employed one or more subordinate officials or employees who shall, directly or indirectly, receive or demand, for himself or another, any part of the compensation of any such subordinate, as the price of appointment or retention of such subordinate, shall be guilty of a Class 1 misdemeanor: Provided, that this section shall not apply in cases in which an official or employee is given an allowance for the conduct of his office from which he is to compensate himself and his subordinates in such manner as he sees fit. Any person convicted of violating this section, in addition to the criminal penalties, shall be subject to removal from office. The procedure for removal shall be the same as that provided for removal of certain local officials from office by G.S. 128-16 to 128-20, inclusive. (1937, c. 32, ss. 1, 2; 1993, c. 539, s. 942; 1994, Ex. Sess., c. 24, s. 14(c).)

§ 128-5. Oath required before acting; penalty.

Every officer and other person required to take an oath of office, or an oath for the faithful discharge of any duty imposed on him, and also the oath appointed for such as hold any office of trust or profit in the State, shall take all said oaths before entering on the duties of the office, or the duties imposed on such person, on pain of forfeiting five hundred dollars ($500.00) to the use of the poor of the county in or for which the office is to be used, and of being ejected from his office or place by proper proceedings for that purpose. (R.C., c. 77, s. 4; Code, s. 1873; Rev., s. 2367; C.S., s. 3203.)

§ 128-6. Persons admitted to office deemed to hold lawfully.

Any person who shall, by the proper authority, be admitted and sworn into any office, shall be held, deemed, and taken, by force of such admission, to be rightfully in such office until, by judicial sentence, upon a proper proceeding, he shall be ousted therefrom, or his admission thereto be, in due course of law, declared void. (Const., art. 4, s. 25; 1844, c. 38, s. 2; 1848, c. 64, s. 1; R.C., c. 77, s. 3; Code, s. 1872; Rev., s. 2368; C.S., s. 3204.)

§ 128-7. Officer to hold until successor qualified.

All officers shall continue in their respective offices until their successors are elected or appointed, and duly qualified. (1848, c. 64, s. 2; R.C., c. 77, s. 3; Code, s. 1872; Rev., s. 2368; C.S., s. 3205.)

§ 128-7.1. Failure to qualify creates vacancy.

If any person who has been elected to public office (i) dies or becomes disqualified for the office before qualifying for the office, or (ii) for any reason refuses to qualify for the office, the office shall be declared vacant. Unless otherwise provided by law, such vacancy shall be filled by appointment by the authority having the power to fill vacancies as prescribed by law. (1971, c. 183.)

§ 128-7.2. Qualifications for appointment to fill vacancy in elective office.

No person is eligible for appointment to fill a vacancy in any elective office, whether State or local, unless that person would have been qualified to vote as an elector for that office if an election were to be held on the date of appointment. This section is intended to implement the provisions of Section 8 of Article VI of the Constitution. (2007-391, s. 27(a).)

§ 128-8: Repealed by Session Laws 1981, c. 884, s. 13.

§ 128-9: Repealed by Session Laws 1979, c. 650.

§ 128-10. Citizen to recover funds of county or town retained by delinquent official.

When an official of a county, city or town is liable upon his bond for unlawfully and wrongfully retaining by virtue of his office a fund, or a part thereof, to which the county, city or town is entitled, any citizen and taxpayer may, in his own name for the benefit of the county, city or town, institute suit and recover from the delinquent official the fund so retained. Any county commissioners, aldermen, councilmen or governing board who fraudulently, wrongfully and unlawfully permit an official so to retain funds shall be personally liable therefor; any citizen and taxpayer may, in his own name for the benefit of the county, city or town, institute suit and recover from such county commissioners, aldermen, councilmen, or governing board, the fund so retained. Before instituting suit under this section, the citizen and taxpayer shall file a statement before the county commissioners, treasurer, or other officers authorized by law to institute the suit, setting forth the fund alleged to be retained or permitted to be retained, and demanding that suit be instituted by the authorities authorized to sue within 60 days. The citizen and taxpayer so suing shall receive one-third part, up to the sum of five hundred dollars ($500.00), of the amount recovered, to indemnify him for his services, but the amount received by the taxpayer and citizen as indemnity shall in no case exceed five hundred dollars ($500.00). (1913, c. 80; C.S., s. 3206.)

§ 128-11. Trust funds to be kept separate.

Any sheriff, treasurer or other officer of any county, city, town or other political subdivision of the State, receiving, by virtue of his office, public money or money to be held by him in trust shall keep or deposit such money or the credits or other evidence thereof separate and apart from his own funds and shall not, at any time, apply such money to his own use or benefit or intermingle the same in any manner with credits or funds of his own. (1931, c. 77, s. 1.)

§ 128-12. Violations to be reported; misdemeanors.

It shall be the duty of the director of the Local Government Commission to report to the district attorney of the district any violation of G.S. 128-11 of which he may have knowledge, and any violation of such section shall be unlawful and shall constitute a Class 1 misdemeanor. (1931, c. 60, s. 3; 1931, c. 77, s. 2; 1973, c. 47, s. 2; 1993, c. 539, s. 943; 1994, Ex. Sess., c. 24, s. 14(c).)

§ 128-13. Officers compensated from fees in certain counties to render statement; penalty; proceeds to school fund.

Every clerk of the superior court, register of deeds, sheriff, coroner, surveyor, or other county officer, whose compensation or services performed shall be derived from fees, shall render to the board of county commissioners of their respective counties, on the first Monday in December of each year, a statement, verified under oath, showing: first, the total gross amount of all fees collected during the preceding fiscal year; second, the total amount paid out during the preceding fiscal year for clerical or office assistance. Any county officer, subject to this section, who refuses or fails to file such report as above provided, on or before the first Monday in December, shall be subject to a fine of twenty-five dollars ($25.00) and ten dollars ($10.00) additional for each day or fraction of a day such failure shall continue. The board of county commissioners shall assess and collect the penalty above provided for, and supply same to the general school fund of the county. The first report under this section shall be for the fiscal year beginning December 12, 1913.

This section applies only to the Counties of Anson, Bertie, Bladen, Cabarrus, Carteret, Chowan, Currituck, Duplin, Halifax, Harnett, Haywood, Hertford, Johnston, Jones, Moore, Pender, Perquimans, Pitt, Randolph, Richmond, Rowan, Scotland, Union, Vance, Warren, Washington, Wayne, Wilson. (1913, c. 97; Ex. Sess., 1913, c. 10; 1935, c. 390.)

§ 128-14. Identification cards for field agents or deputies of State departments.

Every field agent or deputy of the various State departments who is authorized to collect money, audit books, inspect premises of individual or business firms and/or any other field work pertaining to the department which he represents, shall be furnished with an identification card signed by the head of the department represented by him, certifying that the said field agent or deputy has authority to represent the department, and such identification card shall carry a photographic likeness of said representative. (1937, c. 236.)

§ 128-15. Employment preference for veterans and their spouses or surviving spouses.

(a)   It shall be the policy of the State of North Carolina that, in appreciation for their service to this State and this country during a period of war, and in recognition of the time and advantage lost toward the pursuit of a civilian career, veterans shall be granted preference in employment with every State department, agency, and institution.

(b)   As used in this section:

(1)   "A period of war" includes World War I (April 16, 1917, through November 11, 1918), World War II (December 7, 1941, through December 31, 1946), the Korean Conflict (June 27, 1950, through January 31, 1955), the period of time between January 31, 1955, and the end of the hostilities in Vietnam (May 7, 1975), or any other campaign, expedition, or engagement for which a campaign badge or medal is authorized by the United States Department of Defense.

(2)   "Veteran" means a person who served in the Armed Forces of the United States on active duty, for reasons other than training, and has been discharged under other than dishonorable conditions.

(3)   "Eligible veteran" means:

a.   A veteran who served during a period of war; or

b.   The spouse of a disabled veteran; or

c.   The surviving spouse or dependent of a veteran who dies on active duty during a period of war either directly or indirectly as the result of such service; or

d.   A veteran who suffered a disabling injury for service-related reasons during peacetime; or

e.   The spouse of a veteran described in subdivision d. of this subsection; or

f.   The surviving spouse or dependent of a person who served in the Armed Forces of the United States on active duty, for reasons other than training, who dies for service-related reasons during peacetime.

(c)   Hereafter, in all evaluations of applicants for positions with this State or any of its departments, institutions or agencies, a preference shall be awarded to all eligible veterans who are citizens of the State and who served the State or the United States honorably in the military forces of this State or of the United States during a period of war. This preference applies to initial employment with the State and extends to other employment events including subsequent hirings, promotions, reassignments, and horizontal transfers.

(d)   The provisions of this section shall be subject to the provisions of Article 1 of Chapter 165 of the General Statutes, and Parts 13 and 19 of Article 9 of Chapter 143B of the General Statutes. (1939, c. 8; 1953, c. 1332; 1967, c. 536; 1987 (Reg. Sess., 1988), c. 1064, s. 2; 2007-286, s. 1; 2011-183, s. 96.)

§ 128-15.1: Repealed by 1987 (Reg. Sess., 1988), c. 1064, s. 4.

§ 128-15.2. Appointment of acting heads of certain agencies.

In every case where a State board or commission is authorized by statute to appoint the executive head of a State agency or institution, that board or commission may appoint an acting executive head of that agency or institution to serve

(1)   During the physical or mental incapacity of the regular holder of the office to discharge the duties of his office,

(2)   During the continued absence of the regular holder of the office, or

(3)   During a vacancy in the office and pending the selection and qualification of a person to serve for the unexpired term.

An acting executive head of a State agency or institution appointed in accordance with this section may perform any act and exercise any power which a regularly selected holder of such office could lawfully perform and exercise. All powers granted to an acting executive head of a State agency or institution under this section shall expire immediately

(1)   Upon the termination of the incapacity of the officer in whose stead he acts,

(2)   Upon the return of the officer in whose stead he acts, or

(3) Upon the selection and qualification of a person to serve for the unexpired term.

Each State board or commission may determine (after such inquiry as it deems appropriate) that the executive head of a State agency or institution whom it is authorized by statute to appoint is physically or mentally incapable of performing the duties of his office. Each such board or commission may also determine that such incapacity has terminated. (1959, c. 284, s. 1.)

§ 128-15.3. Discrimination against handicapped prohibited in hiring; recruitment, etc., of handicapped persons.

There shall be no discrimination in the hiring policies of the State Personnel System [State Human Resources System] against any applicant for employment based upon any physical defect or impairment of the applicant unless the defect or impairment to some degree prevents the applicant from performing the duties required by the employment sought.

It shall be the policy of this State to give positive emphasis to the recruitment, evaluation, and employment of physically handicapped persons in State government. To carry out the provisions of this section, the Office of State Human Resources shall develop methods and programs to assist and encourage the departments, institutions, and agencies of State government in carrying out this policy and to provide for appropriate study and review of the employment of handicapped persons. (1971, c. 748; 1973, c. 1299; 2013-382, s. 9.1(c).)

Article 2.

Removal of Unfit Officers.

§ 128-16. Officers subject to removal; for what offenses.

Any sheriff or police officer shall be removed from office by the judge of the superior court, resident in or holding the courts of the district where said officer is resident upon charges made in writing, and hearing thereunder, for the following causes:

(1)　For willful or habitual neglect or refusal to perform the duties of his office.

(2)　For willful misconduct or maladministration in office.

(3)　For corruption.

(4)　For extortion.

(5)　Upon conviction of a felony.

(6)　For intoxication, or upon conviction of being intoxicated. (P.L. 1913, c. 761, s. 20; 1919, c. 288; C.S., s. 3208; 1959, c. 1286; 1961, c. 991; 1973, c. 108, s. 82.)

§ 128-17. Petition for removal; county attorney to prosecute.

The complaint or petition shall be entitled in the name of the State of North Carolina, and may be filed upon the relation of any five qualified electors of the county in which the person charged is an officer, upon the approval of the county attorney of such county, or the district attorney of the district, or by any such officer upon his own motion. It shall be the duty of the county attorney or district attorney to appear and prosecute this proceeding. (P.L. 1913, c. 761, s. 21; 1919, c. 288; C.S., s. 3209; 1973, c. 47, s. 2.)

§ 128-18. Petition filed with clerk; what it shall contain; answer.

The accused shall be named as defendant, and the petition shall be signed by some elector, or by such officer. The petition shall state the charges against the accused, and may be amended, and shall be filed in the office of the clerk of the superior court of the county in which the person charged is an officer. The accused may at any time prior to the time fixed for hearing file in the office of the clerk of the superior court his answer, which shall be verified. (P.L. 1913, c. 761, s. 22; 1919, c. 288; C.S., s. 3210.)

§ 128-19. Suspension pending hearing; how vacancy filled.

Upon the filing of the petition in the office of the clerk of the superior court, and the presentation of the same to the judge, the judge may suspend the accused from office if in his judgment sufficient cause appear from the petition and affidavit, or affidavits, which may be presented in support of the charges contained therein. In case of suspension, as herein provided, the temporary vacancy shall be filled in the manner provided by law for filling of the vacancies in such office. (P.L. 1913, c. 761, s. 23; 1919, c. 288; C.S., s. 3211.)

§ 128-20. Precedence on calendar; costs.

In the trial of the cause in the superior court the cause shall be advanced and take precedence over all other causes upon the court calendar, and shall be heard at the next session after the petition is filed, provided the proceedings are filed in said court in time for said action to be heard. The superior court shall fix the time of hearing. If the final termination of such proceedings be favorable to any accused officer, said officer shall be allowed the reasonable and necessary expense, including a reasonable attorney fee, to be fixed by the judge, he has incurred in making his defense, by the county, if he be a county officer, or by the city or town in which he holds office, if he be a city officer. If the action is instituted upon the complaint of citizens as herein provided, and it appears to the court that there was no reasonable cause for filing the complaint, the costs may be taxed against the complaining parties. (P.L. 1913, c. 761, s. 24; 1919, c. 288; C.S., s. 3212; 1973, c. 108, s. 83.)

Article 3.

Retirement System for Counties, Cities and Towns.

§ 128-21. Definitions.

The following words and phrases as used in this Article, unless a different meaning is plainly required by the context, shall have the following meanings:

(1)   "Accumulated contribution" shall mean the sum of all amounts deducted from the compensation of a member and credited to his individual account in the

annuity savings fund, together with regular interest thereon, as provided in G.S. 128-30, subsection (b).

(2) "Actuarial equivalent" shall mean a benefit of equal value when computed at regular interest upon the basis of such mortality tables as shall be adopted by the Board of Trustees.

(3) "Annuity" shall mean payments for life derived from the accumulated contribution of a member. All annuities shall be payable in equal monthly installments.

(4) "Annuity reserve" shall mean the present value of all payments to be made on account of any annuity or benefit in lieu of any annuity computed at regular interest upon the basis of such mortality tables as shall be adopted by the Board of Trustees.

(4a) "Authorized representatives who are assisting the Retirement Systems Division staff" means only other staff of the Department of State Treasurer, staff of the Department of Justice, or persons providing internal auditing assistance required under G.S. 143-746(b).

(5) "Average final compensation" shall mean the average annual compensation, not including any terminal payments for unused sick leave, of a member during the four consecutive calendar years of creditable service producing the highest such average; but shall not include any compensation, as determined by the Board of Trustees, for the reimbursement of expenses or payments for housing or any other allowances whether or not classified as salary and wages.

(6) "Beneficiary" shall mean any person in receipt of a pension, an annuity, a retirement allowance or other benefit as provided by this Article.

(7) "Board of Trustees" shall mean the Board provided for in G.S. 128-28 to administer the Retirement System.

(7a) a. "Compensation" shall mean all salaries and wages prior to any reduction pursuant to sections 125, 401(k), 403(b), 414(h)(2), and 457 of the Internal Revenue Code, not including any terminal payments for unused sick leave, derived from public funds which are earned by a member of the Retirement System for service as an employee in the unit of the Retirement

System for which he is performing full-time work. In addition to the foregoing, "compensation" shall include:

1. Performance-based compensation (regardless of whether paid in a lump sum, periodic installments, or on a monthly basis);

2. Conversion of additional benefits to salary (additional benefits such as health, life, or disability plans), so long as the benefits are other than mandated by State law or regulation;

3. Payment of tax consequences for benefits provided by the employer so long as they constitute an adjustment or increase in salary and not a "reimbursement of expenses";

4. Payout of vacation leave so long as such payouts are permitted by applicable law and regulation;

5. Employee contributions to eligible deferred compensation plans; and

6. Effective July 1, 2009, payment of military differential wages.

b. "Compensation" shall not include any payment, as determined by the Board of Trustees, for the reimbursement of expenses or payments for housing or any other allowances whether or not classified as salary and wages. Notwithstanding any other provision of this Chapter, "compensation" shall not include:

1. Supplement/allowance provided to employee to purchase additional benefits such as health, life, or disability plans;

2. Travel supplement/allowance (nonaccountable allowance plans);

3. Employer contributions to eligible deferred compensation plans;

4. Employer-provided fringe benefits (additional benefits such as health, life, or disability plans);

5. Reimbursement of uninsured medical expenses;

6. Reimbursement of business expenses;

7. Reimbursement of moving expenses;

8. Reimbursement/payment of personal expenses;

9. Incentive payments for early retirement;

10. Bonuses paid incident to retirement;

11. Contract buyout/severance payments; and

12. Payouts for unused sick leave.

c. In the event an employer reports as "compensation" payments not specifically included or excluded as "compensation", such payments shall be "compensation" for retirement purposes only if the employer pays the Retirement System the additional actuarial liability created by such payments.

(8) "Creditable service" shall mean the total of "prior service" plus "membership service" plus service, both noncontributory and purchased, for which credit is allowable as provided in G.S. 128-26. In no event, however, shall "creditable service" be deemed "membership service" for the purpose of determining eligibility for benefits accruing under this Chapter.

(9) "Earnable compensation" shall mean the full rate of the compensation that would be payable to an employee if he worked the full normal working time, including any allowance of maintenance or in lieu thereof received by the member.

(10) "Employee" shall mean any person who is regularly employed in the service of and whose salary or compensation is paid by the employer as defined in subdivision (11) of this section, whether employed or appointed for stated terms or otherwise, except teachers in the public schools and except such employees who hold office by popular election as are not required to devote a major portion of their time to the duties of their office. "Employee" also means all full-time, paid firemen who are employed by any fire department that serves a city or county or any part of a city or county and that is supported in whole or in part by municipal or county funds. "Employee" also includes any participant whose employment is interrupted by reason of service in the Uniformed Services, as that term is defined in section 4303(16) of the Uniformed Services Employment and Reemployment Rights Act, Public Law 103-353, if that participant was an employee at the time of the interruption; if the participant

does not return immediately after that service to employment with a covered employer in this System, then the participant shall be deemed "in service" until the date on which the participant was first eligible to be separated or released from his or her involuntary military service. In all cases of doubt the Board of Trustees shall decide who is an employee. On and after August 1, 2001, a person who is a nonimmigrant alien and who otherwise meets the requirements of this subdivision shall not be excluded from the definition of "employee" solely because the person holds a temporary or time-limited visa.

(11)   "Employer" shall mean any county, incorporated city or town, the board of alcoholic control of any county or incorporated city or town, the North Carolina League of Municipalities, and the State Association of County Commissioners. "Employer" shall also mean any separate, juristic political subdivision of the State as may be approved by the Board of Trustees upon the advice of the Attorney General.

(11a)   "Filing" when used in reference to an application for retirement shall mean the receipt of an acceptable application on a form provided by the Retirement System.

(11b)   "Firefighter" means a person (i) who is a full-time paid employee of an employer that participates in the Local Governmental Employees' Retirement System and maintains a fire department certified by the North Carolina Department of Insurance and (ii) who is actively serving in a position with assigned primary duties and responsibilities for the prevention, detection, and suppression of fire.

(11c)   "Fraud investigation" means an independent review or examination by Retirement Systems Division staff or authorized representatives who are assisting the Retirement Systems Division staff of activities, actions, or decisions by employers or other affiliated or associated entities having an impact on the Retirement System. The purpose of a fraud investigation is to help detect and prevent fraud and to ensure full accountability in the use of pension funds.

(11d)   "Law Enforcement Officer" means a full-time paid employee of an employer, who possesses the power of arrest, who has taken the law enforcement oath administered under the authority of the State as prescribed by G.S. 11-11, and who is certified as a law enforcement officer under the provisions of Chapter 17C of the General Statutes or certified as a deputy sheriff under the provisions of Chapter 17E of the General Statutes. "Law enforcement officer" also means the sheriff of the county. The number of paid personnel employed as law enforcement officers by a law enforcement agency may not exceed the number of law enforcement positions approved by the applicable local governing board.

(12) "Medical board" shall mean the board of physicians provided for in G.S. 128-28, subsection (l).

(13) "Member" shall mean any person included in the membership of the Retirement System as provided in G.S. 128-24.

(14) "Membership service" shall mean service as an employee rendered while a member of the Retirement System or membership service in a North Carolina Retirement System that has been transferred into this system.

(15) "Pension" shall mean payments for life derived from money provided by the employer. All pensions shall be payable in equal monthly installments.

(16) "Pension reserve" shall mean the present value of all payments to be made on account of any pension or benefit in lieu of any pension computed at regular interest upon the basis of such mortality tables as shall be adopted by the Board of Trustees.

(17) "Prior service" shall mean the service of a member rendered before the date he becomes a member of the System, certified on his prior service certificate and allowable as provided by G.S. 128-26.

(18) "Regular interest" shall mean interest compounded annually at such rate as shall be determined by the Board of Trustees in accordance with G.S. 128-29, subsection (b).

(18a) "Rescue squad worker" means a person (i) who is a full-time paid employee of an employer that participates in the Local Governmental Employees' Retirement System and maintains a rescue squad or emergency medical services team certified by the North Carolina Department of Insurance or the Department of Health and Human Services and (ii) who is actively serving in a position with assigned primary duties and responsibilities for the alleviation of human suffering and assistance to persons who are in difficulty, who are injured, or who become suddenly ill, by providing proper and efficient care or emergency medical services.

(19) "Retirement" under this Article shall mean the commencement of monthly retirement benefits, along with the termination of employment and the complete separation from active service with no intent or agreement, expressed or implied, to return to service. A retirement allowance under the provisions of this Article may only be granted upon retirement of a member. In order for a member's retirement to become effective in any month, the member must perform no work for a participating employer, including part-time, temporary, substitute, or contractor work, at any time during the same month immediately following the effective first day of retirement.

(20) "Retirement allowance" shall mean the sum of the annuity and the pension, or any optional benefit payable in lieu thereof.

(21) "Retirement System" shall mean the North Carolina Local Governmental Employees' Retirement System as defined in this Article.

(22) "Service" shall mean service as an employee as described in subdivision (10) of this section and paid for by the employer as described in subdivision (11) of this section.

(23) "Year" shall mean the regular fiscal year beginning July 1, and ending June 30; in the following calendar year unless otherwise defined by regulation of the Board of Trustees. (1939, c. 390, s. 1; 1941, c. 357, s. 1; 1943, c. 535; 1945, c. 526, s. 1; 1947, c. 833, ss. 1, 2; 1949, c. 231, ss. 1, 2; 1949, c. 1015; 1959, c. 491, ss. 1, 2; 1961, c. 515, s. 5; 1965, c. 781; 1971, c. 325, ss. 1-4; 1975, 2nd Sess., c. 983, s. 125; 1977, c. 316, ss. 1, 2; 1981, c. 557, ss. 1, 2; 1985, c. 479, s. 196(b); c. 649, s. 3; 1991, c. 51, s. 1; 1991 (Reg. Sess., 1992), c. 762, ss. 1, 2; 1997-144, s. 1; 1999-167, ss. 1, 2; 1999-456, s. 37; 2001-426, s. 1; 2003-359, ss. 13, 14; 2009-66, ss. 2(a), 6(f), (j); 2011-92, s. 1; 2011-294, s. 4; 2012-185, s. 2(a); 2013-288, ss. 3(b), 4(b).)

§ 128-22. Name and date of establishment.

A Retirement System is hereby established and placed under the management of the Board of Trustees for the purpose of providing retirement allowances and other benefits under the provisions of this Article for employees of those counties, cities and towns or other eligible employers participating in the said Retirement System. Following the filing of the application as provided in G.S. 128-23(c), the Board shall set a date, effective the first day of a calendar quarter, not more than 90 days thereafter, as of which date participation of the employer may begin, which date shall be known as the date of participation for such employer: Provided, that in the judgment of the Board of Trustees an adequate number of persons have indicated their intention to participate; otherwise at such later date as the Board of Trustees may set.

This Retirement System is a governmental plan, within the meaning of Section 414(d) of the Internal Revenue Code. Therefore, the nondiscrimination rules of Sections 401(a)(5) and 401(a)(26) of the Code do not apply. This System shall have the power and privileges of a corporation and shall be known as the "North Carolina Local Governmental Employees' Retirement System," and by such name all of its business shall be transacted, all of its funds invested, and all of its cash and securities and other property held.

Consistent with Section 401(a)(1) of the Internal Revenue Code, all contributions from participating employers and participating employees to this Retirement System shall be made to funds held in trust through trust instruments that have the purposes of distributing trust principal and income to retired members and their beneficiaries and of paying other definitely determinable benefits under this Chapter, after meeting the necessary expenses of administering this Retirement System. Neither the trust corpus nor income from this trust can be used for purposes other than the exclusive benefit of members or their beneficiaries, except that employer contributions made to the trust under a good faith mistake of fact may be returned to an employer, where the refund can occur within less than one year after the mistaken contribution was made, consistent with the rule adopted by the Board of Trustees. The Retirement System shall have a consolidated Plan document, consisting of Article V, Section 6(2) of the North Carolina Constitution, relevant statutory provisions in this Chapter, associated regulations in the North Carolina Administrative Code, substantive and procedural information on the official forms used by the Retirement System, and policies and minutes of the Board of Trustees. (1939, c. 390, s. 2; 1941, c. 357, s. 2; 1943, c. 535; 1945, c. 526, s. 2; 1959, c. 491, s. 3; 2012-130, s. 7(b).)

§ 128-23. Acceptance by cities, towns and counties.

(a) Pursuant to the favorable vote of a majority of the employees of any incorporated city or town, the governing body may, by resolution legally adopted and approved by the Board of Trustees, elect to have its employees become eligible to participate in the Retirement System, and the said municipal governing body may make the necessary appropriation therefor and if necessary levy annually taxes for payment of the same.

(b)   Pursuant to the favorable vote of a majority of the employees of the county, the board of commissioners of any county may, by resolution legally adopted and approved by the Board of Trustees, elect to have its employees become eligible to participate in the Retirement System. Each county is authorized to make appropriations for these purposes and to fund them by levy of property taxes pursuant to G.S. 153-65 and by the allocation of other revenues whose use is not otherwise restricted by law.

(c)   Any eligible employer desiring to participate in the Retirement System shall file with the Board of Trustees an application for participation under the conditions included in this Article on a form approved by the Board of Trustees. In such application the employer shall agree to make the contributions required of participating employers, to deduct from the salaries of employees who may become members the contributions required of members under this Article, and to transmit such contributions to the Board of Trustees. It shall also agree to make the employer's contributions for the participation in the Retirement System of all employees entering the service of the employer, after its participation begins, who shall become members.

(d)   Such contributions as are made by employers shall be regarded as additions to the compensation of such employees as are members of the Retirement System and deducted therefrom for the purpose of making the employer's contribution, in addition to the deduction from the compensation of employees on account of member contributions.

(e)   The agreement of such employer to contribute on account of its employees shall be irrevocable, but should an employer for any reason become financially unable to make the normal and accrued liability contributions payable on account of its employees, then such employer shall be deemed to be in temporary default. Such temporary default shall not relieve such employer from any liability for its contributions payable on account of its employees.

Notwithstanding anything to the contrary, the Retirement System shall not be liable for the payment of any pensions or other benefits on account of the employees or pensioners of any employer under this Article, for which reserves have not been previously created from funds contributed by such employer or its employees for such benefits.

(f) Effective January 1, 1955, there shall be three classes of employers to be designated Class A, Class B and Class C, respectively. Each employer whose date of participation occurs before July 1, 1951, shall be a Class A employer unless such an employer by written notice filed with the Board of Trustees on or before June 30, 1951, elected to be a Class B employer. Each employer whose date of participation occurs on or after July 1, 1951, but before January 1, 1955, shall be a Class A employer. Each employer whose date of participation occurs on or after January 1, 1955, shall be a Class C employer.

(g) Notwithstanding any other provisions of this Article, any employer who is not a participating employer and who employs law enforcement officers transferred from the Law Enforcement Officers' Retirement System to this Retirement System on January 1, 1986, or who employs law enforcement officers electing to become members of this Retirement System on and after January 1, 1986, shall be employers participating in this Retirement System as this participation pertains to their law enforcement officers. The election of membership in this Retirement System shall be at the sole discretion of law enforcement officers of participating employers described in this subsection. (1939, c. 390, s. 3; 1951, c. 274, s. 1; 1955, c. 1153, s. 1; 1971, c. 325, s. 5; 1973, c. 803, s. 16; 1985, c. 479, s. 196(c); 1991, c. 585, s. 1.)

§ 128-24. Membership.

The membership of this Retirement System shall be composed as follows:

(1) All employees entering or reentering the service of a participating employer after the date of participation in the Retirement System of the employer. On and after July 1, 1965, new extension service employees excluded from coverage under Title II of the Social Security Act in the employ of a county participating in the Local Governmental Employees' Retirement System are hereby excluded from participation in the Teachers' and State Employees' Retirement System to the extent of that part of their compensation derived from a county; provided that on and after July 1, 1965, new extension service employees excluded from coverage under Title II of the Social Security Act who are required to accept a federal Civil Service appointment may elect in writing on a form acceptable to the Retirement System, to be excluded from the Teachers' and State Employees' Retirement System and the local Retirement System. At such time as Cooperative Agricultural Extension Service Employees excluded from coverage under Title II of the Social Security Act become

covered by Title II of the Social Security Act, such employees shall no longer be covered by the provisions of this section, provided no accrued rights of these employees under this section prior to coverage by Title II of the Social Security Act shall be diminished.

(1a) Should any member in any period of eight consecutive years after becoming a member be absent from service more than seven years, or should he withdraw his accumulated contributions or should he become a beneficiary or die, he shall thereupon cease to be a member; provided that on and after July 1, 1971, a member shall cease to be a member only if he withdraws his accumulated contributions, or becomes a beneficiary, or dies.

(2) All persons who are employees of a participating county, city, or town except those who shall notify the Board of Trustees in writing, on or before 30 days following the date of participation in the Retirement System by such county, city or town: Provided, further, that employees of county social services and health departments whose compensation is derived from federal, State, and local funds may be members of the North Carolina Local Governmental Employees' Retirement System to the full extent of their compensation. Any member on or after July 1, 1969, may deposit in the annuity savings fund by a single payment the contributions plus interest which would have been credited to his account had he not signed a nonelection blank, and be entitled to such membership service credits and any prior service credits which became void upon execution of such nonelection blank; provided that the employer will pay the appropriate matching contributions.

(3) Effective January 1, 1955, there shall be three classes of members, to be designated Class A, Class B and Class C respectively. Each member who is an employee of a Class A employer shall be a Class A member; each member who is an employee of a Class B employer shall be a Class B member; and each member who is an employee of a Class C employer shall be a Class C member.

(3a) Repealed by Session Laws 1981 (Regular Session, 1982), c. 1396, s. 1.

(4) The provisions of this subdivision (4) shall apply to any member whose retirement became effective prior to July 1, 1965, and became entitled to benefits hereunder in accordance with the provisions hereof. Such benefits shall be computed in accordance with the provisions of G.S. 128-27(b1) as in effect at the date of such separation from service.

a. Notwithstanding any other provision of this Chapter, any member who separates from service prior to the time he shall have attained the age of 60 years, or if a uniformed policeman or fireman prior to the time he shall have attained the age of 55 years, for any reason other than death or retirement for disability as provided in G.S. 128-27(c), after completing 20 or more years of creditable service, and who leaves his total accumulated contributions in the Retirement System, shall have the right to retire on a deferred retirement allowance upon the date he shall have attained the age of 60 years, or if a uniformed policeman or fireman upon the date he shall have attained the age of 55 years; provided that such member may retire only upon electronic submission or written application to the Board of Trustees setting forth at what time, not less than 30 days nor more than 120 days next following the date of filing such application, he desires to be retired. Such deferred retirement allowance shall be computed in accordance with the provisions of G.S. 128-27(b), paragraphs (1), (2) and (3).

b. In lieu of the benefits provided in paragraph a of this subdivision (4), any member who separates from service prior to the time he shall have attained the age of 60 years, or if a uniformed policeman or fireman prior to the time he shall have attained the age of 55 years, for any reason other than death or retirement for disability as provided in G.S. 128-27(c), after completing 30 or more years of creditable service, and who leaves his total accumulated contributions in the Retirement System, may elect to retire on an early retirement allowance; provided that such a member may so retire only upon electronic submission or written application to the Board of Trustees setting forth at what time, not less than 30 days nor more than 120 days next following the date of filing such application, he desires to be retired; provided further that such application shall be duly filed within 60 days following the date of such separation. Such early retirement allowance so elected shall be the actuarial equivalent of the deferred retirement allowance otherwise payable at the attainment of age 60 years, or if a uniformed policeman or fireman at the attainment of age 55 years, upon proper application therefor.

c. Should an employee who retired on an early or service retirement allowance be restored to service prior to the time he shall have attained the age of 62 years, or if a uniformed policeman or fireman prior to the time he shall have attained the age of 55 years, his allowance shall cease, he shall again become a member of the Retirement System, and he shall contribute thereafter at the uniform contribution rate for his class member. Upon his subsequent retirement, he shall be entitled to an allowance not less than the allowance described in 1 below reduced by the amount in 2 below.

1. The allowance to which he would have been entitled if he were retiring for the first time, calculated on the basis of his total creditable service represented by the sum of his creditable service at the time of his first retirement, and his creditable service after he was restored to service.

2. The actuarial equivalent of the retirement benefits he previously received.

d. Should an employee who retired on an early or service retirement allowance be restored to service after the attainment of the age of 62 years, his retirement allowance shall be reduced to the extent necessary (if any) so that the sum of the retirement allowance at the time of retirement and earnings from employment by a unit of the Retirement System for any year (beginning January 1 and ending December 31) will not exceed the member's compensation received for the 12 months of service prior to retirement. Provided, however, that under no circumstances will the member's retirement allowance be reduced below the amount of his annuity as defined in G.S. 128-21(3).

(5) The provisions of this subdivision (5) shall apply to any member whose membership is terminated on or after July 1, 1965, and who becomes entitled to benefits hereunder in accordance with the provisions hereof.

a. Notwithstanding any other provision of this Chapter, any member who separates from service prior to the attainment of the age of 60 years for any reason other than death or retirement for disability as provided in G.S. 128-27(c), after completing 15 or more years of creditable service, and who leaves his total accumulated contributions in said System shall have the right to retire on a deferred retirement allowance upon attaining the age of 60 years; provided that such member may retire only upon electronic submission or written application to the Board of Trustees setting forth at what time, not less than one day nor more than 120 days subsequent to the execution and filing thereof, he desires to be retired; and further provided that in the case of a member who so separates from service on or after July 1, 1967, the aforestated requirement of 15 or more years of creditable service shall be reduced to 12 or more years of creditable service; and further provided that in the case of a member who so separates from service on or after July 1, 1971, or whose account is active on July 1, 1971, the aforestated requirement of 12 or more years of creditable service shall be reduced to five or more years of creditable service. Such deferred retirement allowance shall be computed in accordance with the service retirement provisions of this Article pertaining to a member who is not a law enforcement officer or eligible former law enforcement officer.

b. In lieu of the benefits provided in paragraph a of this subdivision, any member who separates from service prior to the attainment of the age of 60 years, for any reason other than death or retirement for disability as provided in G.S. 128-27(c), after completing 20 or more years of creditable service, and who leaves his total accumulated contributions in said System may elect to retire on an early retirement allowance upon attaining the age of 50 years or at any time thereafter; provided that such member may so retire only upon electronic submission or written application to the Board of Trustees setting forth at what time, not less than one day nor more than 120 days subsequent to the execution and filing thereof, he desires to be retired. Such early retirement allowance so elected shall be equal to the deferred retirement allowance otherwise payable at the attainment of the age of 60 years reduced by the percentage thereof indicated below.

Age at Retirement	Percentage Reduction
59	7
58	14
57	20
56	25
55	30
54	35
53	39
52	43
51	46
50	50

b1. In lieu of the benefits provided in paragraphs a and b of this subdivision, any member who is a law enforcement officer at the time of separation from service prior to the attainment of the age of 50 years, for any reason other than death or disability as provided in this Article, after completing 15 or more years of creditable service in this capacity immediately prior to separation from service, and who leaves his total accumulated contributions in this System, may elect to retire on a deferred early retirement allowance upon attaining the age of 50 years or at any time thereafter; provided, that the member may commence retirement only upon electronic submission or written application to the Board of Trustees setting forth at what time, as of the first day of a calendar month, not less than one day nor more than 120 days subsequent to the execution and filing thereof, he desires to commence retirement. The deferred early retirement allowance shall be computed in accordance with the service retirement provisions of this Article pertaining to law enforcement officers.

b2. In lieu of the benefits provided in paragraphs a and b of this subdivision, any member who is a law enforcement officer at the time of separation from service prior to the attainment of the age of 55 years, for any reason other than death or disability as provided in this Article, after completing five or more years of creditable service in this capacity immediately prior to separation from service, and who leaves his total accumulated contributions in this System may elect to retire on a deferred service retirement allowance upon attaining the age of 55 years or at any time thereafter; provided, that the member may commence retirement only upon electronic submission or written application to the Board of Trustees setting forth at what time, as of the first day of a calendar month not less than one day nor more than 120 days subsequent to the execution and filing thereof, he desires to commence retirement. The deferred service retirement allowance shall be computed in accordance with the service retirement provisions of this Article pertaining to law enforcement officers.

b3. Deferred retirement allowance of members retiring on or after July 1, 1995. - In lieu of the benefits provided in paragraphs a. and b. of this subdivision, any member who separates from service prior to attainment of age 60 years, after completing 20 or more years of creditable service, and who leaves his total accumulated contributions in said System, may elect to retire on a deferred retirement allowance upon attaining the age of 50 years or any time thereafter; provided that such member may so retire only upon electronic submission or written application to the Board of Trustees setting forth at what time, not less than one day nor more than 120 days subsequent to the execution and filing thereof, he desires to be retired. Such deferred retirement allowance shall be computed in accordance with the service retirement provisions of this Article pertaining to a member who is not a law enforcement officer or an eligible former law enforcement officer.

c. Should a beneficiary who retired on an early or service retirement allowance be reemployed by, or otherwise engaged to perform services for, an employer participating in the Retirement System on a part-time, temporary, interim, or on fee-for-service basis, whether contractual or otherwise, and if such beneficiary earns an amount during the 12-month period immediately following the effective date of retirement or in any calendar year which exceeds fifty percent (50%) of the reported compensation, excluding terminal payments, during the 12 months of service preceding the effective date of retirement, or twenty thousand dollars ($20,000), whichever is greater, as hereinafter indexed, then the retirement allowance shall be suspended as of the first day of the month following the month in which the reemployment earnings exceed the amount above, for the balance of the calendar year, except when the reemployment earnings exceed the amount above in the month of December, in which case the retirement allowance shall not be suspended. The retirement allowance of the beneficiary shall be reinstated as of January 1 of each year following suspension. The amount that may be earned before suspension shall be increased on January 1 of each year by the ratio of the Consumer Price Index to the Index one year earlier, calculated to the nearest tenth of a percent (1/10 of 1%).

c1. Within 90 days of the end of each month in which a beneficiary is reemployed under the provisions of sub-subdivision c. of this subdivision, each employer shall provide a report for that month on each reemployed beneficiary, including the terms of the reemployment, the date of the reemployment, and the amount of the monthly compensation. If such a report is not received within the required 90 days, the Board may assess the employer with a penalty of ten percent (10%) of the compensation of the unreported reemployed beneficiaries during the months for which the employer did not report the reemployed beneficiaries, with a minimum penalty of twenty-five dollars ($25.00). If after being assessed a penalty, an employer provides clear and convincing evidence that the failure to report resulted from a lack of oversight or some other event beyond the employer's control and was not a deliberate attempt to omit the reporting of reemployed beneficiaries, the Board may reduce the penalty to not less than two percent (2%) of the compensation of the unreported reemployed beneficiaries during the months for which the employer failed to report, with a minimum penalty of twenty-five dollars ($25.00). Upon receipt by the employer of notice that a penalty has been assessed under this sub-subdivision, the employer shall remit the payment of the penalty to the Retirement System, in one lump sum, no later than 90 days from the date of the notice.

d. Should a beneficiary who retired on an early or service retirement allowance be restored to service as an employee, then the retirement allowance shall cease as of the first day of the month following the month in which the beneficiary is restored to service and the beneficiary shall become a member of the Retirement System and shall contribute thereafter as allowed by law at the uniform contribution payable by all members.

Upon his subsequent retirement, he shall be paid a retirement allowance determined as follows:

1. For a member who earns at least three years' membership service after restoration to service, the retirement allowance shall be computed on the basis of his compensation and service before and after the period of prior retirement without restriction; provided, that if the prior allowance was based on a social security leveling payment option, the allowance shall be adjusted actuarially for the difference between the amount received under the optional payment and what would have been paid if the retirement allowance had been paid without optional modification. In the alternative, the member may receive a refund of the member's accumulated contributions for the period of service after restoration to service in accordance with G.S. 128-27(f).

2. For a member who does not earn three years' membership service after restoration to service, the retirement allowance shall be equal to the sum of the retirement allowance to which he would have been entitled had he not been restored to service, without modification of the election of an optional allowance previously made, and the retirement allowance that results from service earned since being restored to service; provided, that if the prior retirement allowance was based on a social security leveling payment option, the prior allowance shall be adjusted actuarially for the difference between the amount that would have been paid for each month had the payment not been suspended and what would have been paid if the retirement allowance had been paid without optional modification. In the alternative, the member may receive a refund of the member's accumulated contributions for the period of service after restoration to service in accordance with G.S. 128-27(f), or the member may allow this new account to remain inactive.

(5a) Notwithstanding the provisions of paragraphs c and d of the subdivision (5) to the contrary, a beneficiary who was a beneficiary retired on an early or service retirement with the Law Enforcement Officers' Retirement System at the time of the transfer of law enforcement officers employed by a participating employer and beneficiaries last employed by a participating employer to this

Retirement System on January 1, 1986, and who also was a contributing member of this Retirement System on January 1, 1986, shall continue to be paid his retirement allowance without restriction and may continue as a member of this Retirement System with all the rights and privileges appendant to membership. Any beneficiary who retired on an early or service retirement allowance as an employee of any participating employer under the Law Enforcement Officers' Retirement System and becomes employed as an employee by an employer participating in the Retirement System after January 1, 1986, becomes subject to the provisions of G.S. 128-24(5)c. and G.S. 128-24(5)d. on and after January 1, 1989.

(6) Employees of a sending agency participating in an intergovernmental exchange of personnel under the provisions of Article 10 of Chapter 126 shall remain members entitled to all benefits of the System provided that the requirements of Article 10 of Chapter 126 are met; provided further, that a member may retain membership status while serving as an assigned employee or employee on leave under the provisions of Article 10 of Chapter 126 for purposes of receiving the death benefit regardless of whether he and his employer are contributing to his account during the exchange period except that no duplicate benefits shall be paid. (1939, c. 390, s. 4; 1941, c. 357, s. 3; 1949, cc. 1011, 1013; 1951, c. 274, s. 2; 1955, c. 1153, s. 2; 1957, c. 854; 1959, c. 491, s. 4; 1961, c. 515, s. 1; 1965, c. 781; 1967, c. 978, ss. 1, 2; 1969, c. 442, ss. 1-5, 7; c. 982; 1971, c. 325, ss. 6-8; c. 326, ss. 1, 2; 1973, c. 243, s. 1; 1977, c. 783, s. 2; 1981, c. 979, s. 2; 1981 (Reg. Sess., 1982), c. 1396, ss. 1, 2; 1983, c. 556, ss. 1, 2; 1983 (Reg. Sess., 1984), c. 1106, ss. 1, 2; 1985, c. 479, s. 196(d)-(g); c. 649, s. 2; 1987, c. 513, s. 1; c. 738, s. 38(a); 1993 (Reg. Sess., 1994), c. 769, ss. 7.30(a), 7.31(a), (b); 1995, c. 507, s. 7.22(d); 2002-126, s. 28.13(b); 2007-431, s. 10; 2009-66, ss. 3(g), (h), 8(b), 12(e), (f); 2010-72, s. 4(b); 2011-294, s. 2(b); 2012-130, s. 1.)

§ 128-25. Membership in System.

Should sixty per centum (60%) of the members of any retirement, pension or annuity fund or system of any county, city or town of the State, hereafter referred to as a local pension system, elect to become members of the North Carolina Governmental Employees' Retirement System, by a petition duly signed by such members, the participation of such members in the Retirement System may be approved as provided in G.S. 128-24 as though such local pension system were not in operation, and the provisions of this Article shall also apply, except that the existing pensioners or annuitants of the local pension system who were being paid pensions on the date of the approval shall be continued and paid at their existing rates by the North Carolina Governmental Employees' Retirement System, and the liability on this account shall be included in the computation of the accrued liability by the actuary as provided by G.S. 128-30, subsection (d). Any cash and securities to the credit of the local pension system shall be transferred to the North Carolina Governmental Employees' Retirement System as of the date of the approval. The trustees or other administrative head of the local pension system as of the date of the approval shall certify the proportion, if any, of the funds of the System that represents the accumulated contributions of the members, and the relative shares of the members as of that date. Such shares shall be credited to the respective annuity savings accounts of such members in the North Carolina Governmental Employees' Retirement System. The balance of the funds transferred to the North Carolina Governmental Employees' Retirement System shall be offset against the accrued liability before determining the special accrued liability contribution to be paid by the county, city or town as provided by G.S. 128-30, subsection (d). The operation of the local pension system shall be discontinued as of the date of the approval. (1939, c. 390, s. 5; 1941, c. 357, s. 4.)

§ 128-26. Allowance for service.

(a)   Each person who becomes a member during the first year of his or her employer's participation, and who was an employee of the same employer at any time during the year immediately preceding the date of participation, shall file a detailed statement of all service rendered by him or her to that employer prior to the date of participation for which he or she claims credit.

A participating employer may allow prior service credit to any of its employees on account of: their earlier service to the aforesaid employer; or, their earlier service to any other employer as the term employer is defined in G.S. 128-21(11); or, their earlier service to any state, territory, or other governmental subdivision of the United States other than this State.

A participating employer may allow prior service credit to any of its employees on account of service, as defined in G.S. 135-1(23), to the State of North Carolina to the extent of such service prior to the establishment of the Teachers' and State Employees' Retirement System on July 1, 1941; provided that employees allowed such prior service credit pay in a total lump sum an amount calculated on the basis of compensation the employee earned when the employee first entered membership and the employee contribution rate at that time together with interest thereon from year of first membership to year of payment shall be one half of the calculated cost.

(a1)   With respect to a member retiring on or after July 1, 1967, the governing board of a participating unit may allow credit for any period of military service in the Armed Forces of the United States if the person returned to the service of the person's employer within two years after having been honorably discharged, or becoming entitled to be discharged, released, or separated from such the Armed Forces of the United States; provided that, notwithstanding the above provisions, any member having credit for not less than 10 years of otherwise creditable service may be allowed credit for such military services which are not creditable in any other governmental retirement system; provided further, that a member will receive credit for military service under the provisions of this paragraph only if the member submits satisfactory evidence of the military service claimed and the participating unit of which the member is an employee agrees to grant credit for such military service prior to January 1, 1972.

A member retiring on or after July 1, 1971, who is not granted credit for military service under the provisions of the preceding paragraph will be allowed credit for any period of qualifying service in the Armed Forces of the United States, as defined for purposes of reemployment rights under federal law, provided that the member was an employee as defined in G.S. 128-21(10) at the time the member entered military service, and either (i) the returning member is in service, with the employer by whom the member was employed when the member entered military service, for a period of not less than 10 years after the member is separated or released from that military service under other than dishonorable conditions or (ii) the following conditions are met, in the conjunctive:

(1)   The member did not, prior to leaving for military service, provide clear written notice of an intent not to return to work after military service.

(2)   The member was discharged from uniformed service and returned from the leave of absence for uniformed service to membership service in this system within the time limit mandated by federal law for reporting back to work.

(3) The period of uniformed service, for which additional service credit is sought, has been verified by suitable documentation and is not eligible for receipt of benefits under any other retirement system or pension plan.

(4) All service credit forfeited by a refund pursuant to the provisions of G.S. 128-27(f) has been purchased.

The uniformed service credit allowed under this subsection shall be limited to a maximum of five years unless otherwise specifically exempted from that durational limitation by federal law. The salary or compensation of such an employee during the period of qualifying military service shall be deemed to be that salary or compensation the employee would have received but for the period of service had the employee remained continuously employed, if the determination of that salary or compensation is reasonably certain. If the determination of the salary or compensation is not reasonably certain, then it shall be deemed to be that employee's average rate of compensation during the 12-month period immediately preceding the period of service.

Pursuant to 38 U.S.C. § 4318(b)(1), when a member who has been on military leave returns to work consistent with the provisions of this subsection concerning return to service within two years after the member's earliest eligibility for separation or release from military service, then the member's employer must remit to the System all the employer contributions for the full period of that member's military service.

(b) The Board of Trustees shall fix and determine by appropriate rules and regulations how much service in any year is equivalent to one year of service, but in no case shall more than one year of service be creditable for all service in one calendar year.

(c) Subject to the above restrictions and to such other rules and regulations as the Board of Trustees may adopt, the Board of Trustees shall verify, as soon as practicable after the filing of such statements of service, the service therein claimed.

In lieu of a determination of the actual compensation of the members that was received during such period of prior service, the Board of Trustees may use for the purpose of this Article the compensation rates which if they had progressed with the rates of salary increase shown in the tables as prescribed in subsection (o) of G.S. 128-28 would have resulted in the same average salary of the member for the five years immediately preceding the date of participation of his employer, as the records show the member actually received.

(d)   Any member may, up to his date of retirement and within one year thereafter, request the Board of Trustees to modify or correct his prior service credit.

(e)   Creditable service at retirement on which the retirement allowance of a member shall be based shall consist of the membership service rendered by him since he last became a member, and also if he has a prior service certificate which is in full force and effect, the amount of the service certified on his prior service certificate; and if he has sick leave standing to his credit upon retirement on or after July 1, 1971, one month of credit for each 20 days or portion thereof, but not less than one hour; sick leave shall not be counted in computing creditable service for the purpose of determining eligibility for disability retirement or for a vested deferred allowance. Creditable service for unused sick leave shall be allowed only for sick leave accrued monthly during employment under a duly adopted sick leave policy and for which the member may be able to take credits and be paid for sick leave without restriction. However, in no instance shall unused sick leave be credited to a member's account at retirement if the member's last day of actual service is more than 365 days prior to the effective date of the member's retirement.

On and after July 1, 1971, a member whose account was closed on account of absence from service under the provisions of G.S. 128-24(1a) and who subsequently returns to service for a period of five years, may thereafter repay the amount withdrawn plus regular interest thereon from the date of withdrawal through the year of repayment and thereby increase his creditable service by the amount of creditable service lost when this account was closed.

On and after July 1, 1973, a member whose account in the Teachers' and State Employees' Retirement System was closed on account of absence from service under the provisions of G.S. 135-3(3) and who subsequently became or becomes a member of this System with credit for five years of service, may thereafter repay in a lump sum the amount withdrawn from the Teachers' and State Employees' Retirement System plus regular interest thereon from the date of withdrawal through the year of repayment and thereby increase his creditable service in this System by the amount of creditable service lost when his account was closed.

Notwithstanding any other provision of this Chapter, any member who entered service or was restored to service prior to July 1, 1982, and was excluded from membership service solely on account of having attained the age of 62 years, in accordance with former G.S. 128-24(3a), may purchase membership service credits for such excluded service by making a lump-sum payment equal to the contributions that would have been deducted pursuant to G.S. 128-30(b) had he been a member of the Retirement System, increased by interest calculated at a rate of seven percent (7%) per annum.

On and after January 1, 1986, the creditable service of a member who was a member of the Law Enforcement Officers' Retirement System at the time of the transfer of law enforcement officers employed by participating employers from that System to this Retirement System and whose accumulated contributions are transferred from that System to this Retirement System, includes service that was creditable in the Law Enforcement Officers' Retirement System; and membership service with that System is membership service with this Retirement System; provided, notwithstanding any provisions of this Article to the contrary, any inchoate or accrued rights of such a member to purchase creditable service for military service, withdrawn service and prior service under the rules and regulations of the Law Enforcement Officers' Retirement System may not be diminished and may be purchased as creditable service with this Retirement System under the same conditions that would have otherwise applied.

(f)   Effective January 1, 1955, there shall be three classes of prior service certificates, to be designated as Class A, Class B and Class C respectively. Each such certificate issued on account of service rendered to a Class A employer shall be a Class A prior service certificate; each such certificate issued on account of service rendered to a Class B employer shall be a Class B prior service certificate; and each such certificate issued on account of service rendered to a Class C employer shall be a Class C prior service certificate. Each Class C prior service certificate shall specify a prior service benefit percentage rate which shall be three per centum (3%) in the case of any member entitled to such certificate who is, at the date of participation of his employer, in a position covered by the Social Security Act under a federal-State agreement and which shall be five per centum (5%) in the case of a member entitled to such certificate but who at the date of participation of his employer is in a position not so covered.

(g)   During periods when a member is on leave of absence and is receiving less than his full compensation, he will be deemed to be in service only if he is contributing to the Retirement System as provided in G.S. 128-30(b)(4). If he is so contributing, the annual rate of compensation paid to such employee immediately before the leave of absence began will be deemed to be the actual compensation rate of the employee during the leave of absence.

(h) Creditable service at retirement shall include any service rendered by a member while on leave of absence to serve as a member or officer of the General Assembly which is not creditable toward retirement under the Legislative Retirement Fund provided the allowance of such credit shall be contingent upon the cancellation of service credit in the fund and the transfer of the member's contributions plus accumulated interest from the fund to this System.

(h1) Any member may purchase creditable service for service as a member of the General Assembly not otherwise creditable under this section, provided the service is not credited in the Legislative Retirement Fund nor the Legislative Retirement System, and further provided the member pays a lump sum amount equal to the full cost of the additional service credits calculated on the basis of the assumptions used for the purposes of the actuarial valuation of the System's liabilities, taking into account the additional retirement allowance arising on account of the additional service credits commencing at the earliest age at which a member could retire on an unreduced retirement allowance as determined by the Board of Trustees upon the advice of the consulting actuary, plus an administrative fee to be set by the Board of Trustees. Notwithstanding the foregoing provisions of this subsection that provide for the purchase of service credits, the terms "full cost", "full liability", and "full actuarial cost" include assumed annual post-retirement allowance increases, as determined by the Board of Trustees, from the earliest age at which a member could retire on an unreduced service allowance.

(i) Notwithstanding any other provision of this Chapter, any person who withdrew his contributions in accordance with the provisions of G.S. 128-27(f) or 135-5(f) or the rules and regulations of the Law Enforcement Officers' Retirement System and who subsequently returns to service may, upon completion of five years of prior and current membership service, repay in a total lump sum any and all of the accumulated contributions previously withdrawn with interest compounded annually at the rate of six and one-half percent (6.5%) for each calendar year from the year of withdrawal to the year of repayment plus a fee to cover expense of handling which shall be determined by the Board of Trustees, and receive credit for the service forfeited at time of withdrawal(s). These provisions shall apply equally to retired members who had attained five years of prior and current membership service prior to retirement. The retirement allowance of a retired member who restores service under this subsection shall be increased the month following the month payment is received. The increase in the retirement allowance shall be the difference between the initial retirement allowance, under any optional allowance elected at the time of retirement, and the amount of the retirement allowance, under any optional allowance elected at the time of retirement, to which the retired member would have been entitled had the service not been previously forfeited, adjusted by any increases in the retirement accrual rate occurring between the member's date of retirement and the date of payment. The increase in the retirement allowance shall not include any adjustment for cost-of-living increases granted since the date of retirement.

(j) Repealed by Session Laws 1987, c. 617, s. 3.

(j1) Notwithstanding any other provision of this Chapter, any member and any retired member as herein described may purchase creditable service for service in the Armed Forces of the United States, not otherwise allowed, by paying a total lump sum payment determined as follows:

(1) For members who completed 10 years of membership service, and retired members who completed 10 years of membership service prior to retirement, and whose membership began on or prior to January 1, 1988, and who make such purchase within three years after first becoming eligible, the cost shall be an amount equal to the monthly compensation the member earned when the member first entered membership service times the employee contribution rate at that time times the months of service to be purchased with sufficient interest added thereto so as to equal one-half of the cost of allowing such service, plus an administrative fee to be set by the Board of Trustees.

(2) For members who complete five years of membership service, and retired members who complete five years of membership service prior to retirement, and eligible members and retired members covered by paragraph (1) of this subdivision, whose membership began on or before January 1, 1988, but who did not or do not make such purchase within three years after first becoming eligible, the cost shall be an amount equal to the full liability of the service credits calculated on the basis of the assumptions used for the purposes of the actuarial valuation of the System's liabilities and shall take into account the retirement allowance arising on account of the additional service credits commencing at the earliest age at which the member could retire on an unreduced allowance, as determined by the Board of Trustees upon the advice

of the consulting actuary, plus an administrative fee to be set by the Board of Trustees. Notwithstanding the foregoing provisions of this subsection that provide for the purchase of service credits, the term "full liability" includes assumed post-retirement allowance increases, as determined by the Board of Trustees, from the earliest age at which a member could retire on an unreduced service retirement allowance.

Creditable service allowed under this subdivision shall be only for the initial period of "active duty", as defined in 38 U.S. Code Section 101(21), in the Armed Forces of the United States up to the date the member was first eligible to be separated and released and for subsequent periods of "active duty", as defined in 38 U.S. Code Section 101(21), as required by the Armed Forces of the United States up to the date of first eligibility for separation or release, but shall not include periods of active duty in the Armed Forces of the United States creditable in any other retirement system except the National Guard or any reserve component of the Armed Forces of the United States, and shall not include periods of "active duty for training", as defined in 38 U.S. Code Section 101(22), or periods of "inactive duty training", as defined in 38 U.S. Code Section 101(23), rendered in any reserve component of the Armed Forces of the United States. Provided, creditable service may be allowed only for active duty in the Armed Forces of the United States of a member that resulted in a general or honorable discharge from duty. The member shall submit satisfactory evidence of the service claimed. For purposes of this subsection, membership service may include any membership or prior service credits transferred to this Retirement System pursuant to G.S. 128-24.

(j2)   Notwithstanding any other provision of this Chapter, any member and any retired member as herein described may purchase creditable service previously rendered to any state, territory, or other governmental subdivision of the United States other than this State by paying a total lump-sum payment determined as follows:

(1)   For members who completed 10 years of prior and current membership service, and retired members who completed 10 years of prior and current membership service prior to retirement, and whose membership began on or before January 1, 1988, and who make such purchase within three years after first becoming eligible, the cost shall be an amount equal to the monthly compensation the member earned when he first entered membership service, times the employee contribution rate at that time, times the months of service to be purchased, times two, with sufficient interest added thereto so as to equal

the full cost of allowing such service, plus an administrative fee to be set by the Board of Trustees.

(2) For members who complete five years of prior and current membership service, and retired members who complete five years of prior and current membership service prior to retirement, and eligible members and retired members covered by subdivision (1) of this subsection, whose membership began on or before January 1, 1988, but who did not or do not make such purchase within three years after first becoming eligible, the cost shall be an amount equal to the full liability of the service credits calculated on the basis of the assumptions used for the purposes of the actuarial valuation of the System's liabilities and shall take into account the retirement allowance arising on account of the additional service credits commencing at the earliest age at which the member could retire on an unreduced allowance, as determined by the Board of Trustees upon the advice of the consulting actuary, plus an administrative fee to be set by the Board of Trustees. Notwithstanding the foregoing provisions of this subsection that provide for the purchase of service credits, the term "full liability" includes assumed postretirement allowance increases, as determined by the Board of Trustees, from the earliest age at which a member could retire on an unreduced service retirement allowance. Notwithstanding the requirement of five years of current membership service, a member whose membership began prior to the service the member desires to purchase shall be eligible to purchase creditable service under this subdivision upon returning to service as an employee upon completion of a total of five years of membership service and upon completion of one year of current membership service.

Current membership service shall mean membership service earned since the service previously rendered to any state, territory, or other governmental subdivision of the United States other than this State. Creditable service under this subsection shall be allowed only at the rate of one year of out-of-state service for each year of service in this State, with a maximum allowable of 10 years of out-of-state service. Such service is limited to full-time service which would be allowable under the laws governing this System. Credit will be allowed only if no benefit is allowable in another public retirement system as a result of the service.

(k) Notwithstanding any language to the contrary of any provision of this section, or of any repealed provision of this section that was repealed with the inchoate and accrued rights preserved, all repayments and purchases of service credits, allowed under the provisions of this section or of any repealed provision of this section that was repealed with inchoate and accrued rights preserved, must be made within three years after the member first becomes eligible to make such repayments and purchases. Any member who does not repay or purchase service credits within said three years after first eligibility to make such repayments and purchases may, under the same conditions as are otherwise required, repay or purchase service credits provided that the repayment or purchase equals the full cost of the service credits calculated on the basis of the assumptions used for purchases of the actuarial valuation of the System's liabilities and shall take into account the additional retirement allowance arising on account of such additional service credit commencing at the earliest age at which such member could retire on an unreduced retirement allowance as determined by the Board of Trustees upon the advice of the consulting actuary. Notwithstanding the foregoing provisions of this subsection that provide for the purchase of service credits, the terms "full cost", "full liability", and "full actuarial cost" include assumed annual post-retirement allowance increases, as determined by the Board of Trustees, from the earliest age at which a member could retire on an unreduced service allowance. Notwithstanding the foregoing, on and after January 1, 2003, the provisions of this subsection shall not apply to the repayment of contributions withdrawn pursuant to subsection (i) of this section.

(l)   Notwithstanding any other provision of this Chapter, any member may purchase creditable service for periods of employer approved leaves of absence when in receipt of benefits under the North Carolina Workers' Compensation Act. This service shall be purchased by paying a cost calculated in the following manner:

(1)   Leaves of Absence Terminated Prior to July 1, 1983. - The cost to a member whose employer approved leave of absence, when in receipt of benefits under the North Carolina Workers' Compensation Act, terminated upon return to service prior to July 1, 1983, shall be a lump sum amount payable to the Annuity Savings Fund equal to the full liability of the service credits calculated on the basis of the assumptions used for purposes of the actuarial valuation of the system's liabilities, and shall take into account the retirement allowance arising on account of the additional service credit commencing at the earliest age at which the member could retire on an unreduced retirement allowance, as determined by the board of trustees upon the advice of the consulting actuary, plus an administrative fee to be set by the Board of Trustees. Notwithstanding the foregoing provisions of this subdivision that provide for the purchase of service credits, the terms "full cost", "full liability", and "full actuarial cost" include assumed annual post-retirement allowance

increases, as determined by the Board of Trustees, from the earliest age at which a member could retire on an unreduced service allowance.

(2) Leaves of Absence Terminating On and After July 1, 1983. - The cost to a member whose employer approved leave of absence, when in receipt of benefits under the North Carolina Workers' Compensation Act, terminates upon return to service on and after July 1, 1983, shall be a lump sum amount due and payable to the Annuity Savings Fund within six months from return to service equal to the total employee and employer percentage rates of contribution in effect at the time of purchase and based on the annual rate of compensation of the member immediately prior to the leave of absence; Provided, however, the cost to a member whose amount due is not paid within six months from return to service shall be the amount due plus one percent (1%) per month penalty for each month or fraction thereof the payment is made beyond the six-month period.

Whenever the creditable service purchased pursuant to this subsection is for a period that occurs during the four consecutive calendar years that would have produced the highest average annual compensation pursuant to G.S. 128-21(5) had the member not been on leave of absence without pay, then the compensation that the member would have received during the purchased period shall be included in calculating the member's average final compensation. In such cases, the compensation that the member would have received during the purchased period shall be based on the annual rate of compensation of the member immediately prior to the leave of absence.

In the case of a law enforcement officer electing to purchase service under this section who is in receipt of benefits under the North Carolina Workers' Compensation Act due to serious bodily injury suffered in the line of duty as a result of an intentional or unlawful act of another, as certified by the head of the employing law enforcement agency, and whose approved leave of absence terminates on or before a return to service on and after August 1, 2006, the employer percentage rate of contribution payable under subdivision (2) of this subsection shall be made by the employer that granted the leave of absence. The cost to the law enforcement officer shall be reduced by the amount paid by the employer. For purposes of this subsection, "serious bodily injury" means bodily injury that creates a substantial risk of death, or that causes serious permanent disfigurement, coma, a permanent or protracted condition that causes extreme pain, or permanent or protracted loss or impairment of the function of any bodily member or organ, or that results in prolonged hospitalization.

Nothing in this subsection prevents an employer from voluntarily paying all or a part of the employee portion of the total cost of the service credit purchased, and the employer does not discriminate against any eligible law enforcement officer in this subsection employed by the employer by paying that portion of cost. To the extent paid by the employer, the employee portion paid by the employer shall be credited to the Pension Accumulation Fund; to the extent paid by the member, the employee portion paid by the member shall be credited to the member's annuity savings account. A member shall pay any part of the employee portion of the total cost not paid by the employer.

(m) Omitted Membership Service. - A member who had service as an employee as defined in G.S. 135-1(10) and G.S. 128-21(10) or as a teacher as defined in G.S. 135-1(25) and who was omitted from contributing membership through error may be allowed membership service, after submitting clear and convincing evidence of the error, as follows:

(1) within 90 days of the omission, by the payment of employee and employer contributions that would have been paid; or

(2) after 90 days and prior to three years of the omission, by the payment of the employee and employer contributions that would have been paid plus interest compounded annually at a rate equal to the greater of the average yield on the pension accumulation fund for the preceding calendar year or the actuarial investment rate-of-return assumption, as adopted by the Board of Trustees; or

(3) after three years of the omission, by the payment of an amount equal to the full cost of the service credits calculated on the basis of the assumptions used for the purposes of the actuarial valuation of the System's liabilities, and shall take into account the additional retirement allowance arising on account of such additional service credit commencing at the earliest age at which a member could retire on an unreduced retirement allowance, as determined by the Board of Trustees upon the advice of the consulting actuary, plus an administrative fee to be set by the Board of Trustees. Notwithstanding the foregoing provisions of this subdivision that provide for the purchase of service credits, the terms "full cost", "full liability", and "full actuarial cost" include assumed annual post-retirement allowance increases, as determined by the Board of Trustees, from the earliest age at which a member could retire on an unreduced service allowance.

Nothing contained in this subsection shall prevent an employer or member from paying all or a part of the cost of the omitted membership service; and to the extent paid by the employer, the cost paid by the employer shall be credited to the pension accumulation fund; and to the extent paid by the member, the cost paid by the members shall be credited to the member's annuity savings account; provided, however, an employer does not discriminate against any member or group of members in his employ in paying all or any part of the cost of the omitted membership service. In the event an employer pays all or a part of the full actuarial cost as determined in subdivision (3) of this subsection, the employer may, at its option, pay such amount either in a lump sum or by increasing its "accrued liability contribution" for the remainder of its accrued liability period. In the event an employer has satisfied its accrued liability contribution, the employer may amortize its portion of the full actuarial cost over a period not to exceed ten years. The expense of making an actuarial valuation to determine the accrued liability contribution or the additional accrued liability contribution, required to amortize the portion of the full actuarial cost paid by the employer, shall be paid by the employer in a lump sum at the time of the actuarial valuation.

(n)   Repealed by Session Laws 2002-153, s. 3, effective January 1, 2003.

(o)   Credit at Full Cost for Federal Employment. - Notwithstanding any other provisions of this Chapter, a member, upon the completion of five years of membership service, may purchase creditable service for periods of federal employment, provided that the member is not receiving any retirement benefits resulting from this federal employment, and provided that the member is not vested in the particular federal retirement system to which the member may have belonged while a federal employee. The member shall purchase this service by making a lump sum amount payable to the Annuity Savings Fund equal to the full liability of the service credits calculated on the basis of the assumptions used for purposes of the actuarial valuation of the liabilities of the Retirement System; and the calculation of the amount payable shall take into account the retirement allowance arising on account of the additional service credit commencing at the earliest age at which the member could retire on an unreduced retirement allowance, as determined by the Board of Trustees upon the advice of the consulting actuary, plus an administrative fee to be set by the Board of Trustees. Members may also purchase creditable service for periods of employment with public community service entities within the State funded entirely with federal funds, other than the federal government, that are not covered by the provisions of G.S. 128-21(11) or G.S. 135-1(11), under the same terms and conditions that are applicable to the purchase of creditable service for periods of federal employment in accordance with this subsection. "Public community service entities" as used in this subsection shall mean community action, human relations, manpower development, and community development programs as defined in Articles 19 and 21 of Chapter 160A and Article 18 of Chapter 153A of the General Statutes and any other similar programs that the Board of Trustees may adopt. Notwithstanding the foregoing provisions of this subsection that provide for the purchase of service credits, the terms "full cost", "full liability", and "full actuarial cost" include assumed annual post-retirement allowance increases, as determined by the Board of Trustees, from the earliest age at which a member could retire on an unreduced service allowance.

(p) Part-Time Service Credit. -

(1) Notwithstanding any other provision of this Chapter, upon completion of five years of membership service, any member may purchase service previously rendered as a part-time employee of a participating employer as defined in G.S. 128-21(11) or G.S. 135-1(11), except for temporary or part-time service rendered while a full-time student in pursuit of a degree or diploma in a degree-granting program. Payment shall be made in a single lump sum in an amount equal to the full actuarial cost of providing credit for the service, together with interest and an administrative fee, as determined by the Board of Trustees on the advice of the Retirement System's actuary. Notwithstanding the provisions of G.S. 128-26(b), the Board of Trustees shall fix and determine by appropriate rules and regulations how much service in any year, as based on compensation, is equivalent to one year of service in proportion to "earnable compensation", but in no case shall more than one year of service be creditable for all service in one year. Notwithstanding the foregoing provisions of this subdivision that provide for the purchase of service credits, the terms "full cost", "full liability", and "full actuarial cost" include assumed annual post-retirement allowance increases, as determined by the Board of Trustees, from the earliest age at which a member could retire on an unreduced service allowance.

(2) Under all requirements and conditions set forth in the preceding subdivision of this subsection, except for the requirement that the completion of five years of membership service be subsequent to service rendered as a part-time employee, any member with five or more years of membership service standing to his credit may purchase additional membership service for service rendered as a part-time employee of an employer as defined in G.S. 128-21(11) if (i) the member terminates or has terminated employment in any capacity as an employee, (ii) the purchase of the additional membership service causes the member to become eligible to commence an early or service retirement

allowance, and (iii) the member immediately elects to commence retirement and become a beneficiary.

(q) Credit at Full Cost for Probationary Employment. - Notwithstanding any other provision of this Chapter, a member may purchase creditable service, prior to retirement, for employment with an employer as defined in this Article when considered to be in a probationary or employer imposed waiting period status and thereby not regularly employed, between date of employment and date of membership service with the retirement system, provided that the employer or former employer of such a member has revoked this probationary employment or waiting period policy.

Provided, the member shall purchase this service by making a lump sum amount payable to the Annuity Savings Fund equal to the full liability of the service credits calculated on the basis of the assumptions used for purposes of the actuarial valuation of the liabilities of the retirement system, and the calculation of the amount payable shall take into account the retirement allowance arising on account of the additional service credit commencing at the earliest age at which the member could retire on an unreduced retirement allowance, as determined by the Board of Trustees upon the advice of the consulting actuary, plus an administrative fee to be set by the Board of Trustees. In no instance shall the amount payable be less than the contributions a member would have made during the employment plus four percent (4%) interest compounded annually.

Notwithstanding the foregoing provisions of this subsection that provide for the purchase of service credits, the terms "full cost", "full liability", and "full actuarial cost" include assumed annual post-retirement allowance increases, as determined by the Board of Trustees, from the earliest age at which a member could retire on an unreduced service allowance.

Nothing contained in this subsection shall prevent an employer or member from paying all or a part of the cost of the probationary employment; and to the extent paid by the employer, the cost paid by the employer shall be credited to the pension accumulation fund; and to the extent paid by the member, the cost paid by the member shall be credited to the member's annuity savings account; provided, however, an employer does not discriminate against any member or group of members in its current employ in paying all or any part of the cost of the probationary employment. In the event an employer pays all or a part of the full actuarial cost, the employer may, at its option, pay such amount either in a lump sum or by increasing its "accrued liability contribution" for the remainder of its accrued liability period. In the event an employer has satisfied its accrued liability contribution, the employer may amortize its portion of the full actuarial cost over a period not to exceed 10 years. The expense of making an actuarial valuation to determine the accrued liability contribution or the additional accrued liability contribution, required to amortize the portion of the full actuarial cost paid by the employer, shall be paid by the employer in a lump sum at the time of the actuarial valuation.

(r)   Credit at Full Cost for Temporary Government Employment. - Notwithstanding any other provisions of this Chapter, any member may purchase creditable service for government employment when classified as a temporary employee subject to the conditions that:

(1)   The member was employed by an employer as defined in G.S. 128-21(11) or G.S. 135-1(11);

(2)   The member's temporary employment met all other requirements of G.S. 128-21(10), or G.S. 135-1(10) or (25);

(3)   The member has completed five years or more of membership service;

(4)   The member acquires from the employer such certifications of temporary employment as are required by the Board of Trustees; and

(5)   The member makes a lump sum payment into the Annuity Savings Fund equal to the full liability of the service credits calculated on the basis of the assumptions used for purposes of the actuarial valuation of the retirement system's liabilities, and the calculation of the amount payable shall take into account the retirement allowance arising on account of the additional service credit commencing at the earliest age at which the member could retire on an unreduced retirement allowance, as determined by the Board of Trustees upon the advice of the actuary, plus an administrative fee to be determined by the Board of Trustees. Notwithstanding the foregoing provisions of this subdivision that provide for the purchase of service credits, the terms "full cost", "full liability", and "full actuarial cost" include assumed annual post-retirement allowance increases, as determined by the Board of Trustees, from the earliest age at which a member could retire on an unreduced service allowance.

(s)   Credit at Full Cost for Employment Not Otherwise Creditable. - Notwithstanding any other provisions of this Chapter, any member may purchase creditable service for any employment as an employee, as defined in

G.S. 128-21(10), of a local government employer not creditable in any other retirement system or plan, upon completion of five years of membership service by making a lump sum payment into the Annuity Savings Fund. The payment by the member shall be equal to the full liability of the service credits calculated on the basis of the assumptions used for purposes of the actuarial valuation of the retirement system's liabilities, and the calculation of the amount payable shall take into account the additional retirement allowance arising on account of the additional service credits commencing at the earliest age at which the member could retire with an unreduced retirement allowance, as determined by the Board of Trustees upon the advice of the actuary plus an administrative fee to be determined by the Board of Trustees. Notwithstanding the foregoing provisions of this subsection that provide for the purchase of service credits, the terms "full cost", "full liability", and "full actuarial cost" include assumed annual post-retirement allowance increases, as determined by the Board of Trustees, from the earliest age at which a member could retire on an unreduced service allowance.

(t) Purchase of Service Credits Through Rollover Contributions From Certain Other Plans. - Notwithstanding any other provision of this Article, and without regard to any limitations on contributions otherwise set forth in this Article, a member, who is eligible to restore or purchase membership or creditable service pursuant to the provisions of G.S. 128-26, may, subject to such rules and regulations established by the Board of Trustees, purchase such service credits through rollover contributions to the Annuity Savings Fund from (i) an annuity contract described in Section 403(b) of the Internal Revenue Code, (ii) an eligible plan under Section 457(b) of the Internal Revenue Code which is maintained by a state, political subdivision of a state, or any agency or instrumentality of a state or political subdivision of a state, (iii) an individual retirement account or annuity described in Section 408(a) or 408(b) of the Internal Revenue Code that is eligible to be rolled over and would otherwise be includible in gross income, or (iv) a qualified plan described in Section 401(a) or 403(a) of the Internal Revenue Code. Notwithstanding the foregoing, the Retirement System shall not accept any amount as a rollover contribution unless such amount is eligible to be rolled over to a qualified trust in accordance with applicable law and the member provides evidence satisfactory to the Retirement System that such amount qualifies for rollover treatment. Unless received by the Retirement System in the form of a direct rollover, the rollover contribution must be paid to the Retirement System on or before the 60th day after the date it was received by the member.

Purchase of Service Credits Through Plan-to-Plan Transfers. - Notwithstanding any other provision of this Article, and without regard to any limitations on contributions otherwise set forth in this Article, a member, who is eligible to restore or purchase membership or creditable service pursuant to the provisions of G.S. 128-26, may, subject to such rules and regulations established by the Board of Trustees, purchase such service credits through a direct transfer to the Annuity Savings Fund of funds from (i) an annuity contract described in Section 403(b) of the Internal Revenue Code or (ii) an eligible plan under Section 457(b) of the Code which is maintained by a state, political subdivision of a state, or any agency or instrumentality of a state or political subdivision of a state.

(u) Purchase of Service Credits Through Plan-to-Plan Transfers. - Notwithstanding any other provision of this Article, and without regard to any limitations on contributions otherwise set forth in this Article, a member, who is eligible to restore or purchase membership or creditable service pursuant to the provisions of G.S. 128-26, may, subject to such rules and regulations established by the Board of Trustees, purchase such service credits through a direct transfer to the Annuity Savings Fund of funds from (i) the Supplemental Retirement Income Plans A, B, or C of North Carolina or (ii) any other defined contribution plan qualified under Section 401(a) of the Internal Revenue Code which is maintained by the State of North Carolina, a political subdivision of a state, or any agency or instrumentality of a state or political subdivision of a state.

(u1) Expired.

(v) Retroactive Membership Service. - A member who is reinstated to service as an employee as defined in G.S. 128-21(10) retroactively to the date of prior involuntary termination with back pay and associated benefits may be allowed membership service, after submitting clear and convincing evidence of the reinstatement, payment of back pay, and restoration of associated benefits, as follows:

(1) When the reinstatement to service is by court order and is:

a. Within 90 days of the involuntary termination, by the payment of employee and employer contributions that would have been paid; or

b. After 90 days of the involuntary termination, by the payment of the employee and employer contributions that would have been paid plus interest compounded annually at a rate equal to the greater of the average yield on the pension accumulation fund for the preceding calendar year or the actuarial investment rate-of-return assumption, as adopted by the Board of Trustees.

(2) When the reinstatement to service is by settlement agreement voluntarily entered into by the affected parties, by the payment of a lump-sum amount equal to the full liability of the service credits calculated on the basis of the assumptions used for purposes of the actuarial valuation of the system's liabilities, taking into account the retirement allowance arising on account of the additional service credit commencing at the earliest age at which the member could retire on an unreduced retirement allowance, as determined by the Board of Trustees upon the advice of the consulting actuary, plus an administrative fee to be set by the Board of Trustees. Notwithstanding the foregoing provisions of this subsection that provide for the purchase of service credits, the terms "full cost," "full liability," and "full actuarial cost" include assumed annual postretirement allowance increases, as determined by the Board of Trustees, from the earliest age at which a member could retire on an unreduced service allowance.

Nothing contained in this subsection shall prevent an employer or member from paying all or a part of the cost of the retroactive membership service; and to the extent paid by the employer, the cost paid by the employer shall be credited to the pension accumulation fund; and to the extent paid by the member, the cost paid by the member shall be credited to the member's annuity savings account; provided, however, an employer does not discriminate against any member or group of members in his employ in paying all or any part of the cost of the retroactive membership service.

In the event a member received a return of accumulated contributions subsequent to an involuntary termination as provided in G.S. 128-27(f), the member may redeposit, within 90 days of reinstatement retroactive to the date of prior involuntary termination, in the annuity savings fund by single payment, an amount equal to the total amount he previously withdrew plus regular interest and restore the creditable service forfeited upon receiving his return of accumulated contributions.

(w) If a member who is an elected government official and has not vested in this System on July 1, 2007, is convicted of an offense listed in G.S. 128-38.4 for acts committed after July 1, 2007, then that member shall forfeit all benefits under this System, except for a return of member contributions plus interest. If a member who is an elected government official and has vested in this System on July 1, 2007, is convicted of an offense listed in G.S. 128-38.4 for acts committed after July 1, 2007, then that member is not entitled to any creditable service that accrued after July 1, 2007. No member shall forfeit any benefit or creditable service earned from a position not as an elected government official.

(x) If a member who is in service and has not vested in this System on December 1, 2012, is convicted of an offense listed in G.S. 128-38.4A for acts committed after December 1, 2012, then that member shall forfeit all benefits under this System, except for a return of member contributions plus interest. If a member who is in service and has vested in this System on December 1, 2012, is convicted of an offense listed in G.S. 128-38.4A for acts committed after December 1, 2012, then that member is not entitled to any creditable service that accrued after December 1, 2012. (1939, c. 390, s. 6; 1941, c. 357, s. 5; 1943, c. 535; 1945, c. 526, s. 3; 1951, c. 274, s. 3; 1955, c. 1153, s. 3; 1967, c. 978, ss. 11, 12; 1969, c. 442, s. 6; 1971, c. 325, ss. 9-11, 19; 1973, c. 243, s. 2; c. 667, s. 1; c. 816, s. 3; c. 1310, ss. 1-4; 1975, c. 205, s. 1; c. 485, ss. 1-3; 1977, c. 973; 1979, c. 866, s. 1; c. 868, ss. 1, 2; c. 1059, s. 1; 1981, c. 557, s. 3; 1981 (Reg. Sess., 1982), c. 1283, s. 1; c. 1396, s. 3; 1983, c. 533, s. 2; 1983 (Reg. Sess., 1984), c. 1034, s. 231; 1985, c. 407, s. 1; c. 479, s. 196(h); c. 649, ss. 1, 4; 1987, c. 533, s. 2; c. 617, ss. 1-4; c. 717, s. 1; 1987 (Reg. Sess., 1988), c. 1088, ss. 5, 6; c. 1110, s. 8; 1989, c. 255, ss. 1-10; c. 762, s. 2; 1989 (Reg. Sess., 1990), c. 1024, s. 28; 1991, c. 753, s. 1; 1991 (Reg. Sess., 1992), c. 1017, s. 1; 1995, c. 507, s. 7.23D(a); 1998-71, ss. 1, 2; 1998-214, s. 1; 1999-158, s. 1; 2001-487, s. 82; 2002-71, s. 3; 2002-153, ss. 1-3; 2003-359, ss. 17-19, 22; 2005-91, s. 8; 2006-29, s. 1; 2007-179, s. 2(b); 2007-304, s. 1; 2009-281, s. 1; 2009-392, s. 1; 2010-72, s. 5(b); 2011-183, ss. 97(a), (b); 2011-294, s. 5(b); 2012-130, s. 3(a); 2012-193, s. 4; 2013-288, ss. 2(a), 11; 2013-405, s. 6(b).)

§ 128-26A. Reciprocity of creditable service with other State-administered retirement systems.

(a) Only for the purpose of determining eligibility for benefits accruing under this Article, creditable service standing to the credit of a member of the Legislative Retirement System, Consolidated Judicial Retirement System, or the Teachers' and State Employees' Retirement System shall be added to the creditable service standing to the credit of a member of this System; provided, that in the event a person is a retired member of any of the foregoing retirement systems, such creditable service standing to the credit of the retired member prior to retirement shall be likewise counted. In no instance shall service credits maintained in the aforementioned retirement systems be added to the creditable service in this System for application of this System's benefit accrual rate in computing a service retirement benefit unless specifically authorized by this Article.

(b)   A person who was a former member of this System and who has forfeited his creditable service in this System by receiving a return of contributions and who has creditable service in the Legislative Retirement System, Consolidated Judicial Retirement System, or the Teachers' and State Employees' Retirement System may count such creditable service for the purpose of restoring the creditable service forfeited in this System under the terms and conditions as set forth in this Article and reestablish membership in this System.

(c)   Creditable service under this section shall not be counted twice for the same period of time whether earned as a member, purchased, or granted as prior service credits. (1989 (Reg. Sess., 1990), c. 1066, s. 35(b).)

§ 128-27. Benefits.

(a)   Service Retirement Benefits. -

(1)   Any member may retire upon electronic submission or written application to the Board of Trustees setting forth at what time, as of the first day of a calendar month, not less than one day nor more than 120 days subsequent to the execution and filing thereof, he desires to be retired: Provided, that the said member at the time so specified for his retirement shall have attained the age of 60 years and have at least five years of creditable service or shall have completed 30 years of creditable service, or if a fireman, he shall have attained the age of 55 years and have at least five years of creditable service.

(2)   Repealed by Session Laws 1983 (Regular Session, 1984), c. 1019, s. 1.

(3)   Repealed by Session Laws 1971, c. 325, s. 12.

(4)   Any member who was in service October 8, 1981, who had attained 60 years of age, may retire upon electronic submission or written application to the Board of Trustees setting forth at what time, as of the first day of a calendar month, not less than one day nor more than 120 days subsequent to the execution and filing thereof, he desires to be retired.

(5) Any member who is a law enforcement officer, and who attains age 50 and completes 15 or more years of creditable service in this capacity or who attains age 55 and completes five or more years of creditable service in this capacity, may retire upon electronic submission or written application to the Board of Trustees setting forth at what time, as of the first day of a calendar month, not less than one day nor more than 120 days subsequent to the execution and filing thereof, he desires to be retired; provided, also, any member who has met the conditions required by this subdivision but does not retire, and later becomes an employee other than as a law enforcement officer, continues to have the right to commence retirement.

(a1) Early Service Retirement Benefits. - Any member may retire and receive a reduced retirement allowance upon electronic submission or written application to the Board of Trustees setting forth at what time, as of the first day of a calendar month, not less than one day nor more than 120 days subsequent to the execution and filing thereof, he desires to be retired: Provided, that the said member at the time so specified for his retirement shall have attained the age of 50 years and have at least 20 years of creditable service.

(a2) Discontinued Service Retirement Allowance. - A member whose employment with a participating employer is involuntarily terminated as a result of a termination event as defined in this subsection may be allowed a discontinued service retirement allowance, provided that the discontinued service retirement allowance is approved by the terminated member's participating employer, and provided that reemployment with that participating employer is not available to the member at the time of the termination event. For purposes of this section, "termination event" means termination of employment as a result of (i) the participating employer's cessation of operations; (ii) the participating employer's dissolution; (iii) the merger of a participating employer with and into an unrelated entity, other than another participating employer; (iv) the acquisition of the participating employer by an unrelated entity, other than another participating employer; or (v) the determination by the participating employer that a reduction in force will accomplish economies in the participating employer's budget resulting from either the elimination of a job and its responsibilities or from lack of funds to support the job. Final action approving the discontinued service retirement allowance for a terminated member by the member's participating employer shall be taken in an open meeting.

Upon the occurrence of a termination event, and subject to the provisions of this subsection, an unreduced discontinued service retirement allowance, not otherwise allowed under this Chapter, may be approved for terminated members with 20 or more years of creditable service who are at least 55 years of age. Alternatively, upon the occurrence of a termination event, a discontinued service retirement allowance, not otherwise allowed under this Chapter, may be approved for terminated members with 20 or more years of creditable service who are at least 50 years of age, reduced by one-fourth of one percent (¼ of 1%) for each month that retirement precedes the member's fifty-fifth birthday.

In cases in which a discontinued service retirement allowance is approved, the terminated member's employer shall be responsible for making a lump-sum payment to the Retirement System's Board of Trustees equal to the actuarial present value of the additional liabilities imposed upon the Retirement System, to be determined by the Retirement System's consulting actuary, as a result of the discontinued service retirement allowance, plus an administrative fee to be determined by the Board of Trustees. An employer shall not discriminate against any member or group of members employed by the employer in the approval or disapproval of a discontinued service retirement allowance.

(b) Service Retirement Allowance of Persons Retiring on or after July 1, 1959, but prior to July 1, 1965. - Upon retirement from service on or after July 1, 1959, but prior to July 1, 1965, a member shall receive a service retirement allowance which shall consist of:

(1) An annuity which shall be the actuarial equivalent of his accumulated contributions at the time of his retirement; and

(2) A pension equal to the annuity allowable at the age of 65 years or at his retirement age, whichever is the earlier, on the basis of contributions made prior to such earlier age; and

(3) If he has a prior service certificate in full force and effect, an additional pension which shall be equal to the annuity which would have been provided at the age of 65 years, or at the earlier age of retirement if prior thereto, by twice the contributions which he would have made during such period of service had the System been in operation and he contributed thereunder at the rate of

a. Six and twenty-five hundredths percent (6.25%) of his compensation if such certificate is a Class A certificate, or

b. Five percent (5%) of his compensation if such certificate is a Class B certificate, or

c. Four percent (4%) of his compensation if such certificate is a Class C certificate.

(b1) Service Retirement Allowances of Persons Retiring on or after July 1, 1965, but prior to July 1, 1967. - Upon retirement from service on or after July 1, 1965, but prior to July 1, 1967, a member shall receive a service retirement allowance which shall consist of:

(1) If the member's service retirement date occurs on or after his sixty-fifth birthday, such allowance shall be equal to the sum of (i) one percent (1%) of the portion of his average final compensation not in excess of forty-eight hundred dollars ($4,800), plus one and one-half percent (1½%) of the portion of such compensation in excess of forty-eight hundred dollars ($4,800) multiplied by the number of years of his creditable service rendered prior to January 1, 1966, and (ii) one percent (1%) of the portion of his average final compensation not in excess of forty-eight hundred dollars ($4,800), plus one and one-half percent (1½%) of the portion of such compensation in excess of fifty-six hundred dollars ($5,600), multiplied by the number of years of his creditable service rendered after January 1, 1966.

(2a) If the member's service retirement date occurs on or after his sixtieth birthday but before his sixty-fifth birthday, his service retirement allowance shall be computed as in (1) above but shall be reduced by five twelfths of one percent (5/12 of 1%) thereof for each month by which his retirement date precedes the first day of the month coincident with or next following his sixty-fifth birthday.

(2b) If the member's service retirement date occurs before his sixtieth birthday, his service retirement allowance shall be the actuarial equivalent of the allowance payable at the age of 60 years as computed in (2a) above.

(3) Notwithstanding the foregoing provisions, any member whose creditable service commenced prior to July 1, 1965, and uniformed policemen or firemen not covered under the Social Security Act employed thereafter, shall receive not less than the benefit provided by G.S. 128-27(b).

(b2) Service Retirement Allowances of Persons Retiring on or after July 1, 1967, but prior to July 1, 1969. - Upon retirement from service on or after July 1, 1967, but prior to July 1, 1969, a member shall receive a service retirement allowance which shall consist of:

(1) If the member's service retirement date occurs on or after his sixty-fifth birthday, such allowance shall be equal to one and one-quarter percent (1¼%) of the portion of his average final compensation not in excess of five thousand six hundred dollars ($5,600) plus one and one-half percent (1½%) of the portion of such compensation in excess of five thousand six hundred dollars ($5,600), multiplied by the number of years of his creditable service.

(2a) If the member's service retirement date occurs before his sixty-fifth birthday, his service retirement allowance shall be computed as in (1) above, but shall be reduced by one third of one percent (1/3 of 1%) thereof for each month by which his retirement date precedes the first day of the month coincident with or next following his sixty-fifth birthday.

(2b) If the member's service retirement date occurs before his sixtieth birthday, his service retirement allowance shall be the actuarial equivalent of the allowance payable at the age of 60 years as computed in (2a) above.

(3) Notwithstanding the foregoing provision, any member whose creditable service commenced prior to July 1, 1965, and policemen or firemen not covered under the Social Security Act employed thereafter, shall receive not less than the benefits provided by G.S. 128-27(b).

(b3) Service Retirement Allowances of Persons Retiring on or after July 1, 1969, but prior to July 1, 1973. - Upon retirement from service on or after July 1, 1969, but prior to July 1, 1973, a member shall receive a service retirement allowance which shall consist of:

(1) If the member's service retirement date occurs on or after his sixty-fifth birthday, regardless of his years of creditable service, or on or after his sixty-second birthday and the completion of 30 years of creditable service, such allowance shall be equal to one and one-quarter percent (1¼%) of the portion of his average final compensation not in excess of fifty-six hundred dollars ($5,600) plus one and one-half percent (1½%) of the portion of such compensation in excess of fifty-six hundred dollars ($5,600), multiplied by the number of years of his creditable service.

(2a) If the member's service retirement date occurs before his sixty-fifth birthday and prior to his completion of 30 or more years of creditable service, his service retirement allowance shall be computed as in (1) above, but shall be reduced by one quarter of one percent (¼ of 1%) thereof for each month by which his retirement date precedes the first day of the month coincident with or next following his sixty-fifth birthday.

(2b)   If the member's service retirement date occurs before his sixtieth birthday and prior to his completion of 30 or more years of creditable service, his service retirement allowance shall be the actuarial equivalent of the allowance payable at the age of 60 years as computed in (2a) above.

(3a)   If the member's service retirement date occurs before his sixty-second birthday but on or after his sixtieth birthday and on or after completion of 30 or more years of creditable service, his service retirement allowance shall be computed as in (1) above, but shall be reduced by one quarter of one percent (¼ of 1%) thereof for each month by which his retirement date precedes the first day of the month coincident with or next following his sixty-second birthday.

(3b)   If the member's service retirement date occurs before his sixtieth birthday but on or after completion of 30 or more years of creditable service, his service retirement allowance shall be the actuarial equivalent of the allowance payable at the age of 60 years as computed in (3a) above.

(4)   Notwithstanding the foregoing provisions, any member whose creditable service commenced prior to July 1, 1965, and uniformed policemen or firemen not covered under the Social Security Act employed thereafter, shall receive not less than the benefits provided by G.S. 128-27(b).

(b4)   Service Retirement Allowances of Members Retiring on or after July 1, 1973, but prior to July 1, 1976. - Upon retirement from service, in accordance with subsection (a) above, on or after July 1, 1973, but prior to July 1, 1976, a member shall receive a service retirement allowance computed as follows:

(1)   If the member's service retirement date occurs on or after his sixty-fifth birthday, regardless of his years of creditable service, or after the completion of 30 years of creditable service, such allowance shall be equal to one and one-quarter percent (1¼%) of the portion of his average final compensation not in excess of fifty-six hundred dollars ($5,600) plus one and one-half percent (1½%) of the portion of such compensation in excess of fifty-six hundred dollars ($5,600), multiplied by the number of years of his creditable service.

(2a)   If the member's service retirement date occurs on or after his sixtieth birthday but before his sixty-fifth birthday and prior to his completion of 30 or more years of creditable service, his service retirement allowance shall be computed as in (1) above, but shall be reduced by one quarter of one percent (¼ of 1%) thereof for each month by which his retirement date precedes the first day of the month coincident with or next following his sixty-fifth birthday.

(2b) If the member's service retirement date occurs before his sixtieth birthday and prior to his completion of 30 or more years of creditable service, his service retirement allowance shall be the actuarial equivalent of the allowance payable at the age of 60 years as computed in (2a) above.

(3) Notwithstanding the foregoing provisions, any member whose creditable service commenced prior to July 1, 1965, and uniformed policemen or firemen not covered under the Social Security Act employed thereafter, shall receive not less than the benefits provided by G.S. 128-27(b).

(b5) Service Retirement Allowances of Members Retiring on or after July 1, 1976, but prior to July 1, 1978. - Upon retirement from service, in accordance with subsection (a) above, on or after July 1, 1976, but prior to July 1, 1978, a member shall receive a service retirement allowance computed as follows:

(1) If the member's service retirement date occurs on or after his sixty-fifth birthday, regardless of his years of creditable service, or after the completion of 30 years of creditable service, such allowance shall be equal to one and one-half percent (1½%) of his average final compensation, multiplied by the number of years of his creditable service.

(2a) If the member's service retirement date occurs on or after his sixtieth birthday but before his sixty-fifth birthday and prior to his completion of 30 or more years of service, his service retirement allowance shall be computed as in (1) above, but shall be reduced by one quarter of one percent (¼ of 1%) thereof for each month by which his retirement date precedes the first day of the month coincident with or next following his sixty-fifth birthday.

(2b) If the member's service retirement date occurs before his sixtieth birthday and prior to his completion of 30 or more years of creditable service, his service retirement allowance shall be the actuarial equivalent of the allowance payable at the age of 60 years as computed in (2a) above.

(3) Notwithstanding the foregoing provisions, any member whose creditable service commenced prior to July 1, 1965, and uniformed policemen or firemen not covered under the Social Security Act employed thereafter, shall receive not less than the benefits provided by G.S. 128-27(b).

(b6) Service Retirement Allowance of Members Retiring on or after July 1, 1978, but prior to July 1, 1983. - Upon retirement from service, in accordance with subsection (a) above, on or after July 1, 1978, but prior to July 1, 1983, a member shall receive a service retirement allowance computed as follows:

(1) If the member's service retirement date occurs on or after his sixty-fifth birthday or after the completion of 30 years of creditable service, such allowance shall be equal to one and fifty-five one-hundredths percent (1.55%) of his average final compensation, multiplied by the number of years of his creditable service.

(2a) If the member's service retirement date occurs after his sixtieth and before his sixty-fifth birthday and prior to his completion of 30 or more years of creditable service, his retirement allowance shall be computed as in (1) above, but shall be reduced by one quarter of one percent (1/4 of 1%) thereof for each month by which his retirement date precedes the first day of the month coincident with or next following his sixty-fifth birthday.

(2b) If the member's service retirement date occurs before his sixtieth birthday and prior to his completion of 30 or more years of creditable service, his retirement allowance shall be the actuarial equivalent of the allowance payable at the age of 60 years as computed in (2a) above.

(3) Notwithstanding the foregoing provisions, any member whose creditable service commenced prior to July 1, 1965, and uniformed policemen or firemen not covered under the Social Security Act employed thereafter, shall receive not less than the benefits provided by G.S. 128-27(b).

(b7) Service Retirement Allowances of Members Retiring on or after July 1, 1983, but prior to July 1, 1985. - Upon retirement from service, in accordance with subsection (a) above, on or after July 1, 1983, but prior to July 1, 1985, a member shall receive a service retirement allowance computed as follows:

(1) If the member's service retirement date occurs on or after his sixty-fifth birthday, regardless of his years of creditable service, or after the completion of 30 years of creditable service, such allowance shall be equal to one and fifty-seven one-hundredths percent (1.57%) of his average final compensation, multiplied by the number of years of his creditable service.

(2a) If the member's service retirement date occurs after his sixtieth and before his sixty-fifth birthday and prior to his completion of 30 or more years of creditable service, his retirement allowance shall be computed as in (1) above, but shall be reduced by one quarter of one percent (1/4 of 1%) thereof for each month by which his retirement date precedes the first day of the month coincident with or next following his sixty-fifth birthday.

(2b)   If the member's service retirement date occurs before his sixtieth birthday and prior to his completion of 30 or more years of creditable service, his retirement allowance shall be the actuarial equivalent of the allowance payable at the age of 60 years as computed in (2a) above.

(3)   Notwithstanding the foregoing provisions, any member whose creditable service commenced prior to July 1, 1965, and uniformed policemen or firemen not covered under the Social Security Act employed thereafter, shall receive not less than the benefits provided by G.S. 128-27(b).

(b8)   Service Retirement Allowance of Law Enforcement Officers Retiring on or after January 1, 1986, but before July 1, 1988. - Upon retirement from service, in accordance with subsection (a) above, on or after January 1, 1986, but before July 1, 1988, a member who is a law enforcement officer or an eligible former law enforcement officer shall receive the following service retirement allowance:

(1)   If the member's service retirement date occurs on or after his 55th birthday, and completion of five years of creditable service as a law enforcement officer, or after the completion of 30 years of creditable service, the allowance shall be equal to one and fifty-eight one hundredths percent (1.58%) of his average final compensation, multiplied by the number of years of his creditable service.

(2)   If the member's service retirement date occurs after his 50th and before his 55th birthday with 15 or more years of creditable service as a law enforcement officer and prior to his completion of 30 years of creditable service, his retirement allowance shall be computed as in (1) above, but shall be reduced by one-third of one percent (1/3 of 1%) for each month by which his retirement date precedes the first day of the month coincident with or next following his 55th birthday.

(b9)   Service Retirement Allowance of Members Retiring on or after July 1, 1985, but before July 1, 1988. - Upon retirement from service, in accordance with subsection (a) above, on or after July 1, 1985, but before July 1, 1988, a member shall receive the following service retirement allowance:

(1) If the member's service retirement date occurs on or after his 65th birthday, regardless of his years of creditable service, or after the completion of 30 years of creditable service, such allowance shall be equal to one and fifty-eight one hundredths percent (1.58%) of his average final compensation, multiplied by the number of years of his creditable service.

(2) Such allowance shall also be governed by the provisions of G.S. 128-27(b7)(2a), (2b), and (3).

(b10) Service Retirement Allowance of Members Retiring on or after July 1, 1988, but before July 1, 1989. - Upon retirement from service in accordance with subsection (a) above, on or after July 1, 1988, but before July 1, 1989, a member shall receive the following service retirement allowance:

(1) A member who is a law enforcement officer or an eligible former law enforcement officer shall receive a service retirement allowance computed as follows:

a. If the member's service retirement date occurs on or after his 55th birthday, and completion of five years of creditable service as a law enforcement officer, or after the completion of 30 years of creditable service, the allowance shall be equal to one and sixty hundredths percent (1.60%) of his average final compensation, multiplied by the number of years of his creditable service.

b. Such allowance shall also be governed by the provisions of G.S. 128-27(b8)(2).

(2) A member who is not a law enforcement officer or an eligible former law enforcement officer shall receive a service retirement allowance computed as follows:

a. If the member's service retirement date occurs on or after his 65th birthday upon the completion of five years of creditable service or after the completion of 30 years of creditable service, or on or after his 60th birthday upon the completion of 25 years of creditable service, such allowance shall be equal to one and sixty-hundredths percent (1.60%) of his average final compensation, multiplied by the number of years of his creditable service.

b. Such allowance shall also be governed by the provisions of G.S. 128-27(b7)(2a), (2b) and (3).

(b11) Service Retirement Allowance of Members Retiring on or after July 1, 1989, but before July 1, 1990. - Upon retirement from service in accordance with subsection (a) above, on or after July 1, 1989, but before July 1, 1990, a member shall receive the following service retirement allowance:

(1) A member who is a law enforcement officer or an eligible former law enforcement officer shall receive a service retirement allowance computed as follows:

a. If the member's service retirement date occurs on or after his 55th birthday, and completion of five years of creditable service as a law enforcement officer, or after the completion of 30 years of creditable service, the allowance shall be equal to one and sixty-three hundredths percent (1.63%) of his average final compensation, multiplied by the number of years of his creditable service.

b. This allowance shall also be governed by the provisions of G.S. 128-27(b8)(2).

(2) A member who is not a law enforcement officer or an eligible former law enforcement officer shall receive a service retirement allowance computed as follows:

a. If the member's service retirement date occurs on or after his 65th birthday upon the completion of five years of creditable service or after the completion of 30 years of creditable service or on or after his 60th birthday upon the completion of 25 years of creditable service, the allowance shall be equal to one and sixty-three hundredths percent (1.63%) of his average final compensation, multiplied by the number of years of creditable service.

b. This allowance shall also be governed by the provisions of G.S. 128-27(b7)(2a) and (3).

(b12) Service Retirement Allowance of Members Retiring on or after July 1, 1990, but before July 1, 1992. - Upon retirement from service in accordance with subsection (a) above, on or after July 1, 1990, but before July 1, 1992, a member shall receive the following service retirement allowance:

(1) A member who is a law enforcement officer or an eligible former law enforcement officer shall receive a service retirement allowance computed as follows:

a. If the member's service retirement date occurs on or after his 55th birthday, and completion of five years of creditable service as a law enforcement officer, or after the completion of 30 years of creditable service, the allowance shall be equal to one and sixty-four hundredths percent (1.64%) of his average final compensation, multiplied by the number of years of his creditable service.

b. This allowance shall also be governed by the provisions of G.S. 128-27(b8)(2).

(2) A member who is not a law enforcement officer or an eligible former law enforcement officer shall receive a service retirement allowance computed as follows:

a. If the member's service retirement date occurs on or after his 65th birthday upon the completion of five years of creditable service or after the completion of 30 years of creditable service or on or after his 60th birthday upon the completion of 25 years of creditable service, the allowance shall be equal to one and sixty-four hundredths percent (1.64%) of his average final compensation, multiplied by the number of years of creditable service.

b. This allowance shall also be governed by the provisions of G.S. 128-27(b7)(2a) and (3).

(b13) Service Retirement Allowance of Members Retiring on or after July 1, 1992, but before July 1, 1994. - Upon retirement from service in accordance with subsection (a) above, on or after July 1, 1992, but before July 1, 1994, a member shall receive the following service retirement allowance:

(1) A member who is a law enforcement officer or an eligible former law enforcement officer shall receive a service retirement allowance computed as follows:

a. If the member's service retirement date occurs on or after his 55th birthday, and completion of five years of creditable service as a law enforcement officer, or after the completion of 30 years of creditable service, the allowance shall be equal to one and seventy hundredths percent (1.70%) of his average final compensation, multiplied by the number of years of his creditable service.

b. This allowance shall also be governed by the provisions of G.S. 128-27(b8)(2).

(2) A member who is not a law enforcement officer or an eligible former law enforcement officer shall receive a service retirement allowance computed as follows:

a. If the member's service retirement date occurs on or after his 65th birthday upon the completion of five years of creditable service or after the completion of 30 years of creditable service or on or after his 60th birthday upon the completion of 25 years of creditable service, the allowance shall be equal to one and seventy hundredths percent (1.70%) of his average final compensation, multiplied by the number of years of creditable service.

b. This allowance shall also be governed by the provisions of G.S. 128-27(b7)(2a), (2b), and (3).

(b14) Service Retirement Allowance of Members Retiring on or after July 1, 1994, but before July 1, 1995. - Upon retirement from service in accordance with subsection (a) or (a1) above, on or after July 1, 1994, but before July 1, 1995, a member shall receive the following service retirement allowance:

(1) A member who is a law enforcement officer or an eligible former law enforcement officer shall receive a service retirement allowance computed as follows:

a. If the member's service retirement date occurs on or after his 55th birthday, and completion of five years of creditable service as a law enforcement officer, or after the completion of 30 years of creditable service, the allowance shall be equal to one and seventy-one hundredths percent (1.71%) of his average final compensation, multiplied by the number of years of his creditable service.

b. This allowance shall also be governed by the provisions of G.S. 128-27(b8)(2).

(2) A member who is not a law enforcement officer or an eligible former law enforcement officer shall receive a service retirement allowance computed as follows:

a. If the member's service retirement date occurs on or after his 65th birthday upon the completion of five years of creditable service or after the completion of 30 years of creditable service or on or after his 60th birthday upon the completion of 25 years of creditable service, the allowance shall be equal to one and seventy-one hundredths percent (1.71%) of his average final compensation, multiplied by the number of years of creditable service.

b.   This allowance shall also be governed by the provisions of G.S. 128-27(b7)(2a), (2b), and (3).

(b15)   Service Retirement Allowance of Members Retiring on or after July 1, 1995 but before July 1, 1997. - Upon retirement from service in accordance with subsection (a) or (a1) above, on or after July 1, 1995, but before July 1, 1997, a member shall receive the following service retirement allowance:

(1)   A member who is a law enforcement officer or an eligible former law enforcement officer shall receive a service retirement allowance computed as follows:

a.   If the member's service retirement date occurs on or after his 55th birthday, and completion of five years of creditable service as a law enforcement officer, or after the completion of 30 years of creditable service, the allowance shall be equal to one and seventy-two hundredths percent (1.72%) of his average final compensation, multiplied by the number of years of his creditable service.

b.   If the member's service retirement date occurs on or after his 50th birthday and before his 55th birthday with 15 or more years of creditable service as a law enforcement officer and prior to the completion of 30 years of creditable service, his retirement allowance shall be equal to the greater of:

1.   The service retirement allowance payable under G.S. 128-27(b15)(1)a. reduced by one-third of one percent (1/3 of 1%) thereof for each month by which his retirement date precedes the first day of the month coincident with or next following the month the member would have attained his 55th birthday; or

2.   The service retirement allowance as computed under G.S. 128-27(b15)(1)a. reduced by five percent (5%) times the difference between 30 years and his creditable service at retirement.

(2)   A member who is not a law enforcement officer or an eligible former law enforcement officer shall receive a service retirement allowance computed as follows:

a. If the member's service retirement date occurs on or after his 65th birthday upon the completion of five years of creditable service or after the completion of 30 years of creditable service or on or after his 60th birthday upon the completion of 25 years of creditable service, the allowance shall be equal to one and seventy-two hundredths percent (1.72%) of his average final compensation, multiplied by the number of years of creditable service.

b. If the member's service retirement date occurs after his 60th and before his 65th birthday and prior to his completion of 25 years or more of creditable service, his retirement allowance shall be computed as in G.S. 128-27(b15)(2)a. but shall be reduced by one-quarter of one percent (¼ of 1%) thereof for each month by which his retirement date precedes the first day of the month coincident with or next following his 65th birthday.

c. If the member's early service retirement date occurs on or after his 50th birthday and before his 60th birthday and after completion of 20 years of creditable service but prior to the completion of 30 years of creditable service, his early service retirement allowance shall be equal to the greater of:

1. The service retirement allowance as computed under G.S. 128-27(b15)(2)a. but reduced by the sum of five-twelfths of one percent (5/12 of 1%) thereof for each month by which his retirement date precedes the first day of the month coincident with or next following the month the member would have attained his 60th birthday, plus one-quarter of one percent (¼ of 1%) thereof for each month by which his 60th birthday precedes the first day of the month coincident with or next following his 65th birthday; or

2. The service retirement allowance as computed under G.S. 128-27(b15)(2)a. reduced by five percent (5%) times the difference between 30 years and his creditable service at retirement; or

3. If the member's creditable service commenced prior to July 1, 1995, the service retirement allowance equal to the actuarial equivalent of the allowance payable at the age of 60 years as computed in G.S. 128-27(b15)(2)b.

d. Notwithstanding the foregoing provisions, any member whose creditable service commenced prior to July 1, 1965, shall not receive less than the benefit provided by G.S. 128-27(b).

(b16) Service Retirement Allowance of Member Retiring on or after July 1, 1997, but before July 1, 1998. - Upon retirement from service in accordance with subsection (a) or (a1) above, on or after July 1, 1997, but before July 1, 1998, a member shall receive the following service retirement allowance:

(1)   A member who is a law enforcement officer or an eligible former law enforcement officer shall receive a service retirement allowance computed as follows:

a.   If the member's service retirement date occurs on or after his 55th birthday, and completion of five years of creditable service as a law enforcement officer, or after the completion of 30 years of creditable service, the allowance shall be equal to one and seventy-six hundredths percent (1.76%) of his average final compensation, multiplied by the number of years of his creditable service.

b.   If the member's service retirement date occurs on or after his 50th birthday and before his 55th birthday with 15 or more years of creditable service as a law enforcement officer and prior to the completion of 30 years of creditable service, his retirement allowance shall be equal to the greater of:

1.   The service retirement allowance payable under G.S. 128-27(b16)(1)a., reduced by one-third of one percent (1/3 of 1%) thereof for each month by which his retirement date precedes the first day of the month coincident with or next following the month the member would have attained his 55th birthday; or

2.   The service retirement allowance as computed under G.S. 128-27(b16)(1)a. reduced by five percent (5%) times the difference between 30 years and his creditable service at retirement.

(2)   A member who is not a law enforcement officer or an eligible former law enforcement officer shall receive a service retirement allowance computed as follows:

a.   If the member's service retirement date occurs on or after his 65th birthday upon the completion of five years of creditable service or after the completion of 30 years of creditable service or on or after his 60th birthday upon the completion of 25 years of creditable service, the allowance shall be equal to one and seventy-six hundredths percent (1.76%) of average final compensation, multiplied by the number of years of creditable service.

b.   If the member's service retirement date occurs after his 60th birthday and before his 65th birthday and prior to his completion of 25 years or more of creditable service, his retirement allowance shall be computed as in G.S. 128-27(b16)(2)a. but shall be reduced by one-quarter of one percent (¼ of 1%) thereof for each month by which his retirement date precedes the first day of the month coincident with or next following his 65th birthday.

c. If the member's early service retirement date occurs on or after his 50th birthday and before his 60th birthday and after completion of 20 years of creditable service but prior to the completion of 30 years of creditable service, his early service retirement allowance shall be equal to the greater of:

1. The service retirement allowance as computed under G.S. 128-27(b16)(2)a. but reduced by the sum of five-twelfths of one percent (5/12 of 1%) thereof for each month by which his retirement date precedes the first day of the month coincident with or next following the month the member would have attained his 60th birthday, plus one-quarter of one percent (¼ of 1%) thereof for each month by which his 60th birthday precedes the first day of the month coincident with or next following his 65th birthday; or

2. The service retirement allowance as computed under G.S. 128-27(b16)(2)a. reduced by five percent (5%) times the difference between 30 years and his creditable service at retirement; or

3. If the member's creditable service commenced prior to July 1, 1995, the service retirement allowance equal to the actuarial equivalent of the allowance payable at the age of 60 years as computed in G.S. 128-27(b16)(2)b.

d. Notwithstanding the foregoing provisions, any member whose creditable service commenced prior to July 1, 1965, shall not receive less than the benefit provided by G.S. 128-27(b).

(b17) Service Retirement Allowance of Member Retiring on or After July 1, 1998, but before July 1, 2000. - Upon retirement from service in accordance with subsection (a) or (a1) above, on or after July 1, 1998, but before July 1, 2000, a member shall receive the following service retirement allowance:

(1) A member who is a law enforcement officer or an eligible former law enforcement officer shall receive a service retirement allowance computed as follows:

a. If the member's service retirement date occurs on or after his 55th birthday and completion of five years of creditable service as a law enforcement officer, or after the completion of 30 years of creditable service, the allowance shall be equal to one and seventy-seven hundredths percent (1.77%) of his average final compensation, multiplied by the number of years of his creditable service.

b. If the member's service retirement date occurs on or after his 50th birthday and before his 55th birthday with 15 or more years of creditable service as a law enforcement officer and prior to the completion of 30 years of creditable service, his retirement allowance shall be equal to the greater of:

1. The service retirement allowance payable under G.S. 128-27(b17)(1)a. reduced by one-third of one percent (1/3 of 1%) thereof for each month by which his retirement date precedes the first day of the month coincident with or next following the month the member would have attained his 55th birthday; or

2. The service retirement allowance as computed under G.S. 128-27(b17)(1)a. reduced by five percent (5%) times the difference between 30 years and his creditable service at retirement.

(2) A member who is not a law enforcement officer or an eligible former law enforcement officer shall receive a service retirement allowance computed as follows:

a. If the member's service retirement date occurs on or after his 65th birthday upon the completion of five years of creditable service or after the completion of 30 years of creditable service or on or after his 60th birthday upon the completion of 25 years of creditable service, the allowance shall be equal to one and seventy-seven hundredths percent (1.77%) of average final compensation, multiplied by the number of years of creditable service.

b. If the member's service retirement date occurs after his 60th birthday and before his 65th birthday and prior to his completion of 25 years or more of creditable service, his retirement allowance shall be computed as in G.S. 128-27(b17)(2)a. but shall be reduced by one-quarter of one percent (¼ of 1%) thereof for each month by which his retirement date precedes the first day of the month coincident with or next following his 65th birthday.

c. If the member's early service retirement date occurs on or after his 50th birthday and before his 60th birthday and after completion of 20 years of creditable service but prior to the completion of 30 years of creditable service, his early service retirement allowance shall be equal to the greater of:

1. The service retirement allowance as computed under G.S. 128-27(b17)(2)a. but reduced by the sum of five-twelfths of one percent (5/12 of 1%) thereof for each month by which his retirement date precedes the first day of the month coincident with or next following the month the member would have attained his 60th birthday, plus one-quarter of one percent (¼ of 1%) thereof for each month by which his 60th birthday precedes the first day of the month coincident with or next following his 65th birthday; or

2. The service retirement allowance as computed under G.S. 128-27(b17)(2)a. reduced by five percent (5%) times the difference between 30 years and his creditable service at retirement; or

3. If the member's creditable service commenced prior to July 1, 1995, the service retirement allowance equal to the actuarial equivalent of the allowance payable at the age of 60 years as computed in G.S. 128-27(b17)(2)b.

d. Notwithstanding the foregoing provisions, any member whose creditable service commenced prior to July 1, 1965, shall not receive less than the benefit provided by G.S. 128-27(b).

(b18) Service Retirement Allowance of Member Retiring on or After July 1, 2000, but Before July 1, 2001. - Upon retirement from service in accordance with subsection (a) or (a1) above, on or after July 1, 2000, but before July 1, 2001, a member shall receive the following service retirement allowance:

(1) A member who is a law enforcement officer or an eligible former law enforcement officer shall receive a service retirement allowance computed as follows:

a. If the member's service retirement date occurs on or after his 55th birthday and completion of five years of creditable service as a law enforcement officer, or after the completion of 30 years of creditable service, the allowance shall be equal to one and seventy-eight hundredths percent (1.78%) of his average final compensation, multiplied by the number of years of his creditable service.

b. If the member's service retirement date occurs on or after his 50th birthday and before his 55th birthday with 15 or more years of creditable service as a law enforcement officer and prior to the completion of 30 years of creditable service, his retirement allowance shall be equal to the greater of:

1. The service retirement allowance payable under G.S. 128-27(b18)(1)a. reduced by one-third of one percent (1/3 of 1%) thereof for each month by which his retirement date precedes the first day of the month coincident with or next following the month the member would have attained his 55th birthday;

2. The service retirement allowance as computed under G.S. 128-27(b18)(1)a. reduced by five percent (5%) times the difference between 30 years and his creditable service at retirement.

(2) A member who is not a law enforcement officer or an eligible former law enforcement officer shall receive a service retirement allowance computed as follows:

a. If the member's service retirement date occurs on or after his 65th birthday upon the completion of five years of creditable service or after the completion of 30 years of creditable service or on or after his 60th birthday upon the completion of 25 years of creditable service, the allowance shall be equal to one and seventy-eight hundredths percent (1.78%) of average final compensation, multiplied by the number of years of creditable service.

b. If the member's service retirement date occurs after his 60th birthday and before his 65th birthday and prior to his completion of 25 years or more of creditable service, his retirement allowance shall be computed as in G.S. 128-27(b18)(2)a. but shall be reduced by one-quarter of one percent (¼ of 1%) thereof for each month by which his retirement date precedes the first day of the month coincident with or next following his 65th birthday.

c. If the member's early service retirement date occurs on or after his 50th birthday and before his 60th birthday and after completion of 20 years of creditable service but prior to the completion of 30 years of creditable service, his early service retirement allowance shall be equal to the greater of:

1. The service retirement allowance as computed under G.S. 128-27(b18)(2)a. but reduced by the sum of five-twelfths of one percent (5/12 of 1%) thereof for each month by which his retirement date precedes the first day of the month coincident with or next following the month the member would have attained his 60th birthday, plus one-quarter of one percent (¼ of 1%) thereof for each month by which his 60th birthday precedes the first day of the month coincident with or next following his 65th birthday; or

2. The service retirement allowance as computed under G.S. 128-27(b18)(2)a. reduced by five percent (5%) times the difference between 30 years and his creditable service at retirement; or

3. If the member's creditable service commenced prior to July 1, 1995, the service retirement allowance equal to the actuarial equivalent of the allowance payable at the age of 60 years as computed in G.S. 128-27(b18)(2)b.

d. Notwithstanding the foregoing provisions, any member whose creditable service commenced prior to July 1, 1965, shall not receive less than the benefit provided by G.S. 128-27(b).

(b19) Service Retirement Allowance of Member Retiring on or After July 1, 2001, But Before July 1, 2002. - Upon retirement from service in accordance with subsection (a) or (a1) above, on or after July 1, 2001, but before July 1, 2002, a member shall receive the following service retirement allowance:

(1) A member who is a law enforcement officer or an eligible former law enforcement officer shall receive a service retirement allowance computed as follows:

a. If the member's service retirement date occurs on or after his 55th birthday and completion of five years of creditable service as a law enforcement officer, or after the completion of 30 years of creditable service, the allowance shall be equal to one and eighty-one hundredths percent (1.81%) of his average final compensation, multiplied by the number of years of his creditable service.

b. If the member's service retirement date occurs on or after his 50th birthday and before his 55th birthday with 15 or more years of creditable service as a law enforcement officer and prior to the completion of 30 years of creditable service, his retirement allowance shall be equal to the greater of:

1. The service retirement allowance payable under G.S. 128-27(b19)(1)a. reduced by one-third of one percent (1/3 of 1%) thereof for each month by which his retirement date precedes the first day of the month coincident with or next following the month the member would have attained his 55th birthday;

2. The service retirement allowance as computed under G.S. 128-27(b19)(1)a. reduced by five percent (5%) times the difference between 30 years and his creditable service at retirement.

(2) A member who is not a law enforcement officer or an eligible former law enforcement officer shall receive a service retirement allowance computed as follows:

a. If the member's service retirement date occurs on or after his 65th birthday upon the completion of five years of creditable service or after the completion of 30 years of creditable service or on or after his 60th birthday upon the completion of 25 years of creditable service, the allowance shall be equal to one and eighty-one hundredths percent (1.81%) of average final compensation, multiplied by the number of years of creditable service.

b. If the member's service retirement date occurs after his 60th birthday and before his 65th birthday and prior to his completion of 25 years or more of creditable service, his retirement allowance shall be computed as in G.S. 128-27(b19)(2)a. but shall be reduced by one-quarter of one percent (¼ of 1%) thereof for each month by which his retirement date precedes the first day of the month coincident with or next following his 65th birthday.

c. If the member's early service retirement date occurs on or after his 50th birthday and before his 60th birthday and after completion of 20 years of creditable service but prior to the completion of 30 years of creditable service, his early service retirement allowance shall be equal to the greater of:

1. The service retirement allowance as computed under G.S. 128-27(b19)(2)a. but reduced by the sum of five-twelfths of one percent (5/12 of 1%) thereof for each month by which his retirement date precedes the first day of the month coincident with or next following the month the member would have attained his 60th birthday, plus one-quarter of one percent (¼ of 1%) thereof for each month by which his 60th birthday precedes the first day of the month coincident with or next following his 65th birthday; or

2. The service retirement allowance as computed under G.S. 128-27(b19)(2)a. reduced by five percent (5%) times the difference between 30 years and his creditable service at retirement; or

3. If the member's creditable service commenced prior to July 1, 1995, the service retirement allowance equal to the actuarial equivalent of the allowance payable at the age of 60 years as computed in G.S. 128-27(b19)(2)b.

d. Notwithstanding the foregoing provisions, any member whose creditable service commenced prior to July 1, 1965, shall not receive less than the benefit provided by G.S. 128-27(b).

(b20) Service Retirement Allowance of Member Retiring on or After July 1, 2002, but Before July 1, 2003. - Upon retirement from service in accordance with subsection (a) or (a1) above, on or after July 1, 2002, but before July 1, 2003, a member shall receive the following service retirement allowance:

(1) A member who is a law enforcement officer or an eligible former law enforcement officer shall receive a service retirement allowance computed as follows:

a. If the member's service retirement date occurs on or after his 55th birthday and completion of five years of creditable service as a law enforcement officer, or after the completion of 30 years of creditable service, the allowance shall be equal to one and eighty-two hundredths percent (1.82%) of his average final compensation, multiplied by the number of years of his creditable service.

b. If the member's service retirement date occurs on or after his 50th birthday and before his 55th birthday with 15 or more years of creditable service as a law enforcement officer and prior to the completion of 30 years of creditable service, his retirement allowance shall be equal to the greater of:

1. The service retirement allowance payable under G.S. 128-27(b20)(1)a. reduced by one-third of one percent (1/3 of 1%) thereof for each month by which his retirement date precedes the first day of the month coincident with or next following the month the member would have attained his 55th birthday;

2. The service retirement allowance as computed under G.S. 128-27(b20)(1)a. reduced by five percent (5%) times the difference between 30 years and his creditable service at retirement.

(2) A member who is not a law enforcement officer or an eligible former law enforcement officer shall receive a service retirement allowance computed as follows:

a. If the member's service retirement date occurs on or after his 65th birthday upon the completion of five years of creditable service or after the completion of 30 years of creditable service or on or after his 60th birthday upon the completion of 25 years of creditable service, the allowance shall be equal to one and eighty-two hundredths percent (1.82%) of average final compensation, multiplied by the number of years of creditable service.

b.   If the member's service retirement date occurs after his 60th birthday and before his 65th birthday and prior to his completion of 25 years or more of creditable service, his retirement allowance shall be computed as in G.S. 128-27(b20)(2)a. but shall be reduced by one-quarter of one percent (¼ of 1%) thereof for each month by which his retirement date precedes the first day of the month coincident with or next following his 65th birthday.

c.   If the member's early service retirement date occurs on or after his 50th birthday and before his 60th birthday and after completion of 20 years of creditable service but prior to the completion of 30 years of creditable service, his early service retirement allowance shall be equal to the greater of:

1.   The service retirement allowance as computed under G.S. 128-27(b20)(2)a. but reduced by the sum of five-twelfths of one percent (5/12 of 1%) thereof for each month by which his retirement date precedes the first day of the month coincident with or next following the month the member would have attained his 60th birthday, plus one-quarter of one percent (¼ of 1%) thereof for each month by which his 60th birthday precedes the first day of the month coincident with or next following his 65th birthday; or

2.   The service retirement allowance as computed under G.S. 128-27(b20)(2)a. reduced by five percent (5%) times the difference between 30 years and his creditable service at retirement; or

3.   If the member's creditable service commenced prior to July 1, 1995, the service retirement allowance equal to the actuarial equivalent of the allowance payable at the age of 60 years as computed in G.S. 128-27(b20)(2)b.

d.   Notwithstanding the foregoing provisions, any member whose creditable service commenced prior to July 1, 1965, shall not receive less than the benefit provided by G.S. 128-27(b).

(b21)   Service Retirement Allowance of Member Retiring on or After July 1, 2003. - Upon retirement from service in accordance with subsection (a) or (a1) above, on or after July 1, 2003, a member shall receive the following service retirement allowance:

(1) A member who is a law enforcement officer or an eligible former law enforcement officer shall receive a service retirement allowance computed as follows:

a. If the member's service retirement date occurs on or after his 55th birthday and completion of five years of creditable service as a law enforcement officer, or after the completion of 30 years of creditable service, the allowance shall be equal to one and eighty-five hundredths percent (1.85%) of his average final compensation, multiplied by the number of years of his creditable service.

b. If the member's service retirement date occurs on or after his 50th birthday and before his 55th birthday with 15 or more years of creditable service as a law enforcement officer and prior to the completion of 30 years of creditable service, his retirement allowance shall be equal to the greater of:

1. The service retirement allowance payable under G.S. 128-27(b21)(1)a. reduced by one-third of one percent (1/3 of 1%) thereof for each month by which his retirement date precedes the first day of the month coincident with or next following the month the member would have attained his 55th birthday;

2. The service retirement allowance as computed under G.S. 128-27(b21)(1)a. reduced by five percent (5%) times the difference between 30 years and his creditable service at retirement.

(2) A member who is not a law enforcement officer or an eligible former law enforcement officer shall receive a service retirement allowance computed as follows:

a. If the member's service retirement date occurs on or after his 65th birthday upon the completion of five years of creditable service or after the completion of 30 years of creditable service or on or after his 60th birthday upon the completion of 25 years of creditable service, the allowance shall be equal to one and eighty-five hundredths percent (1.85%) of average final compensation, multiplied by the number of years of creditable service.

b. If the member's service retirement date occurs after his 60th birthday and before his 65th birthday and prior to his completion of 25 years or more of creditable service, his retirement allowance shall be computed as in G.S. 128-27(b21)(2) a. but shall be reduced by one-quarter of one percent (¼ of 1%) thereof for each month by which his retirement date precedes the first day of the month coincident with or next following his 65th birthday.

c. If the member's early service retirement date occurs on or after his 50th birthday and before his 60th birthday and after completion of 20 years of creditable service but prior to the completion of 30 years of creditable service, his early service retirement allowance shall be equal to the greater of:

1. The service retirement allowance as computed under G.S. 128-27(b21)(2)a. but reduced by the sum of five-twelfths of one percent (5/12 of 1%) thereof for each month by which his retirement date precedes the first day of the month coincident with or next following the month the member would have attained his 60th birthday, plus one-quarter of one percent (¼ of 1%) thereof for each month by which his 60th birthday precedes the first day of the month coincident with or next following his 65th birthday; or

2. The service retirement allowance as computed under G.S. 128-27(b21)(2)a. reduced by five percent (5%) times the difference between 30 years and his creditable service at retirement; or

3. If the member's creditable service commenced prior to July 1, 1995, the service retirement allowance equal to the actuarial equivalent of the allowance payable at the age of 60 years as computed in G.S. 128-27(b21)(2)b.

d. Notwithstanding the foregoing provisions, any member whose creditable service commenced prior to July 1, 1965, shall not receive less than the benefit provided by G.S. 128-27(b).

(c) Disability Retirement Benefits. - Upon the application of a member or of his employer, any member who has had five or more years of creditable service may be retired by the Board of Trustees, on the first day of any calendar month, not less than one day nor more than 120 days next following the date of filing such application, on a disability retirement allowance: Provided, that the medical board, after a medical examination of such member, shall certify that such member is mentally or physically incapacitated for the further performance of duty, that such incapacity was incurred at the time of active employment and has been continuous thereafter, that such incapacity is likely to be permanent, and that such member should be retired; Provided further the medical board shall determine if the member is able to engage in gainful employment and, if so, the member may still be retired and the disability retirement allowance as a result thereof shall be reduced as in subsection (e) below. Provided further, that the Medical Board shall not certify any member as disabled who:

(1) Applies for disability retirement based upon a mental or physical incapacity which existed when the member first established membership in the system; or

(2) Is in receipt of any payments on account of the same disability which existed when the member first established membership in the system.

The Board of Trustees shall require each employee upon enrolling in the retirement system to provide information on the membership application concerning any mental or physical incapacities existing at the time the member enrolls.

Notwithstanding the requirement of five or more years of creditable service to the contrary, a member who is a law enforcement officer, an eligible fireman as defined in G.S. 58-86-25, or an eligible rescue squad worker as defined in G.S. 58-86-30 and becomes incapacitated for duty as the natural and proximate result of injuries incurred while in the actual performance of his or her duties, and meets all other requirements for disability retirement benefits, may be retired by the Board of Trustees on a disability retirement allowance.

Notwithstanding the foregoing to the contrary, any beneficiary who commenced retirement with an early or service retirement benefit has the right, within three years of his retirement, to convert to an allowance with disability retirement benefits without modification of any election of optional allowance previously made; provided, the beneficiary would have met all applicable requirements for disability retirement benefits while still in service as a member. The allowance on account of disability retirement benefits to the beneficiary shall be retroactive to the effective date of early or service retirement.

Notwithstanding the foregoing, effective April 1, 1991, the surviving designated beneficiary of a deceased member who met all other requirements for disability retirement benefits, except whose death occurred before the first day of the calendar month in which the member's disability retirement allowance was to be due and payable, may elect to receive the reduced retirement allowance provided by a one hundred percent (100%) joint and survivor payment option in lieu of a return of accumulated contributions, provided the following conditions apply:

(1) At the time of the member's death, one and only one beneficiary is eligible to receive a return of accumulated contributions, and

(2) The member had not instructed the Board of Trustees in writing that he did not wish the provision of this subsection to apply.

(d) Allowance on Disability Retirement of Persons Retiring prior to July 1, 1965. - Upon retirement for disability, in accordance with subsection (c) above, prior to July 1, 1965, a member shall receive a service retirement allowance if he has attained the age of 60 years, otherwise he shall receive a disability retirement allowance which shall consist of:

(1) An annuity which shall be the actuarial equivalent of his accumulated contributions at the time of the retirement;

(2) A pension equal to seventy-five percent (75%) of the pension that would have been payable upon service retirement at the age of 65 years had the member continued in service to the age of 65 years without further change in compensation.

Supplemental disability benefits heretofore provided are hereby made a permanent part of disability benefits after age 65, and shall not be discontinued at age 65.

(d1) Allowance on Disability Retirement of Persons Retiring on or after July 1, 1965, but prior to July 1, 1969. - Upon retirement for disability, in accordance with subsection (c) above, on or after July 1, 1965, but prior to July 1, 1969, a member shall receive a service retirement allowance if he has attained the age of 60 years, otherwise he shall receive a disability retirement allowance which shall be computed as follows:

(1) Such allowance shall be equal to the service retirement allowance which would have been payable had he continued in service without further change in compensation, to the age of 60 years, minus the actuarial equivalent of the contributions he would have made during such continued service.

(2) Notwithstanding the foregoing provisions, any member whose creditable service commenced prior to July 1, 1965, and uniformed policemen or firemen not covered under the Social Security Act employed thereafter, shall receive not less than the benefit provided by G.S. 128-27(d).

(d2) Allowance on Disability Retirement of Persons Retiring on or after July 1, 1969, but prior to July 1, 1971. - Upon retirement for disability, in accordance with subsection (c) above, on or after July 1, 1969, but prior to July 1, 1971, a member shall receive a service retirement allowance if he has attained the age of 60 years, otherwise he shall receive a disability retirement allowance which shall be computed as follows:

(1) Such allowance shall be equal to the service retirement allowance which would have been payable had he continued in service without further change in compensation to the age of 65 years, minus the actuarial equivalent of the contributions he would have made during such continued service.

(2) Notwithstanding the foregoing provisions, any member whose creditable service commenced prior to July 1, 1965, and uniformed policemen or firemen not covered under the Social Security Act employed thereafter, shall receive not less than the benefit provided by G.S. 128-27(d).

(d3) Allowance on Disability Retirement of Persons Retiring on or after July 1, 1971, but prior to July 1, 1982. - Upon retirement for disability, in accordance with subsection (c) of this section on or after July 1, 1971, but prior to July 1, 1982, a member shall receive a service retirement allowance if he has attained the age of 65 years; otherwise he shall receive a disability retirement allowance which shall be computed as follows:

(1) Such allowance shall be equal to a service retirement allowance calculated on the basis of the member's average final compensation prior to his disability retirement and the creditable service he would have had at the age of 65 years if he had continued in service.

(2) Notwithstanding the foregoing provisions,

a. Any member whose creditable service commenced prior to July 1, 1971, shall receive not less than the benefit provided by G.S. 128-27(d2);

b. The amount of disability allowance payable from the reserve funds of the Retirement System to any member retiring on or after July 1, 1974, who is eligible for and in receipt of a disability benefit under the Social Security Act shall be seventy percent (70%) of the amount calculated under a above, and the balance shall be provided by the employer from time to time during each year in such amounts as may be required to cover such payments as current disbursements; and

c. The amount of disability allowance payable to any member retiring on or after July 1, 1974, who is not eligible for and in receipt of a disability benefit under the Social Security Act shall not be payable from the reserve funds of the Retirement System but shall be provided by the employer from time to time during each year in such amounts as may be required to cover such payments as current disbursements.

(d4) Allowance on Disability Retirement of Persons Retiring on or after July 1, 1982. - Upon retirement for disability, in accordance with subsection (c) of this section on or after July 1, 1982, a member shall receive a service retirement allowance if he has qualified for an unreduced service retirement allowance; otherwise the allowance shall be equal to a service retirement allowance calculated on the member's average final compensation prior to his disability retirement and the creditable service he would have had had he continued in service until the earliest date on which he would have qualified for an unreduced service retirement allowance.

(e) Reexamination of Beneficiaries Retired on Account of Disability. - Once each year during the first five years following retirement of a member on a disability allowance, and once in every three-year period thereafter, the Board of Trustees may, and upon his application shall, require any disability beneficiary who has not yet attained the age of 60 years to undergo a medical examination, such examination to be made at the place of residence of said beneficiary or other place mutually agreed upon, by the physician or physicians designated by the Board of Trustees. Should any disability beneficiary who has not yet attained the age of 60 years refuse to submit to at least one medical examination in any such year by a physician or physicians designated by the Board of Trustees, his allowance may be discontinued until his withdrawal of such refusal, and should his refusal continue for one year, all his rights in and to his pension may be revoked by the Board of Trustees.

(1) The Board of Trustees shall determine whether a disability beneficiary is engaged in or is able to engage in a gainful occupation paying more than the difference, as hereinafter indexed, between his disability retirement allowance and the gross compensation earned as an employee during the 12 consecutive months in the final 48 months of service prior to retirement producing the highest gross compensation excluding any compensation received on account of termination. If the disability beneficiary is earning or is able to earn more than the difference, the portion of his disability retirement allowance not provided by his contributions shall be reduced to an amount which, together with the portion of the disability retirement allowance provided by his contributions and the amount earnable by him shall equal the amount of his gross compensation prior to retirement. This difference shall be increased on January 1 each year by the

ratio of the Consumer Price Index to the Index one year earlier, calculated to the nearest tenth of a percent (1/10 of 1%). Should the earning capacity of the disability beneficiary later change, the portion of his disability retirement allowance not provided by his contributions may be further modified. In lieu of the reductions on account of a disability beneficiary earning more than the aforesaid difference, he may elect to convert his disability retirement allowance to a service retirement allowance calculated on the basis of his average final compensation and creditable service at the time of disability retirement and his age at the time of conversion to service retirement. This election is irrevocable.

The provisions of this subdivision shall not apply to beneficiaries of the Law Enforcement Officers' Retirement System transferred to this Retirement System who commenced retirement on and before July 1, 1981.

(2)   Should a disability beneficiary under the age of 62 years be restored to active service at a compensation not less than his average final compensation, his retirement allowance shall cease, he shall again become a member of the Retirement System and he shall contribute thereafter at the contribution rate which is applicable during his subsequent membership service. Any prior service certificate on the basis of which his service was computed at the time of his retirement shall be restored to full force and effect, and in addition, upon his subsequent retirement he shall be credited with all his service as a member, but should he be restored to active service on or after the attainment of the age of 50 years his pension upon subsequent retirement shall not exceed the sum of the pension which he was receiving immediately prior to his last restoration after June 30, 1951, and the pension that he would have received on account of his service since such last restoration had he entered service at that time as a new entrant.

(3)   Notwithstanding the foregoing, a member retired on a disability retirement allowance who is restored to service and subsequently retires on or after July 1, 1971, shall be entitled to an allowance not less than the allowance prescribed in a below reduced by the amount in b below.

a.   The allowance to which he would have been entitled if he were retiring for the first time, calculated on the basis of his total creditable service represented by the sum of his creditable service at the time of his first retirement and his creditable service after he was restored to service.

b.   The actuarial equivalent of the retirement benefits he previously received.

(3a)   Notwithstanding the foregoing, should a beneficiary who retired on a disability retirement allowance be restored to service as an employee, then the retirement allowance shall cease as of the first day of the month following the month in which the beneficiary is restored to service and the beneficiary shall become a member of the Retirement System and shall contribute thereafter as allowed by law at the uniform contribution payable by all members. Upon the subsequent retirement of the beneficiary, he shall be entitled to an allowance to which he would have been entitled if he were retiring for the first time, calculated on the basis of his total creditable service represented by the sum of his creditable service at the time of his first retirement and his creditable service after he was restored to service. Provided, however, any election of an optional allowance cannot be changed unless the member subsequently completes three years of membership service after being restored to service.

(4)   As a condition to the receipt of the disability retirement allowance provided for in G.S. 128-27(d), (d1), (d2) and (d3) each member retired on a disability retirement allowance shall, on or before April 15 of each calendar year, provide the Board of Trustees with a statement of his or her income received as compensation for services, including fees, commissions or similar items, and income received from business, for the previous calendar year. Such statement shall be filed on a form as required by the Board of Trustees. The benefit payable to a beneficiary who does not or refuses to provide the information requested within 60 days after such request shall not be paid a benefit until the information so requested is provided, and should such refusal or failure to provide such information continue for 240 days after such request, the right of a beneficiary to a benefit under the Article may be terminated.

The Director of the State Retirement Systems shall contact any State or federal agency which can provide information to substantiate the statement required to be submitted by this subdivision and may enter into agreements for the exchange of information.

(5)   Notwithstanding any other provisions of this Article to the contrary, a beneficiary who was a beneficiary retired on a disability retirement with the Law Enforcement Officers' Retirement System at the time of the transfer of law enforcement officers employed by a participating employer and beneficiaries last employed by a participating employer to this Retirement System and who also was a contributing member of this Retirement System at that time, shall continue to be paid his retirement allowance without restriction and may continue as a member of this Retirement System with all the rights and

privileges appendant to membership. Any beneficiary who retired on a disability retirement allowance as an employee of any participating employer under the Law Enforcement Officers' Retirement System and becomes employed as an employee other than as a law enforcement officer by an employer participating in the Retirement System after the aforementioned transfer shall continue to be paid his retirement allowance without restriction and may continue as a member of this Retirement System with all the rights and privileges appendant to membership until January 1, 1989, at which time his retirement allowance shall cease and his subsequent retirement shall be determined in accordance with the preceding subdivision (3a) of this section. Any beneficiary as hereinbefore described who becomes employed as a law enforcement officer by an employer participating in the Retirement System shall cease to be a beneficiary and shall immediately commence membership and his subsequent retirement shall be determined in accordance with subdivision (3a) of this section.

(6) Notwithstanding any other provision to the contrary, a beneficiary in receipt of a disability retirement allowance until the earliest date on which he would have qualified for an unreduced service retirement allowance shall thereafter (i) not be subject to further reexaminations as to disability, (ii) not be subject to any reduction in allowance on account of being engaged in a gainful occupation other than with an employer participating in the Retirement System, and (iii) be considered a beneficiary in receipt of a service retirement allowance. Provided, however, a beneficiary in receipt of a disability retirement allowance whose allowance is reduced on account of reexamination as to disability or to ability to engage in a gainful occupation prior to the date on which he would have qualified for an unreduced service retirement allowance shall have only the right to elect to convert to an early or service retirement allowance as permitted under subdivision (1) above.

(f) Return of Accumulated Contributions. - Should a member cease to be an employee except by death or retirement under the provisions of this Chapter, he shall upon submission of an application be paid, not earlier than 60 days from the date of termination of service, his contributions and, if he has attained at least five years of membership service or if termination of his membership service is involuntary as certified by the employer, the accumulated regular interest thereon, provided that he has not in the meantime returned to service. Upon payment of such sum his membership in the System shall cease and, if he thereafter again becomes a member, no credit shall be allowed for any service previously rendered except as provided in G.S. 128-26; and such payment shall be in full and complete discharge of any rights in or to any benefits otherwise payable hereunder. Upon receipt of proof satisfactory to the Board of Trustees of the death, prior to retirement, of a member or former member there shall be paid to such person or persons as he shall have nominated by electronic submission prior to completing 10 years of service in a form approved by the Board of Trustees or by written designation duly acknowledged and filed with the Board of Trustees, if such person or persons are living at the time of the member's death, otherwise to the member's legal representatives, the amount of his accumulated contributions at the time of his death, unless the beneficiary elects to receive the alternate benefit under the provisions of (m) below. An extension service employee who made contributions to the Local Governmental Employees' Retirement System and the Teachers' and State Employees' Retirement System as a result of dual employment may not be paid his accumulated contributions unless he is eligible to be paid his accumulated contributions in both systems for the same period of service.

Pursuant to the provisions of G.S. 135-56.2, a member who is also a member of the Consolidated Judicial Retirement System may irrevocably elect to transfer any accumulated contributions to the Consolidated Judicial Retirement System or to the Supplemental Retirement Income Plan and forfeit any rights in or to any benefits otherwise payable hereunder.

(f1)   Notwithstanding the foregoing provisions, upon or after retirement any member who was a uniformed fireman and any surviving beneficiary of a member who was a uniformed fireman, shall upon submission of an application, be paid the sum of accumulated contributions, with regular interest thereon, made under those provisions of G.S. 128-30(b)(1) that applied from July 1, 1965, through June 30, 1971, to the extent of the contributions required of the member that were in excess of the contributions required of other members of the Local Governmental Employees' Retirement System covered under the Social Security Act as was from time to time in effect; provided that, the return of contributions shall be payable only if the contributions did not increase the retirement allowance of the member or surviving beneficiary under the provisions of this Chapter.

(f2)   Expired.

(g)   (See Editor's note) Election of Optional Allowance. - With the provision that until the first payment on account of any benefit becomes normally due, or his first retirement check has been cashed, any member may elect to receive his benefits in a retirement allowance payable throughout life, or he may elect to receive the actuarial equivalent of such retirement allowance, including any special retirement allowance, in a reduced allowance payable throughout life under the provisions of one of the Options set forth below. The election of Option 2, 3, or 6 or nomination of the person thereunder shall be revoked if such person nominated dies prior to the date the first payment becomes normally due or the first retirement check has been cashed. Such election may be revoked by the member prior to the date the first payment becomes normally due or his first retirement check has been cashed. Provided, however, in the event a member has elected Option 2, 3, or 5 and nominated his or her spouse to receive a retirement allowance upon the member's death, and the spouse predeceases the member after the first payment becomes normally due or the first retirement check has been cashed, if the member remarries he or she may request to nominate a new spouse to receive the retirement allowance under the previously elected option, within 90 days of the remarriage, and may nominate a new spouse to receive the retirement allowance under the previously elected option by written designation duly acknowledged and filed with the Board of Trustees within 120 days of the remarriage. The new nomination shall be effective on the first day of the month in which it is made and shall provide for a retirement allowance computed to be the actuarial equivalent of the retirement allowance in effect immediately prior to the effective date of the new nomination. Any member having elected Option 2, 3, 5, or 6 and nominated his or her spouse to receive a retirement allowance upon the member's death may, after divorce from his or her spouse, revoke the nomination and elect a new option, effective on the first day of the month in which the new option is elected, providing for a retirement allowance computed to be the actuarial equivalent of the retirement allowance in effect immediately prior to the effective date of the new option. Except as provided in this section, the member may not change the member's retirement benefit option or the member's designated beneficiary for survivor benefits, if any, after the member has cashed the first retirement check or after the 25th day of the month following the month in which the first check is mailed, whichever comes first.

Option one.

(a)   In the Case of a Member Who Retires prior to July 1, 1965. - If he dies before he has received in annuity payments the present value of his annuity as it was at the time of his retirement, the balance shall be paid to such person as he shall nominate by written designation duly acknowledged and filed with the Board of Trustees or, if none, to his legal representative.

(b)   In the Case of a Member Who Retires on or after July 1, 1965, but prior to July 1, 1993. - If he dies within 10 years from his retirement date, an amount equal to his accumulated contributions at retirement, less one one-hundred-twentieth thereof for each month for which he has received a retirement allowance payment, shall be paid to such person as he shall nominate by written designation duly acknowledged and filed with the Board of Trustees or, if none, to his legal representative; or

Option two. Upon his death his reduced retirement allowance shall be continued throughout the life of and paid to such person as he shall nominate by written designation duly acknowledged and filed with the Board of Trustees at the time of his retirement, provided that if the person selected is other than his spouse the reduced retirement allowance payable to the member shall not be less than one half of the retirement allowance without optional modification which would otherwise be payable to him; or

Option three. Upon his death, one half of his reduced retirement allowance shall be continued throughout the life of, and paid to such person as he shall nominate by written designation duly acknowledged and filed with the Board of Trustees at the time of his retirement; or

Option four. Adjustment of Retirement Allowance for Social Security Benefits. - Until the first payment on account of any benefit becomes normally due, any member may elect to convert his benefit otherwise payable on his account after retirement into a retirement allowance of equivalent actuarial value of such amount that with his benefit under Title II of the Federal Social Security Act, he will receive, so far as possible, approximately the same amount per year before and after the earliest age at which he becomes eligible, upon application therefor, to receive a social security benefit.

Option five. For Members Retiring prior to July 1, 1993. - The member may elect to receive a reduced retirement allowance under the conditions of Option two or Option three, as provided for above, with the modification that if both he and the person nominated die within 10 years from his retirement date, an amount equal to his accumulated contributions at retirement, less 1/120th thereof for each month for which a retirement allowance has been paid, shall be paid to his legal representatives or to such person as he shall nominate by written designation duly acknowledged and filed with the Board of Trustees.

Option six. A member may elect either Option two or Option three with the added provision that in the event the designated beneficiary predeceases the member, the retirement allowance payable to the member after the designated beneficiary's death shall be equal to the retirement allowance which would have been payable had the member not elected the option.

Upon the death of a member after the effective date of a retirement for which the member has been approved and following receipt by the Board of Trustees of an election of benefits (Form 6-E or Form 7-E) but prior to the cashing of the first benefit check, the retirement benefit shall be payable as provided by the member's election of benefits under this subsection.

Upon the death of a member after the effective date of a retirement for which the member has been approved but prior to the receipt by the Board of Trustees of an election of benefits (Form 6-E or Form 7-E), properly acknowledged and filed by the member, the member's designated beneficiary for a return of accumulated contributions may elect to receive the benefit, if only one beneficiary is eligible to receive the return of accumulated contributions. If more than one beneficiary is eligible to receive the return of accumulated contributions, the administrator or executor of the member's estate will select an option and name the beneficiary or beneficiaries.

(g1) In the event of the death of a retired member while in receipt of a retirement allowance under the provisions of this Article, there shall be paid to such person or persons as the retiree shall have nominated by electronic submission in a form approved by the Board of Trustees or by written designation duly acknowledged and filed with the Board of Trustees, if such person or persons are living at the time of the retiree's death, otherwise to the retiree's legal representatives, a death benefit equal to the excess, if any, of the accumulated contributions of the retiree at the date of retirement over the total of the retirement allowances paid prior to the death of the retiree. In the event that a retiree is receiving a Special Retirement Allowance under subsection (m1) of this section, there shall be paid to such person or persons as the retiree shall have nominated by electronic submission in a form approved by the Board of Trustees or by written designation duly acknowledged and filed with the Board of Trustees, if such person or persons are living at the time of the retiree's death, otherwise to the retiree's legal representatives, an additional death benefit equal to the excess, if any, of the employee voluntary contributions that were transferred from the Supplemental Retirement Income Plan of North Carolina or the North Carolina Public Employee Deferred Compensation Plan to this Retirement System over the total of the Special Retirement Allowances paid prior to the death of the retiree. For purposes of this paragraph, the term "accumulated contributions" excludes any amount transferred under subsection (m2) of this section.

In the event that a retirement allowance becomes payable to the designated survivor of a retired member under the provisions above and such retirement allowance to the survivor shall terminate upon the death of the survivor before the total of the retirement allowances paid to the retiree and the designated survivor combined equals the amount of the accumulated contributions of the retiree at the date of retirement, the excess, if any, of such accumulated contributions over the total of the retirement allowances paid to the retiree and the survivor combined shall be paid in a lump sum to such person or persons as the retiree shall have nominated by electronic submission in a form approved by the Board of Trustees or by written designation duly acknowledged and filed with the Board of Trustees, if such person or persons are living at the time such payment falls due, otherwise to the retiree's legal representative. For purposes of this paragraph, the term "accumulated contributions" includes amounts of employee voluntary contributions that were transferred from the Supplemental Retirement Income Plan of North Carolina to this Retirement System at retirement by eligible law enforcement officers.

In the event that a retirement allowance becomes payable to the principal beneficiary designated to receive a return of accumulated contributions pursuant to subsection (m) of this section and that beneficiary dies before the total of the retirement allowances paid equals the amount of the accumulated contributions of the member at the date of the member's death, the excess of those accumulated contributions over the total of the retirement allowances paid to the beneficiary shall be paid in a lump sum to the person or persons the member has designated as the contingent beneficiary for return of accumulated contributions, if the person or persons are living at the time the payment falls due, otherwise to the principal beneficiary's legal representative. For purposes of this paragraph, the term "accumulated contributions" includes amounts of employee voluntary contributions that were transferred from the Supplemental Retirement Income Plan of North Carolina to this Retirement System at retirement by eligible law enforcement officers.

In the event a retiree purchases creditable service as provided in G.S. 128-26, there shall be paid to such person or persons as the retiree shall have nominated by electronic submission in a form approved by the Board of Trustees or by written designation duly acknowledged and filed with the Board of Trustees, if such person or persons are living at the time of the retiree's death, otherwise to the retiree's legal representatives, an additional death benefit equal to the excess, if any, of the cost of the creditable service purchased less the administrative fee, if any, over the total of the increase in the retirement allowance attributable to the additional creditable service, paid from the month following the month in which payment was received to the death of the retiree.

In the event that a retirement allowance becomes payable to the designated survivor of a retired member under the provisions above, and such retirement allowance to the survivor shall terminate upon the death of the survivor before the total of the increase in the retirement allowance attributable to the additional creditable service paid to the retiree and the designated survivor combined equals the cost of the creditable service purchased less the administrative fee, the excess, if any, shall be paid in a lump sum to such person or persons as the retiree shall have nominated by electronic submission in a form approved by the Board of Trustees or by written designation duly acknowledged and filed with the Board of Trustees, if such person or persons are living at the time such payment falls due, otherwise to the retiree's legal representative.

In the event that a retiree dies without having designated a beneficiary to receive a benefit under the provisions of this subsection, any such benefit that becomes payable shall be paid to the member's estate.

(h)   Until June 30, 1951, all benefits payable to or on account of any beneficiary retired before such date shall be computed on the basis of the provisions of Chapter 128 as they existed at the date of establishment of the Retirement System. On and after July 1, 1951, all such benefits shall be adjusted to take into account, under such rules as the Board of Trustees may adopt, the provisions of Chapter 128 and all amendments thereto in effect on July 1, 1951, and no further contributions on account of such adjustments shall be required of such beneficiaries. The Board of Trustees may authorize such transfers of reserves between the funds of the Retirement System as may be required on account of such adjustments.

(i)   No action shall be commenced against the State or the Retirement System by any retired member or beneficiary respecting any deficiency in the payment of benefits more than three years after such deficient payment was made, and no action shall be commenced by the State or the Retirement System against any retired member or former member or beneficiary respecting any overpayment of benefits or contributions more than three years after such overpayment was made.

(j)   Increase in Benefits to Those Persons Who Were in Receipt of Benefits prior to July 1, 1967. - From and after July 1, 1967, the monthly benefits, to or on account of persons who commenced receiving benefits from the System prior to July 1, 1967, shall be increased by a percentage thereof. Such percentage shall be determined in accordance with the following schedule:

Period in Which Benefits Commenced	Percentage
January 1, 1966, to June 30, 1967	5%
Year 1965	6%
Year 1964	7%
Year 1963	8%
Year 1962	9%
Year 1961	10%
Year 1960	11%
Year 1959	12%
Year 1958	13%
Year 1957	14%
Year 1956	15%
Year 1955	16%
Year 1954	17%
Year 1953	18%
Year 1952	19%
Year 1951	20%
Year 1950	21%
Year 1949	22%
Year 1948	23%
Year 1947	24%

Year 1946... 25%

The minimum increase pursuant to this subsection (j) shall be five dollars ($5.00) per month; provided that, if an optional benefit has been elected, said minimum shall be reduced actuarially as determined by the Board and shall be applicable to a retired member, if surviving, otherwise to his designated beneficiary under the option elected.

(k)   Post-Retirement Increases in Allowances. - As of December 31, 1969, the ratio of the Consumer Price Index to such index one year earlier shall be determined. If such ratio indicates an increase that equals or exceeds three per centum (3%), each beneficiary receiving a retirement allowance as of December 31, 1968, shall be entitled to have his allowance increased three per centum (3%) effective July 1, 1970.

As of December 31, 1970, the ratio of the Consumer Price Index to such index one year earlier shall be determined. If such ratio indicates an increase of at least one per centum (1%), each beneficiary on the retirement rolls as of July 1, 1970, shall be entitled to have his allowance increased effective July 1, 1971, as follows:

Increase In Index	Increase In Allowance
1.00 to 1.49%	1%
1.50 to 2.49%	2%
2.50 to 3.49%	3%
3.50% or more	4%

As of December 31, 1971, an increase in retirement allowances shall be calculated and made effective July 1, 1972, in the manner described in the preceding paragraph. As of December 31 of each year after 1971, the ratio (R) of the Consumer Price Index to such index one year earlier shall be determined, and each beneficiary on the retirement rolls as of July 1 of the year of determination shall be entitled to have his allowance increased effective on July 1 of the year following the year of determination by the same percentage of increase indicated by the ratio (R) calculated to the nearest tenth of one per centum (1/10 of 1%), but not more than four per centum (4%); provided that any such increase in allowances shall be contingent upon the total fund providing sufficient investment gains to cover the additional actuarial liabilities on account of such increase. The determination of whether there are sufficient investment gains to cover the possible postretirement increase in allowance shall reside exclusively within the discretion of the Board of Trustees and shall be informed by the findings within the annual actuarial valuation reports. In considering whether to grant a postretirement increase, the Board of Trustees shall take into account both the rate of inflation as determined by the Consumer Price Index and the record of investment gains or losses during the preceding three-year period.

The allowance of a surviving annuitant of a beneficiary whose allowance is increased under this subsection shall, when and if payable, be increased by the same per centum.

Any increase in allowance granted hereunder shall be permanent, irrespective of any subsequent decrease in the Consumer Price Index, and shall be included in determining any subsequent increase.

Notwithstanding the foregoing linkage between increases in the Consumer Price Index and correlative contingent increases in retirement benefits determined by the availability of sufficient investment gains to cover the additional actuarial liabilities arising from those increased benefits, the Board of Trustees, may in any year, considering an increase, if any, in the Consumer Price Index, fund a cost-of-living increase in a percentage amount, measured in tenths of one percent (1/10 of 1%), of up to four percent (4%), provided that the Board may use only investment gains to fund such an increase.

For purposes of this subsection, Consumer Price Index shall mean the Consumer Price Index (all items - United States city average), as published by the United States Department of Labor, Bureau of Labor Statistics.

(l) Death Benefit Plan. - The provisions of this subsection shall become effective for any employer only after an agreement to that effect has been executed by the employer and the Director of the Retirement System. There is hereby created a Group Life Insurance Plan (hereinafter called the "Plan") which is established as an employee welfare benefit plan that is separate and apart from the Retirement System and under which the members of the Retirement System shall participate and be eligible for group life insurance benefits. Upon receipt of proof, satisfactory to the Board of Trustees in their capacity as trustees under the Group Life Insurance Plan, of the death, in service, of a member who had completed at least one full calendar year of membership in the Retirement System, there shall be paid to such person as he shall have nominated by electronic submission prior to completing 10 years of service in a form approved by the Board of Trustees or by written designation duly acknowledged and filed with the Board of Trustees, if such person is living at the time of the member's death, otherwise to the member's legal representatives, a death benefit. Such death benefit shall be equal to the greater of:

(1)   The compensation on which contributions were made by the member during the calendar year preceding the year in which his death occurs, or

(2)   The greatest compensation on which contributions were made by the member during a 12-month period of service within the 24-month period of service ending on the last day of the month preceding the month in which his last day of actual service occurs;

(3)   Repealed by Session Laws 1983 (Regular Session, 1984), c. 1049, s. 2;

subject to a minimum of twenty-five thousand dollars ($25,000) and a maximum of fifty thousand dollars ($50,000). Such death benefit shall be payable apart and separate from the payment of the member's accumulated contributions under the System on his death pursuant to the provisions of subsection (f) of this section. For the purpose of the Plan, a member shall be deemed to be in service at the date of his death if his death occurs within 180 days from the last day of his actual service.

The death benefit provided in this subsection shall not be payable, notwithstanding the member's compliance with all the conditions set forth in the preceding paragraph, if his death occurs

(1)   After June 30, 1969 and after he has attained age 70; or

(2)   After December 31, 1969 and after he has attained age 69; or

(3)   After December 31, 1970 and after he has attained age 68; or

(4)   After December 31, 1971 and after he has attained age 67; or

(5)   After December 31, 1972 and after he has attained age 66; or

(6) After December 31, 1973 and after he has attained age 65; or

(7) After December 31, 1978, but before January 1, 1987, and after he has attained age 70.

Notwithstanding the above provisions, the death benefit shall be payable on account of the death of any member who died or dies on or after January 1, 1974, but before January 1, 1979, after attaining age 65, if he or she had not yet attained age 65, if he or she had not yet attained age 66, was at the time of death completing the work year for those individuals under specific contract, or during the fiscal year for those individuals not under specific contract, in which he or she attained age 65, and otherwise met all conditions for payment of the death benefit.

Notwithstanding the above provisions, the Board of Trustees may and is specifically authorized to provide the death benefit according to the terms and conditions otherwise appearing in this Plan in the form of group life insurance, either (i) by purchasing a contract or contracts of group life insurance with any life insurance company or companies licensed and authorized to transact business in this State for the purpose of insuring the lives of members in service, or (ii) by establishing a separate trust fund qualified under section 501(c)(9) of the Internal Revenue Code of 1954, as amended, for such purpose. To that end the Board of Trustees is authorized, empowered and directed to investigate the desirability of utilizing group life insurance by either of the foregoing methods for the purpose of providing the death benefit. If a separate trust fund is established, it shall be operated in accordance with rules and regulations adopted by the Board of Trustees and all investment earnings on the trust fund shall be credited to such fund.

In administration of the death benefit the following shall apply:

(1) For the purpose of determining eligibility only, in this subsection "calendar year" shall mean any period of 12 consecutive months. For all other purposes in this subsection "calendar year" shall mean the 12 months beginning January 1 and ending December 31.

(2) Last day of actual service shall be:

a. When employment has been terminated, the last day the member actually worked.

b. When employment has not been terminated, the date on which an absent member's sick and annual leave expire.

c. When a participant's employment is interrupted by reason of service in the Uniformed Services, as that term is defined in section 4303(16) of the Uniformed Services Employment and Reemployment Rights Act, Public Law 103-353, and the participant does not return immediately after that service to employment with a covered employer in this System, the date on which the participant was first eligible to be separated or released from his or her involuntary military service.

(3) For a period when a member is on leave of absence, his status with respect to the death benefit will be determined by the provisions of G.S. 128-26(g).

(4) A member on leave of absence from his position as a local governmental employee for the purpose of serving as a member or officer of the General Assembly shall be deemed to be in service during sessions of the General Assembly and thereby covered by the provisions of the death benefit, if applicable. The amount of the death benefit for such member shall be the equivalent of the salary to which the member would have been entitled as a local governmental employee during the 12-month period immediately prior to the month in which death occurred, not to be less than twenty-five thousand dollars ($25,000) nor to exceed fifty thousand dollars ($50,000).

The provisions of the Retirement System pertaining to administration, G.S. 128-28, and management of funds, G.S. 128-29, are hereby made applicable to the Plan.

(l1) Death Benefit Plan for Law Enforcement Officers. - Under all requirements and conditions as otherwise provided for in subsection (l), except for the requirement that the provisions are effective only after an agreement has been executed by the employer and the Director of the Retirement System, all law enforcement officers who are members of the Retirement System shall participate and be eligible for group life insurance benefits under the Plan, and employers shall fund the cost of these benefits.

(l2) Death Benefit for Retired Members. - Upon receipt of proof, satisfactory to the Board of Trustees in its capacity under this subsection, of the death of a retired member of the Retirement System on or after July 1, 1988, but before January 1, 1999, there shall be paid a death benefit to the surviving spouse of the deceased retired member or to the deceased retired member's legal representative if not survived by a spouse; provided the retired member has elected, when first eligible, to make, and has continuously made, in advance of his death required contributions as determined by the Board of Trustees on a fully contributory basis through retirement allowance deductions or other methods adopted by the Board of Trustees, to a group death benefit trust fund administered by the Board of Trustees separate and apart from the Retirement System's Annuity Savings Fund and Pension Accumulation Fund. This death benefit shall be a lump-sum payment in the amount of five thousand dollars ($5,000) upon the completion of 24 months of contributions required under this subsection. Should death occur before the completion of 24 months of contributions required under this subsection, the deceased retired member's surviving spouse or legal representative if not survived by a spouse shall be paid the sum of the retired member's contributions required by this subsection plus interest to be determined by the Board of Trustees.

(I3) Death Benefit for Retired Members. - Upon receipt of proof, satisfactory to the Board of Trustees in its capacity under this subsection, of the death of a retired member of the Retirement System on or after January 1, 1999, but before July 1, 2004, there shall be paid a death benefit to the surviving spouse of the deceased retired member or to the deceased retired member's legal representative if not survived by a spouse; provided the retired member has elected, when first eligible, to make, and has continuously made, in advance of his death required contributions as determined by the Board of Trustees on a fully contributory basis through retirement allowance deductions or other methods adopted by the Board of Trustees, to a group death benefit trust fund administered by System's Annuity Savings Fund and Pension Accumulation Fund. This death benefit shall be a lump sum payment in the amount of six thousand dollars ($6,000) upon the completion of 24 months of contributions required under this subsection. Should death occur before the completion of 24 months of contributions required under this subsection, the deceased retired member's surviving spouse or legal representative if not survived by a spouse shall be paid the sum of the retired member's contributions required by this subsection plus interest to be determined by the Board of Trustees.

(I4) Death Benefit for Retired Members. - Upon receipt of proof, satisfactory to the Board of Trustees in its capacity under this subsection, of the death of a retired member of the Retirement System on or after July 1, 2004, but before July 1, 2007, there shall be paid a death benefit to the surviving spouse of the deceased retired member or to the deceased retired member's legal representative if not survived by a spouse; provided the retired member has elected, when first eligible, to make, and has continuously made, in advance of his death required contributions as determined by the Board of Trustees on a fully contributory basis through retirement allowance deductions or other methods adopted by the Board of Trustees, to a group death benefit trust fund administered by the Board of Trustees separate and apart from the Retirement System's Annuity Savings Fund and Pension Accumulation Fund. This death benefit shall be a lump-sum payment in the amount of nine thousand dollars ($9,000) upon the completion of 24 months of contributions required under this subsection. Should death occur before the completion of 24 months of contributions required under this subsection, the deceased retired member's surviving spouse or legal representative if not survived by a spouse shall be paid the sum of the retired member's contributions required by this subsection plus interest to be determined by the Board of Trustees.

Upon receipt of proof, satisfactory to the Board of Trustees in its capacity under this subsection, of the death of a retired member of the Retirement System on or after July 1, 2007, there shall be paid a death benefit to the surviving spouse of the deceased retired member or to the deceased retired member's legal representative if not survived by a spouse; provided the retired member has elected, when first eligible, to make, and has continuously made, in advance of his death required contributions as determined by the Board of Trustees on a fully contributory basis through retirement allowance deductions or other methods adopted by the Board of Trustees, to a group death benefit trust fund administered by the Board of Trustees separate and apart from the Retirement System's Annuity Savings Fund and Pension Accumulation Fund. This death benefit shall be a lump-sum payment in the amount of ten thousand dollars ($10,000) upon the completion of 24 months of contributions required under this subsection. Should death occur before the completion of 24 months of contributions required under this subsection, the deceased retired member's surviving spouse or legal representative if not survived by a spouse shall be paid the sum of the retired member's contributions required by this subsection plus interest to be determined by the Board of Trustees.

(m)   Survivor's Alternate Benefit. - Upon the death of a member in service, the beneficiary designated to receive a return of accumulated contributions shall have the right to elect to receive in lieu thereof the reduced retirement allowance provided by Option two of subsection (g) above computed by assuming that the member had retired on the first day of the month following the date of his death, provided that all four of the following conditions apply:

(1) a. The member had attained such age and/or creditable service to be eligible to commence retirement with an early or service retirement allowance, or

b. The member had obtained 20 years of creditable service in which case the retirement allowance shall be computed in accordance with G.S. 128-27(b21)(1)b. or G.S. 128-27(b21)(2)c., notwithstanding the requirement of obtaining age 50, or

b1. The member was a law enforcement officer who had obtained 15 years of service as a law enforcement officer and was killed in the line of duty, or the member was a firefighter or a rescue squad worker who had obtained 15 years of service as a firefighter or a rescue squad worker and was killed in the line of duty, in which cases the retirement allowance shall be computed in accordance with G.S. 128-27(b21)(1)b., notwithstanding the requirement of obtaining age 50.

c. Repealed by Session Laws 2010-72, s. 2(b), effective July 1, 2010.

(2) At the time of the member's death, one and only one beneficiary is eligible to receive a return of his accumulated contributions.

(3) The member had not instructed the Board of Trustees in writing that he did not wish the provisions of this subsection apply.

(4) The member had not commenced to receive a retirement allowance as provided under this Chapter.

For the purpose of this benefit, a member is considered to be in service at the date of his death if his death occurs within 180 days from the last day of his actual service. The last day of actual service shall be determined as provided in subsection (l) of this section. Upon the death of a member in service, the surviving spouse may make all purchases for creditable service as provided for under this Chapter for which the member had made application in writing prior to the date of death, provided that the date of death occurred prior to or within 60 days after notification of the cost to make the purchase.

For the purpose of calculating this benefit, any terminal payouts made after the date of death that meet the definition of compensation shall be credited to the month prior to the month of death. These terminal payouts do not include salary or wages paid for work performed during the month of death.

(m1) Special Retirement Allowance for Law Enforcement Officers. - Upon retirement, a member who is a law enforcement officer vested as of June 30, 2010, may elect to transfer any portion of his eligible accumulated contributions, not including any Roth after-tax contributions and the earnings thereon, from the Supplemental Retirement Income Plan of North Carolina to this Retirement System and receive, in addition to his basic service, early or disability retirement allowance, a special retirement allowance which shall be based upon his eligible accumulated account balance at the date of the transfer of the assets to this System. For the purpose of determining the special retirement allowance, the Board of Trustees shall adopt straight life annuity factors on the basis of mortality tables, such other tables as may be necessary and the interest assumption rate recommended by the actuary based upon actual experience including an assumed annual post-retirement allowance increase of four percent (4%). The Board of Trustees shall modify such factors every five years, as shall be deemed necessary, based upon the five year experience study as required by G.S. 128-28(o). Provided, however, a member who transfers his eligible accumulated contributions from the Supplemental Retirement Income Plan of North Carolina shall be taxed for North Carolina State Income tax purposes on the special retirement allowance the same as if that special retirement allowance had been paid directly by the Supplemental Retirement Income Plan of North Carolina. The Local Governmental Employees' Retirement System shall be responsible to determine the taxable amount, if any, and report accordingly.

(m2) Special Retirement Allowance. - At any time coincident with or following retirement, a member may make a one-time election to transfer any portion of the member's eligible accumulated contributions, not including any Roth after-tax contributions and the earnings thereon, from the Supplemental Retirement Income Plan of North Carolina or the North Carolina Public Employee Deferred Compensation Plan to this Retirement System and receive, in addition to the member's basic service, early or disability retirement allowance, a special retirement allowance which shall be based upon the member's transferred balance. Notwithstanding anything to the contrary, a member may not transfer such amounts as will cause the member's retirement allowance under the System to exceed the amount allowable under G.S. 128-38.2(b). The Board of Trustees may establish a minimum amount that must be transferred if a transfer is elected. The member may elect a special retirement allowance with no postretirement increases or a special retirement allowance with annual postretirement increases equal to the annual increase in the U.S. Consumer Price Index. Postretirement increases on any other allowance will not apply to the special retirement allowance. The Board of Trustees shall provide educational materials to the members who apply for the transfer authorized by this section. Those materials shall describe the special retirement allowance and shall explain (i) the relationship between the transferred balance and the monthly benefit; and (ii) how the member's heirs may be impacted by the election to make this transfer and any costs and fees involved.

For the purpose of determining the special retirement allowance, the Board of Trustees shall adopt straight life annuity factors on the basis of yields on U.S. Treasury Bonds and mortality and such other tables as may be necessary based upon actual experience. A single set of mortality and such other tables will be used for all members, with factors differing only based on the age of the member and the election of postretirement increases. The Board of Trustees shall modify the mortality and such other tables every five years, as shall be deemed necessary, based upon the five-year experience study as required by G.S. 128-28(o). Provided, however, a member who transfers the member's eligible accumulated contributions from the Supplemental Retirement Income Plan of North Carolina or the North Carolina Public Employee Deferred Compensation Plan to this Retirement System shall be taxed for North Carolina State Income Tax purposes on the special retirement allowance the same as if that special retirement allowance had been paid directly by the Supplemental Retirement Income Plan of North Carolina. The Local Governmental Employees' Retirement System shall be responsible to determine the taxable amount, if any, and report accordingly.

The special retirement allowance shall continue for the life of the member and the beneficiary designated to receive a monthly survivorship benefit under Option 2, 3 or 6 as provided in G.S. 128-27(g), if any. The Board of Trustees, however, shall establish two payment options that guarantee payments as follows:

(1) A member may elect to receive the special retirement allowance for life but with payments guaranteed for a number of months to be specified by the Board of Trustees. Under this plan, if the member dies before the expiration of the specified number of months, the special retirement allowance will continue to be paid to the member's designated beneficiary for the life of the beneficiary, if Option 2, 3 or 6 is selected. If Option 2, 3 or 6 is not selected, the member's designated beneficiary will receive the benefit only for the remainder of the specified number of months. If the member's designated beneficiary dies before receiving payments for the specified number of months, any remaining payments will be paid to the member's estate.

(2) A member may elect to receive the special retirement allowance for life but is guaranteed that the sum of the special allowance payments will equal the total of the transferred amount. Under this payment option, if the member dies before receiving the total transferred amount, the special retirement allowance will continue to be paid to the member's designated beneficiary for the life of the beneficiary, if Option 2, 3 or 6 is selected. If Option 2, 3 or 6 is not selected, the member's designated beneficiary or the member's estate shall be paid any remaining balance of the transferred amount.

The Supplemental Retirement Board of Trustees established under G.S. 135-96 may assess a one-time flat administrative fee not to exceed the actual cost of the administrative expenses relating to these transfers.

The Board of Trustees shall report annually to the Joint Legislative Commission on Governmental Operations on the number of persons who made an election in the previous calendar year, with any recommendations it might make on amendment or repeal based on any identified problems.

The General Assembly reserves the right to repeal or amend this subsection, but such repeal or amendment shall not affect any person who has already made the one-time election provided in this subsection.

(n)   Increases in Benefits Paid in Respect to Members Retired prior to July 1, 1967. - From and after July 1, 1971, the monthly benefits to or on account of persons who commenced receiving benefits prior to July 1, 1965, shall be increased by twenty percent (20%) thereof; the monthly benefits to or on account of persons who commenced receiving benefits after June 30, 1965 and before July 1, 1967, shall be increased by five percent (5%) thereof. These increases shall be calculated after monthly retirement allowances as of July 1, 1971 have been increased to the extent provided for in subsection (k) above.

(o)   Increases in Benefits to Those Persons Who Were Retired prior to January 1, 1969. - From and after July 1, 1973, the monthly benefits to or on account of persons who commenced receiving benefits from the System prior to January 1, 1969, shall be increased by a percentage thereof. Such percentage shall be determined in accordance with the following schedule:

Year(s) in Which

Benefits Commenced   Percentage

1959 through 1968   10

1946 through 1958   25

These increases shall be calculated after monthly retirement allowances as of July 1, 1973, have been increased to the extent provided for in the preceding subsection (k).

(p)   Increases in Benefits to Those Persons on Disability Retirement Who Were Retired prior to July 1, 1971. - From and after July 1, 1974, the monthly benefits to members who commenced receiving disability benefits prior to July 1, 1965, shall be increased by one percent (1%) thereof for each year by which the member retired prior to the age of 65 years; the monthly benefits to members who commenced receiving disability benefits after June 30, 1965, and before July 1, 1971, shall be increased by five percent (5%) thereof. These increases shall be calculated before monthly retirement allowances as of June 30, 1974, have been increased to the extent provided for in the preceding subsection (k).

(q)   Notwithstanding any of the foregoing provisions, the increase in allowance to each beneficiary on the retirement rolls as of July 1, 1973, which shall become effective on July 1, 1974, as otherwise provided in G.S. 128-27(k), shall be the current maximum four percent (4%) plus an additional two percent (2%) to a total of six percent (6%) for the year 1974 only. The provisions of this subsection shall apply also to the allowance of a surviving annuitant of a beneficiary.

(r)   Notwithstanding any of the foregoing provisions, the increase in allowance to each beneficiary on the retirement rolls as of July 1, 1974, which shall become payable on July 1, 1975, and to each beneficiary on the retirement rolls as of July 1, 1975, which shall become payable on July 1, 1976, as otherwise provided in G.S. 128-27(k), shall be the current maximum four percent (4%) plus an additional four percent (4%) to a total of eight percent (8%) for the years 1975 and 1976 only, provided that the increases do not exceed the actual percentage increase in the Consumer Price Index as determined in G.S. 128-27(k). The provisions of this subsection shall apply also to the allowance of a surviving annuitant of a beneficiary.

(s)   Notwithstanding any other provision of this section, the increase in the allowance to each beneficiary on the retirement rolls as otherwise provided in G.S. 128-27(k) shall be the current maximum of four per centum (4%) plus an additional four per centum (4%) to a total of eight per centum (8%) on July 1, 1975, and July 1, 1976, provided the increases do not exceed the actual percentage increase in the cost of living as determined in G.S. 128-27(k). The provisions of this subsection shall apply also to the allowance of a surviving annuitant of a beneficiary. The cost of these increases shall be borne from the funds of the Retirement System.

(t) Increases in Benefits to Those Persons on Disability Retirement Who Were Retired prior to July 1, 1971. - From and after July 1, 1975, the monthly benefits to members who commenced receiving disability benefits prior to July 1, 1965, shall be increased one percent (1%) thereof for each year by which the member retired prior to age 65 years; the monthly benefits to members who commenced receiving disability benefits after June 30, 1965, and before July 1, 1971, shall be increased by five percent (5%) thereof. These increases shall be calculated before monthly retirement allowances as of June 30, 1975, have been increased to the extent provided in the preceding provisions of this Chapter.

(u) Notwithstanding the foregoing provisions, the increase in allowance to each beneficiary on the retirement rolls as of July 1, 1977, which shall become payable on July 1, 1978, as otherwise provided in G.S. 128-27(k), shall be the current maximum four percent (4%) plus an additional two and one-half percent (2 ½%) for the year beginning July 1, 1978. The provisions of this subsection shall apply also to the allowance of a surviving annuitant of a beneficiary.

(v) Increases in Allowances Paid Beneficiaries Retired prior to July 1, 1976. - From and after July 1, 1978, the monthly allowances paid to or on account of beneficiaries who commenced receiving such allowances prior to July 1, 1976, shall be increased by seven percent (7%) thereof. This increase shall be calculated before monthly allowances, as of July 1, 1978, have been increased to the extent provided for in the preceding subsections (k) and (u). The provisions of this subsection shall apply also to the allowance of a surviving annuitant of a beneficiary.

(w) Notwithstanding the foregoing provisions, the increase in allowance to each beneficiary on the retirement rolls as of July 1, 1978, which shall become payable on July 1, 1979, as otherwise provided in G.S. 128-27(k), shall be five percent (5%) for the year beginning July 1, 1979. Provisions of this subsection shall apply also to the allowance of a surviving annuitant of a beneficiary.

(x) Increases in Benefits to Those Persons Who Were Retired prior to July 1, 1978. - From and after July 1, 1980, the monthly benefits to or on account of persons who commenced receiving benefits from the system prior to July 1, 1978, shall be increased by a percentage in accordance with the following schedule:

Period in Which Benefits Commenced	Percentage
On or before June 30, 1959	10%
July 1, 1959, to June 30, 1968	7%
July 1, 1968, to June 30, 1978	2%

This increase shall be calculated independent of any other post-retirement increase, without compounding, otherwise payable from and after July 1, 1980.

(y) Notwithstanding the foregoing provisions, the increase in allowance to each beneficiary on the retirement rolls as of July 1, 1980, which shall become payable on January 1, 1982, as otherwise provided in G.S. 128-27(h), shall be the percentage available therefrom plus an additional six and six-tenths percent (6.6%); provided that in no case shall the increase exceed a total of seven percent (7%). The provisions of this subsection shall apply also to the allowance of a surviving annuitant of the beneficiary.

(z) Notwithstanding the foregoing provisions, the increase in allowance to each beneficiary as of July 1, 1983, which shall become payable on July 1, 1984, shall be three and eight-tenths percent (3.8%) as provided in G.S. 128-27(k) plus an additional four and two-tenths percent (4.2%) to a total of eight percent (8%). The provision of this subsection shall apply also to the allowance of a surviving annuitant of a beneficiary. The cost of these increases shall be borne from the funds of the Retirement System.

(z1) Notwithstanding the foregoing provisions, from and after July 1, 1985, the retirement allowance to or on account of beneficiaries whose retirement commenced on or before July 1, 1984, shall be increased by four percent (4%) of the allowance payable on July 1, 1984, in accordance with G.S. 128-27(k). Furthermore, from and after July 1, 1985, the retirement allowance to or on account of beneficiaries whose retirement commenced after July 1, 1984, but before June 30, 1985, shall be increased by a prorated amount of four percent (4%) of the allowance payable as determined by the Board of Trustees based upon the number of months that a retirement allowance was paid between July 1, 1984, and June 30, 1985.

(aa) From and after July 1, 1985, the retirement allowance to or on account of beneficiaries on the retirement rolls as of June 1, 1985, shall be increased by six-tenths percent (0.6%) of the allowance payable on June 1, 1985. This allowance shall be calculated on the basis of the allowance payable and in effect on June 30, 1985, so as not to be compounded on any other increases payable on allowances in effect on June 30, 1985.

(bb) From and after July 1, 1986, the retirement allowance to or on account of beneficiaries whose retirement commenced on or before July 1, 1985, shall be increased by three and eight-tenths percent (3.8%) of the allowance payable on July 1, 1985, in accordance with G.S. 128-27(k). Furthermore, from and after July 1, 1986, the retirement allowance to or on account of beneficiaries whose retirement commenced after July 1, 1985, but before June 30, 1986, shall be increased by a prorated amount of three and eight-tenths percent (3.8%) of the allowance payable as determined by the Board of Trustees based upon the number of months that a retirement allowance was paid between July 1, 1985, and June 30, 1986.

(cc) From and after July 1, 1987, the retirement allowance to or on account of beneficiaries whose retirement commenced on or before July 1, 1986, shall be increased by four percent (4.0%) of the allowance payable on July 1, 1986, in accordance with G.S. 128-27(k). Furthermore, from and after July 1, 1987, the retirement allowance to or on account of beneficiaries whose retirement commenced after July 1, 1986, but before June 30, 1987, shall be increased by a prorated amount of four percent (4.0%) of the allowance payable as determined by the Board of Trustees based upon the number of months that a retirement allowance was paid between July 1, 1986, and June 30, 1987.

(dd) From and after July 1, 1988, the retirement allowance to or on account of beneficiaries whose retirement commenced on or before July 1, 1987, shall be increased by three and six-tenths percent (3.6%) of the allowance payable on July 1, 1987, in accordance with G.S. 128-27(k). Furthermore, from and after July 1, 1988, the retirement allowance to or on account of beneficiaries whose retirement commenced after July 1, 1987, but before June 30, 1988, shall be increased by a prorated amount of three and six-tenths percent (3.6%) of the allowance payable as determined by the Board of Trustees based upon the number of months that a retirement allowance was paid between July 1, 1987, and June 30, 1988.

(ee) Increase in Allowance as to Persons on Retirement Rolls as of June 1, 1988. - From and after July 1, 1988, the retirement allowance to or on account of beneficiaries on the retirement rolls as of June 1, 1988, shall be increased by one and two-tenths percent (1.2%) of the allowance payable on June 1, 1988. This allowance shall be calculated on the basis of the allowance payable and in effect on June 30, 1988, so as not to be compounded on any other increase payable under subsection (k) of this section or otherwise granted by act of the 1987 Session of the General Assembly.

(ff) From and after July 1, 1989, the retirement allowance to or on account of beneficiaries whose retirement commenced on or before July 1, 1988, shall be increased by three and one-half percent (3.5%) of the allowance payable on July 1, 1988, in accordance with G.S. 128-27(k). Furthermore, from and after July 1, 1989, the retirement allowance to or on account of beneficiaries whose retirement commenced after July 1, 1988, but before June 30, 1989, shall be increased by a prorated amount of three and one-half percent (3.5%) of the allowance payable as determined by the Board of Trustees based upon the number of months that a retirement allowance was paid between July 1, 1988, and June 30, 1989.

(gg) Increase in Allowance as to Persons on Retirement Rolls as of June 1, 1989. - From and after July 1, 1989, the retirement allowance to or on account of beneficiaries on the retirement rolls as of June 1, 1989, shall be increased by one and nine-tenths percent (1.9%) of the allowance payable on June 1, 1989. This allowance shall be calculated on the basis of the allowance payable and in effect on June 30, 1989, so as not to be compounded on any other increase payable under subsection (k) of this section or otherwise granted by act of the 1989 Session of the General Assembly.

(hh) Increase in Allowance as to Persons on Retirement Rolls as of June 1, 1990. - From and after July 1, 1990, the retirement allowance to or on account of beneficiaries on the retirement rolls as of June 1, 1990, shall be increased by six-tenths of one percent (0.6%) of the allowance payable on June 1, 1990. This allowance shall be calculated on the basis of the allowance payable and in effect on June 30, 1990, so as not to be compounded on any other increase granted by act of the 1989 Session of the General Assembly (1990 Regular Session).

(ii) From and after July 1, 1990, the retirement allowance to or on account of beneficiaries whose retirement commenced on or before July 1, 1989, shall be increased by six and one-tenth percent (6.1%) of the allowance payable on

July 1, 1989, in accordance with G.S. 128-27(k). Furthermore, from and after July 1, 1990, the retirement allowance to or on account of beneficiaries whose retirement commenced after July 1, 1989, but before June 30, 1990, shall be increased by a prorated amount of six and one-tenth percent (6.1%) of the allowance payable as determined by the Board of Trustees based upon the number of months that a retirement allowance was paid between July 1, 1989, and June 30, 1990.

(jj) Increase in Allowance as to Persons on Retirement Rolls as of June 1, 1992. - From and after July 1, 1992, the retirement allowance to or on account of beneficiaries on the retirement rolls as of June 1, 1992, shall be increased by three and six-tenths percent (3.6%) of the allowance payable on June 1, 1992. This allowance shall be calculated on the allowance payable and in effect on June 30, 1992, so as not to be compounded on any other increase payable under subsection (k) of this section or otherwise granted by act of the 1991 Session of the General Assembly, 1992 Regular Session.

(kk) From and after July 1, 1992, the retirement allowance to or on account of beneficiaries whose retirement commenced on or before July 1, 1991, shall be increased by one and six-tenths percent (1.6%) of the allowance payable on July 1, 1991, in accordance with G.S. 128-27(k). Furthermore, from and after July 1, 1992, the retirement allowance to or on account of beneficiaries whose retirement commenced after July 1, 1991, but before June 30, 1992, shall be increased by a prorated amount of one and six-tenths percent (1.6%) of the allowance payable as determined by the Board of Trustees based upon the number of months that a retirement allowance was paid between July 1, 1991 and June 30, 1992.

(ll) From and after July 1, 1993, the retirement allowance to or on account of beneficiaries whose retirement commenced on or before July 1, 1992, shall be increased by one and six-tenths percent (1.6%) of the allowance payable on July 1, 1992, in accordance with G.S. 128-27(k). Furthermore, from and after July 1, 1993, the retirement allowance to or on account of beneficiaries whose retirement commenced after July 1, 1992, but before June 30, 1993, shall be increased by a prorated amount of one and six-tenths percent (1.6%) of the allowance payable as determined by the Board of Trustees based upon the number of months that a retirement allowance was paid between July 1, 1992, and June 30, 1993.

(mm) Increase in Allowance as to Persons on Retirement Rolls as of June 1, 1994. - From and after July 1, 1994, the retirement allowance to or on account of beneficiaries on the retirement rolls as of June 1, 1994, shall be increased by six-tenths of one percent (.6%) of the allowance payable on June 1, 1994. This allowance shall be calculated on the allowance payable and in effect on June 30, 1994, so as not to be compounded on any other increase payable under subsection (k) of this section or otherwise granted by act of the 1993 General Assembly in 1994.

(nn) From and after July 1, 1994, the retirement allowance to or on account of beneficiaries whose retirement commenced on or before July 1, 1993, shall be increased by two and eight-tenths percent (2.8%) of the allowance payable on July 1, 1993, in accordance with G.S. 128-27(k). Furthermore, from and after July 1, 1994, the retirement allowance to or on account of beneficiaries whose retirement commenced after July 1, 1993, but before June 30, 1994, shall be increased by a prorated amount of two and eight-tenths percent (2.8%) of the allowance payable as determined by the Board of Trustees based upon the number of months that a retirement allowance was paid between July 1, 1993, and June 30, 1994.

(oo) From and after July 1, 1995, the retirement allowance to or on account of beneficiaries whose retirement commenced on or before July 1, 1994, shall be increased by two percent (2%) of the allowance payable on July 1, 1994, in accordance with G.S. 128-27(k). Furthermore, from and after July 1, 1995, the retirement allowance to or on account of beneficiaries whose retirement commenced after July 1, 1994, but before June 30, 1995, shall be increased by a prorated amount of two percent (2%) of the allowance payable as determined by the Board of Trustees based upon the number of months that a retirement allowance was paid between July 1, 1994, and June 30, 1995.

(pp) Increase in Allowance as to Persons on Retirement Rolls as of June 1, 1995. - From and after July 1, 1995, the retirement allowance to or on account of beneficiaries on the retirement rolls as of June 1, 1995, shall be increased by six-tenths of one percent (0.6%) of the allowance payable on June 1, 1995. This allowance shall be calculated on the allowance payable and in effect on June 30, 1995, so as not to be compounded on any other increase payable under subsection (k) of this section or otherwise granted by act of the 1995 General Assembly.

(qq) From and after July 1, 1995, the retirement allowance to or on account of beneficiaries whose retirement commenced on or before July 1, 1993, shall be increased by seven-tenths of one percent (0.7%) of the allowance payable on July 1, 1993, in accordance with G.S. 128-27(k). Furthermore, from and after

July 1, 1995, the retirement allowance to or on account of beneficiaries whose retirement commenced after July 1, 1993, but before June 30, 1994, shall be increased by a prorated amount of seven-tenths of one percent (0.7%) of the allowance payable as determined by the Board of Trustees based upon the number of months that a retirement allowance was paid between July 1, 1993, and June 30, 1994.

(rr) From and after September 1, 1996, the retirement allowance to or on account of beneficiaries whose retirement commenced on or before July 1, 1995, shall be increased by four and four-tenths percent (4.4%) of the allowance payable on July 1, 1995, in accordance with G.S. 128-27(k). Furthermore, from and after September 1, 1996, the retirement allowance to or on account of beneficiaries whose retirement commenced after July 1, 1995, but before June 30, 1996, shall be increased by a prorated amount of four and four-tenths percent (4.4%) of the allowance payable as determined by the Board of Trustees based upon the number of months that a retirement allowance was paid between July 1, 1995, and June 30, 1996.

(ss) From and after July 1, 1997, the retirement allowance to or on account of beneficiaries whose retirement commenced on or before July 1, 1996, shall be increased by four percent (4%) of the allowance payable on June 1, 1997, in accordance with G.S. 128-27(k). Furthermore, from and after July 1, 1997, the retirement allowance to or on account of beneficiaries whose retirement commenced after July 1, 1996, but before June 30, 1997, shall be increased by a prorated amount of four percent (4%) of the allowance payable as determined by the Board of Trustees based upon the number of months that a retirement allowance was paid between July 1, 1996, and June 30, 1997.

(tt) Increase in Allowance as to Persons on Retirement Rolls as of June 1, 1997. - From and after July 1, 1997, the retirement allowance to or on account of beneficiaries on the retirement rolls as of June 1, 1997, shall be increased by two and three-tenths percent (2.3%) of the allowance payable on June 1, 1997. This allowance shall be calculated on the allowance payable and in effect on June 30, 1997, so as not to be compounded on any other increase payable under subsection (k) of this section or otherwise granted by act of the 1997 General Assembly.

(uu) From and after July 1, 1998, the retirement allowance to or on account of beneficiaries whose retirement commenced on or before July 1, 1997, shall be increased by two and one-half percent (2.5%) of the allowance payable on June 1, 1998, in accordance with subsection (k) of this section. Furthermore, from and after July 1, 1998, the retirement allowance to or on account of beneficiaries whose retirement commenced after July 1, 1997, but before June 30, 1998, shall be increased by a prorated amount of two and one-half percent (2.5%) of the allowance payable as determined by the Board of Trustees based upon the number of months that a retirement allowance was paid between July 1, 1997, and June 30, 1998.

(vv) Increase in Allowance as to Persons on Retirement Rolls as of June 1, 1998. - From and after July 1, 1998, the retirement allowance to or on account of beneficiaries on the retirement rolls as of June 1, 1998, shall be increased by six-tenths of one percent (0.6%) of the allowance payable on June 1, 1998. This allowance shall be calculated on the allowance payable and in effect on June 30, 1998, so as not to be compounded on any other increase payable under subsection (k) of this section or otherwise granted by act of the 1997 General Assembly.

(ww) From and after July 1, 1999, the retirement allowance to or on account of beneficiaries whose retirement commenced on or before July 1, 1998, shall be increased by one percent (1.0%) of the allowance payable on June 1, 1999, in accordance with subsection (k) of this section. Furthermore, from and after July 1, 1999, the retirement allowance to or on account of beneficiaries whose retirement commenced after July 1, 1998, but before June 30, 1999, shall be increased by a prorated amount of one percent (1.0%) of the allowance payable as determined by the Board of Trustees based upon the number of months that a retirement allowance was paid between July 1, 1998, and June 30, 1999.

(xx) Increase in Allowance as to Persons on Retirement Rolls as of June 1, 2000. - From and after July 1, 2000, the retirement allowance to or on account of beneficiaries on the retirement rolls as of June 1, 2000, shall be increased by six-tenths of one percent (0.6%) of the allowance payable on June 1, 2000. This allowance shall be calculated on the allowance payable and in effect on June 30, 2000, so as not to be compounded on any other increase payable under subsection (k) of this section or otherwise granted by act of the 1999 General Assembly, 2000 Regular Session.

(yy) From and after July 1, 2000, the retirement allowance to or on account of beneficiaries whose retirement commenced on or before July 1, 1999, shall be increased by three and eight-tenths percent (3.8%) of the allowance payable on June 1, 2000, in accordance with subsection (k) of this section. Furthermore, from and after July 1, 2000, the retirement allowance to or on account of beneficiaries whose retirement commenced after July 1, 1999, but before June

30, 2000, shall be increased by a prorated amount of three and eight-tenths percent (3.8%) of the allowance payable as determined by the Board of Trustees based upon the number of months that a retirement allowance was paid between July 1, 1999, and June 30, 2000.

(zz)	From and after July 1, 2001, the retirement allowance to or on account of beneficiaries whose retirement commenced on or before July 1, 2000, shall be increased by two percent (2%) of the allowance payable on June 1, 2001, in accordance with subsection (k) of this section. Furthermore, from and after July 1, 2001, the retirement allowance to or on account of beneficiaries whose retirement commenced after July 1, 2000, but before June 30, 2001, shall be increased by a prorated amount of two percent (2%) of the allowance payable as determined by the Board of Trustees based upon the number of months that a retirement allowance was paid between July 1, 2000, and June 30, 2001.

(aaa)	Increase in Allowance as to Persons on Retirement Rolls as of June 1, 2001. - From and after July 1, 2001, the retirement allowance to or on account of beneficiaries on the retirement rolls as of June 1, 2001, shall be increased by one and seven-tenths percent (1.7%) of the allowance payable on June 1, 2001. This allowance shall be calculated on the allowance payable and in effect on June 30, 2001, so as not to be compounded on any other increase payable under subsection (k) of this section or otherwise granted by act of the 2001 General Assembly.

(bbb)	From and after July 1, 2002, the retirement allowance to or on account of beneficiaries whose retirement commenced on or before July 1, 2001, shall be increased by one and four-tenths percent (1.4%) of the allowance payable on June 1, 2002, in accordance with subsection (k) of this section. Furthermore, from and after July 1, 2002, the retirement allowance to or on account of beneficiaries whose retirement commenced after July 1, 2001, but before June 30, 2002, shall be increased by a prorated amount of one and four-tenths percent (1.4%) of the allowance payable as determined by the Board of Trustees based upon the number of months that a retirement allowance was paid between July 1, 2001, and June 30, 2002.

(ccc)	Increase in Allowance as to Persons on Retirement Rolls as of June 1, 2002. - From and after July 1, 2002, the retirement allowance to or on account of beneficiaries on the retirement rolls as of June 1, 2002, shall be increased by six-tenths of one percent (0.6%) of the allowance payable on June 1, 2002. This allowance shall be calculated on the allowance payable and in effect on June 30, 2002, so as not to be compounded on any other increase payable under subsection (k) of this section or otherwise granted by act of the 2002 Regular Session of the 2001 General Assembly.

(ddd)   From and after July 1, 2003, the retirement allowance to or on account of beneficiaries whose retirement commenced on or before July 1, 2002, shall be increased by two percent (2.0%) of the allowance payable on June 1, 2003, in accordance with subsection (k) of this section. Furthermore, from and after July 1, 2003, the retirement allowance to or on account of beneficiaries whose retirement commenced after July 1, 2002, but before June 30, 2003, shall be increased by a prorated amount of two percent (2.0%) of the allowance payable as determined by the Board of Trustees based upon the number of months that a retirement allowance was paid between July 1, 2002, and June 30, 2003.

(eee)   From and after July 1, 2003, the retirement allowance to or on account of beneficiaries whose retirement commenced on or before June 1, 1982, shall be increased by six percent (6.0%) of the allowance payable on June 1, 2003, in accordance with subsection (k) of this section. Furthermore, from and after July 1, 2003, the retirement allowance to or on account of beneficiaries whose retirement commenced on or after July 1, 1982, but before July 1, 1993, shall be increased by one and one-tenth percent (1.1%) of the allowance payable on June 1, 2003, in accordance with subsection (k) of this section. This allowance shall be calculated on the allowance payable and in effect on June 30, 2003, so as not to be compounded on any other increase payable under subsection (k) of this section or otherwise granted by act of the 2003 Regular Session of the 2003 General Assembly.

(fff)   Increase in Allowance as to Persons on Retirement Rolls as of June 1, 2003. - From and after July 1, 2003, the retirement allowance to or on account of beneficiaries on the retirement rolls as of June 1, 2003, shall be increased by one and one-half percent (1.5%) of the allowance payable on June 1, 2003. This allowance shall be calculated on the allowance payable and in effect on June 30, 2003, so as not to be compounded on any other increase payable under subsection (k) of this section or otherwise granted by act of the 2003 General Assembly.

(ggg)   From and after July 1, 2005, the retirement allowance to or on account of beneficiaries whose retirement commenced on or before July 1, 2004, shall be increased by two and one-half percent (2.5%) of the allowance payable on June 1, 2005, in accordance with subsection (k) of this section. Furthermore, from and after July 1, 2005, the retirement allowance to or on account of beneficiaries whose retirement commenced after July 1, 2004, but before June

30, 2005, shall be increased by a prorated amount of two and one-half percent (2.5%) of the allowance payable as determined by the Board of Trustees based upon the number of months that a retirement allowance was paid between July 1, 2004, and June 30, 2005. (1939, c. 390, s. 7; 1945, c. 526, s. 4; 1951, c. 274, ss. 4-6; 1955, c. 1153, ss. 4-6; 1957, c. 855, ss. 1-4; 1959, c. 491, ss. 5-8; 1961, c. 515, ss. 2, 6, 7; 1965, c. 781; 1967, c. 978, ss. 3-7; 1969, c. 442, ss. 7-14; c. 898; 1971, c. 325, ss. 12-16, 19; c. 326, ss. 3-7; 1973, c. 243, ss. 3-7; c. 244, ss. 1-3; c. 816, s. 4; c. 994, ss. 2, 4; c. 1313, ss. 1, 2; 1975, c. 486, ss. 1, 2; c. 621, ss. 1, 2; 1975, 2nd Sess., c. 983, ss. 126-128; 1977, 2nd Sess., c. 1240; 1979, c. 862, ss. 2, 6, 7; c. 974, s. 1; c. 1063, s. 2; 1979, 2nd Sess., c. 1196, s. 2; cc. 1213, 1240; 1981, c. 672, s. 2; c. 689, s. 1; c. 940, s. 1; c. 975, s. 2; c. 978, ss. 3, 4; c. 980, ss. 1, 2; c. 981, ss. 1, 2; 1981 (Reg. Sess., 1982), c. 1284, ss. 1, 2; 1983, c. 467; c. 761, ss. 226, 227; 1983 (Reg. Sess., 1984), c. 1019, s. 1; c. 1044; c. 1049, ss. 1-3; c. 1086; 1985, c. 138; c. 348, s. 2; c. 479, s. 196(i)-(n); c. 520, s. 2; c. 649, ss. 8, 10; c. 751, ss. 1-4, 6; c. 791, s. 56; 1985 (Reg. Sess., 1986), c. 1014, s. 49(d); 1987, c. 181, s. 1; c. 513, s. 1; c. 738, ss. 27(c), 37(b); c. 824, s. 2; 1987 (Reg. Sess., 1988), c. 1061, s. 2; c. 1086, s. 22(c); c. 1108, s. 3; c. 1110, ss. 4-7; 1989, c. 717, ss. 13, 13.1; c. 731, s. 2; c. 752, s. 41(c); c. 792, ss. 3.4-3.6; 1989 (Reg. Sess., 1990), c. 1077, ss. 13-16; c. 1080; 1991, c. 636, s. 20(a); 1991 (Reg. Sess., 1992), c. 766, s. 1; c. 900, ss. 52(e)-(g), 53(a); c. 929, s. 1; c. 1030, s. 51.1; 1993, c. 321, ss. 74(b), 74.1(c), (d); c. 531, s. 3; 1993 (Reg. Sess., 1994), c. 769, ss. 7.30(b)-(d), (l); 1995, c. 507, ss. 7.22(e), (f), 7.23(c), (d), 7.23A(c); 1996, 2nd Ex. Sess., c. 18, s. 28.21(d); 1997-443, s. 33.22(g)-(j); 1998-153, s. 21(d)-(h); 1998-212, ss. 28.26(b), 28.27(e), (f); 1999-237, s. 28.23(d); 2000-67, ss. 26.20(g)-(j); 2001-424, ss. 32.22(d), 32.23(a)-(d); 2001-435, s. 1; 2002-126, ss. 28.8(b), 28.9(e)-(h); 2003-319, ss. 1-4; 2003-359, ss. 15, 16, 21; 2004-136, s. 1; 2004-147, ss. 2, 3; 2005-91, ss. 9, 10; 2005-276, s. 29.25(d); 2007-384, ss. 10.1, 10.2; 2007-431, ss. 2, 6; 2007-496, s. 2; 2009-66, ss. 3(i)-(k), 5(d)-(f), 6(b), 11(h)-(j), 12(g), (h); 2009-109, s. 2; 2010-72, ss. 1(b), 2(b), 9(b), 10(b); 2010-96, s. 40.7; 2010-124, ss. 4-6, 6.1(a), (b); 2011-92, s. 2; 2011-294, s. 3(b); 2011-371, s. 1; 2012-82, s. 1; 2012-178, s. 2.)

Vision Books Order Form

Fax Orders:	1-980-299-5965
Phone Orders:	1-704-898-0770
E-mail Orders:	www.visionbooks.org
Mail Orders:	Vision Books, LLC P.O. Box 42406 Charlotte, NC 28215

Shipp To:
Name_____
Address_____
City_____State_____Zip_____
Phone_____Fax_____
Email_____@_____

Bill To: We can bill a third party on your behalf.
Name_____
Address_____
City_____State_____Zip_____
Phone___(____)_____Fax_____
Email_____@_____

Pamphlet Number ($15.00 Each)	Qty	Total Cost
_____	_____	_____
_____	_____	_____
_____	_____	_____
_____	_____	_____
_____	_____	_____
_____	_____	_____
_____	_____	_____
_____	_____	_____
Full Volume Set 1-92	92 Pamphlets	1,380.00

Free Shipping Shipping & Handling on Full Volume Orders
Add $1.00 Shipping & Handling per pamphlet $_____

Total Cost $_____

Thank you for your support. Management!

DID YOU ENJOY THIS BOOK?

Vision Books, LLC would like to hear from you! If you or someone you know has been fasely imprisoned, we would like to hear your story. If the 'North Carolina Criminal Law and Procedure' has had an effect in your life or if you have suggestions, we would like to hear from you. Send your letters to:

Vision Books, LLC
Attn: Staff Writers
P.O. Box 42406
Charlotte, NC 28215
Email: staff@visionbooks.org

Order Additional Copies:

Fax Orders:	1-980-299-5965
Phone Orders:	1-704-898-0770
E-mail Orders:	www.visionbooks.org
Mail Orders:	Vision Books, LLC P.O. Box 42406 Charlotte, NC 28215

www.ingramcontent.com/pod-product-compliance
Lightning Source LLC
Chambersburg PA
CBHW051628170526
45167CB00001B/101